REA's MATH BUILDER

for Admission & Standardized Tests

by the staff of
Research & Education Association

 RESEARCH & EDUCATION ASSOCIATION
61 Ethel Road West • Piscataway, New Jersey 08854

REA's MATH BUILDER
for Admission & Standardized Tests

Printed in the United States of America

Library of Congress Catalog Card Number 93-85675

International Standard Book Number 0-87891-876-0

Research & Education Association
61 Ethel Road West
Piscataway, NJ 08854

*REA supports the effort to conserve
and protect environmental resources
by using recycled papers.*

ACKNOWLEDGMENTS

We thank the following authors for their contributions to the Math Builder:

Robert A. Bell, Ph.D.
Mathematics Instructor
Cooper-Union School of Engineering
New York, NY

Diane Bohannon, Ed.S.
Chairperson of Mathematics Department
Halls High School, Knoxville, TN

Roger C. Fryer, M.A.T.
Mathematics Instructor
Cosumnes River College, Sacramento, CA

Elaine M. Klett, M.S.
Mathematics Instructor
Brookdale Community College, Lincroft, NJ

Lutfi A. Lutfiyya, Ph.D.
Associate Professor of Mathematics
Kearney State College, Kearney, NE

John S. Robertson, Ph.D.
Associate Professor of Mathematics
U.S. Military Academy, West Point, NY

Vijay K. Rohatgi, Ph.D.
Professor of Mathematics
Bowling Green State University
Bowling Green, OH

Jerry R. Shipman, Ph.D.
Professor and Chairperson
of Mathematics
Alabama A&M University
Normal, AL

Ricardo Simpson-Rivera, M.S.
Visiting Scientist
Oregon State University
Corvallis, OR

Walter Smulson, M.A.
Chairperson of Mathematics Department
Loyola College, Wilmette, IL

Ron Walters, M.Ed.
Chairperson of Mathematics Department
Meade County High School
Bradenburg, KY

Ernest Woodward, Ed.D.
Professor of Mathematics
Austin Peay State University
Clarksville, TN

In addition, special recognition is also extended to the following persons:

Dr. Max Fogiel, President, for his overall guidance which has
brought this publication to completion

Stacey A. Sporer, Managing Editor, for coordinating the editorial
staff throughout each phase of the project

Wade Olsson, Production Editor, and Daniel Sellman, Editorial
Assistant, for their editorial contributions

Bruce Hanson, Graphic Design Manager, for his cover design and
final efforts in getting the book to press

Marty Perzan, for typesetting the book

CONTENTS

CHAPTER 1

About the Math Builder

About Research and Education Association

REA is an organization of educators, scientists, and engineers specializing in various academic fields. REA was founded in 1959 for the purpose of disseminating the most recently developed scientific information to groups in industry, government, high schools, and universities. Since then, REA has become a successful and highly respected publisher of study aids, test preparation books, handbooks, and reference works.

REA's Test Preparation series extensively prepares students and professionals for the Graduate Record Examinations (GRE), Graduate Management Admission Test (GMAT), Scholastic Assessment Test (SAT I), Medical College Admission Test (MCAT), Advanced Placement exams, and the SAT IIs (formerly the College Board Achievement Tests).

REA's publications and educational materials are highly regarded for their significant contribution to the quest for excellence that characterizes today's educational goals. We continually receive an unprecedented amount of praise from professionals, instructors, librarians, parents, and students for our published books. Our authors are as diverse as the subjects and fields represented in the books we publish. They are well-known in their respective fields and serve on the faculties of prestigious universities throughout the United States.

About this Book

REA's staff of authors and educators has prepared material, exercises, and tests based on each of the major standardized exams, including the High School Equivalency Diploma examination (GED), GRE, GMAT, American College Testing Program (ACT), Preliminary SAT (PSAT), SAT I, Elementary Level Mathematics (ELM), National Teacher's Examination (NTE), California Basic Exam Skills Test (CBEST), Pre-Professional Skills Test (PPST), and other teacher certification tests. The types of questions represented on these standardized exams have been analyzed in order to produce the most comprehensive preparatory material possible. You will find review material, helpful strategies, and exercises geared to your level of studying. This book will teach as well as review and refresh math skills needed to score high on standardized tests.

How to Use this Book

If you are preparing to take the GED, GRE, GMAT, ACT, SAT I, PSAT, ELM, NTE, PPST, CBEST or other teacher certification exams, you will be taking a test that requires excellent math ability. This book comprises a comprehensive mathematics review that can be tailored to your specific test preparation needs.

Locate your test on the chart below, and then find the corresponding sections recommended for study. REA suggests that you study the indicated material thoroughly as a review for your test.

	Arithmetic Chapter 2 Pages 7– 70	Algebra Chapter 3 Pages 71– 136	Geometry Chapter 4 Pages 137– 218	Student-Produced Response Chapter 5 Pages 219– 258	Word Problems Chapter 6 Pages 259– 325	Quantitative Ability Chapter 7 Pages 327– 347	Data Sufficiency Chapter 8 Pages 349– 369
PSAT	×	×	×	×	×	×	
SAT I	×	×	×	×	×	×	
ACT	×	×	×		×		
NTE	×	×	×		×		
PPST	×	×	×		×		
CBEST	×	×	×		×		
ELM	×	×	×		×		
GRE	×	×	×		×	×	
GMAT	×	×	×		×		×
GED	×	×	×		×		

This book will help you prepare for your test because it includes different types of questions and drills that are representative of each specific test. The book also includes diagnostic tests so that you can determine your strengths and weaknesses within a specific subject. The explanations are clear and comprehensive, explaining not only why the answer is correct but also, where appropriate, why the incorrect answers are not the best choice. The Math Review gives you practice within a wide range of categories and question types.

The **Arithmetic** chapter prepares students for arithmetic questions on the PSAT, SAT I, ACT, ELM, NTE, PPST, CBEST, GRE, GMAT, and GED. Even if you are not planning to take an exam in which arithmetic is tested, this chapter can be extremely helpful in building your math skills for more difficult problems.

The **Algebra** chapter prepares students for algebra questions on the PSAT, SAT I, ACT, ELM, NTE, PPST, CBEST, GRE, GMAT, and GED. It includes a comprehensive review of algebra skills, from the most basic terms to complex equations that require more in-depth problem-solving skills .

The **Geometry** chapter highlights all the geometry terms, equations, and problem skills needed to succeed on the geometry portion of any standardized test. Students taking the PSAT, SAT I, ACT, NTE, PPST, CBEST, ELM, GRE, GMAT, or GED will encounter geometry questions on their test, and should study this chapter thoroughly.

The **Student Produced Response** chapter should be used when studying for the PSAT and SAT I. Students taking these exams will find a section of questions in which they have to produce their own answers, rather than selecting from five possible correct responses, and enter them on an answer grid.

The **Word Problems** chapter brings together all the building blocks you have already studied in the Arithmetic, Algebra, and Geometry Skills chapters and further teaches how to solve word problems of all kinds, such as algebra, rate, work, mixture, interest, discount, profit, sets, geometry, measurement, and data interpretation. Further, this chapter gives solid strategies in how to solve word problems, which can seem confusing and overwhelming. Students preparing for the following tests can expect to see word problems on their exam: PSAT, SAT I, ACT, NTE, PPST, CBEST, ELM, GRE, GMAT, and GED.

The **Quantitative Ability** chapter is for those studying for the PSAT, SAT I, or GRE exam. In the GRE, Quantitative Ability includes quantitative comparison, discrete quantitative, and data interpretation. Both the SAT and PSAT include only quantitative comparison.

The **Data Sufficiency** chapter is unique to students taking the GMAT exam. This chapter helps you practice for the Data Sufficiency portion of your test.

Finally, before getting started, here are a few guidelines:

- Study full chapters. If, after a few minutes, the material appears rather easy, continue studying anyway. Many chapters (like the tests themselves) become more difficult as they go on.

- Review the arithmetic chapter regardless of whether or not basic arithmetic problems appear on your exam. A solid foundation in arithmetic will improve your ability to solve more complex questions and thus make it easier to grasp more challenging material.

- Use this guide as a supplement to review materials provided by test administrators.

- Take the diagnostic test before each review chapter, even if you feel confident that you already know the material well enough to skip a particular chapter. Often, skills we have not used for a long time become rusty, and unlike riding a bike, they do not come back to us right away. Taking the diagnostic test will put your mind at ease: you will discover either that you absolutely know the material or that you need to review. This will eliminate the panic you might otherwise experience during the test upon discovering that you have forgotten how to approach a certain type of problem.

The Math Review

As you prepare for a standardized math test, you will want to review some of the basic concepts in arithmetic, algebra, geometry, and word problems. The more familiar you are with the fundamental principles, the better you will do on your test. Our math reviews represent the various mathematics topics that appear on the math portions of standardized tests. You will not find calculus, trigonometry, or even imaginary numbers in our math review, because these concepts are not tested on the standardized test you are about to take. The mathematics concepts presented on your test are ones with which you are already familiar and simply need to review in order to score well.

Along with knowledge of these topics, how quickly and accurately you answer math questions will have an effect on your success. All tests have time limits, so the more questions you can answer correctly in the given period of time, the better off you will be. Our suggestion is that you first take each diagnostic test. Pay special attention to both the time it takes to complete the test and the number of correct answers. For extra practice, make sure to complete the drills as you review.

CHAPTER 2

Arithmetic

➤ Diagnostic Test
➤ Arithmetic Review and Drills
➤ Glossary

ARITHMETIC DIAGNOSTIC TEST

1. Ⓐ Ⓑ Ⓒ Ⓓ Ⓔ
2. Ⓐ Ⓑ Ⓒ Ⓓ Ⓔ
3. Ⓐ Ⓑ Ⓒ Ⓓ Ⓔ
4. Ⓐ Ⓑ Ⓒ Ⓓ Ⓔ
5. Ⓐ Ⓑ Ⓒ Ⓓ Ⓔ
6. Ⓐ Ⓑ Ⓒ Ⓓ Ⓔ
7. Ⓐ Ⓑ Ⓒ Ⓓ Ⓔ
8. Ⓐ Ⓑ Ⓒ Ⓓ Ⓔ
9. Ⓐ Ⓑ Ⓒ Ⓓ Ⓔ
10. Ⓐ Ⓑ Ⓒ Ⓓ Ⓔ
11. Ⓐ Ⓑ Ⓒ Ⓓ Ⓔ
12. Ⓐ Ⓑ Ⓒ Ⓓ Ⓔ
13. Ⓐ Ⓑ Ⓒ Ⓓ Ⓔ
14. Ⓐ Ⓑ Ⓒ Ⓓ Ⓔ
15. Ⓐ Ⓑ Ⓒ Ⓓ Ⓔ
16. Ⓐ Ⓑ Ⓒ Ⓓ Ⓔ
17. Ⓐ Ⓑ Ⓒ Ⓓ Ⓔ
18. Ⓐ Ⓑ Ⓒ Ⓓ Ⓔ
19. Ⓐ Ⓑ Ⓒ Ⓓ Ⓔ
20. Ⓐ Ⓑ Ⓒ Ⓓ Ⓔ
21. Ⓐ Ⓑ Ⓒ Ⓓ Ⓔ
22. Ⓐ Ⓑ Ⓒ Ⓓ Ⓔ
23. Ⓐ Ⓑ Ⓒ Ⓓ Ⓔ
24. Ⓐ Ⓑ Ⓒ Ⓓ Ⓔ
25. Ⓐ Ⓑ Ⓒ Ⓓ Ⓔ

26. Ⓐ Ⓑ Ⓒ Ⓓ Ⓔ
27. Ⓐ Ⓑ Ⓒ Ⓓ Ⓔ
28. Ⓐ Ⓑ Ⓒ Ⓓ Ⓔ
29. Ⓐ Ⓑ Ⓒ Ⓓ Ⓔ
30. Ⓐ Ⓑ Ⓒ Ⓓ Ⓔ
31. Ⓐ Ⓑ Ⓒ Ⓓ Ⓔ
32. Ⓐ Ⓑ Ⓒ Ⓓ Ⓔ
33. Ⓐ Ⓑ Ⓒ Ⓓ Ⓔ
34. Ⓐ Ⓑ Ⓒ Ⓓ Ⓔ
35. Ⓐ Ⓑ Ⓒ Ⓓ Ⓔ
36. Ⓐ Ⓑ Ⓒ Ⓓ Ⓔ
37. Ⓐ Ⓑ Ⓒ Ⓓ Ⓔ
38. Ⓐ Ⓑ Ⓒ Ⓓ Ⓔ
39. Ⓐ Ⓑ Ⓒ Ⓓ Ⓔ
40. Ⓐ Ⓑ Ⓒ Ⓓ Ⓔ
41. Ⓐ Ⓑ Ⓒ Ⓓ Ⓔ
42. Ⓐ Ⓑ Ⓒ Ⓓ Ⓔ
43. Ⓐ Ⓑ Ⓒ Ⓓ Ⓔ
44. Ⓐ Ⓑ Ⓒ Ⓓ Ⓔ
45. Ⓐ Ⓑ Ⓒ Ⓓ Ⓔ
46. Ⓐ Ⓑ Ⓒ Ⓓ Ⓔ
47. Ⓐ Ⓑ Ⓒ Ⓓ Ⓔ
48. Ⓐ Ⓑ Ⓒ Ⓓ Ⓔ
49. Ⓐ Ⓑ Ⓒ Ⓓ Ⓔ
50. Ⓐ Ⓑ Ⓒ Ⓓ Ⓔ

ARITHMETIC DIAGNOSTIC TEST

This diagnostic test is designed to help you determine your strengths and your weaknesses in arithmetic. Follow the directions for each part and check your answers.

> ## Study this chapter for the following tests:
> ## PSAT, SAT I, ACT, NTE, PPST, CBEST, GRE, GMAT, GED, and ELM

50 Questions

DIRECTIONS: Choose the correct answer for each of the following problems. Fill in the answer on the answer sheet.

1. What part of three fourths is one tenth?

   (A) $\frac{1}{8}$ (B) $\frac{15}{2}$ (C) $\frac{2}{15}$

   (D) $\frac{3}{40}$ (E) None of the above

2. One number is 2 more than 3 times another. Their sum is 22. Find the numbers.

   (A) 8, 14   (B) 2, 20   (C) 5, 17

   (D) 4, 18   (E) 10, 12

3. What is the median of the following group of scores?

   27, 27, 26, 26, 26, 26, 18, 13, 36, 36, 30, 30, 30, 27, 29

   (A) 30   (B) 26   (C) 25.4

   (D) 27   (E) 36

4. What percent of 260 is 13?

   (A) .05%   (B) 5%   (C) 50%

   (D) .5%   (E) 20%

5. Subtract: $4\frac{1}{3} - 1\frac{5}{6}$

   (A) $3\frac{2}{3}$ (B) $2\frac{1}{2}$ (C) $3\frac{1}{2}$

   (D) $2\frac{1}{6}$ (E) None of the above

6. What is the product of $(\sqrt{3} + 6)$ and $(\sqrt{3} - 2)$?

(A) $9 + 4\sqrt{3}$ (B) -9 (C) $-9 + 4\sqrt{3}$

(D) $-9 + 2\sqrt{3}$ (E) 9

7. The number missing in the series, 2, 6, 12, 20, x, 42, 56 is:

(A) 36   (B) 24   (C) 30

(D) 38   (E) 40

8. What is the value of the following expression: $\dfrac{1}{1 + \dfrac{1}{1 + \dfrac{1}{4}}}$

(A) $^9/_5$ (B) $^5/_9$ (C) $^1/_2$

(D) 2   (E) 4

9. Which of the following has the smallest value?

(A) $^1/_{0.2}$ (B) $^{0.1}/_2$ (C) $^{0.2}/_1$

(D) $^{0.2}/_{0.1}$ (E) $^2/_{0.1}$

10. Which is the smallest number?

(A) $5 \cdot 10^{-3} / 3 \cdot 10^{-3}$ (B) $.3 / .2$

(C) $.3 / 3 \cdot 10^{-3}$ (D) $5 \cdot 10^{-2} / .1$

(E) $.3 / 3 \cdot 10^{-1}$

11. $10^3 + 10^5 =$

(A) 10^8 (B) 10^{15} (C) 20^8

(D) 2^{15} (E) 101,000

12. How many digits are in the standard numeral for $2^{31} \cdot 5^{27}$?

(A) 31   (B) 29   (C) 28

(D) 26   (E) 25

13. $475,826 \cdot 521,653 + 524,174 \cdot 521,653 =$

    (A) 621,592,047,600   (B) 519,697,450,000

    (C) 495,652,831,520   (D) 521,653,000,000

    (E) 524,174,000,000

14. How many ways can you make change for a quarter?

    (A) 8   (B) 9   (C) 10

    (D) 12   (E) 14

15. The sixtieth digit in the decimal representation of $1/7$ is

    (A) 1   (B) 4   (C) 2

    (D) 5   (E) 7

16. What is the least prime number which is a divisor of $7^9 + 11^{25}$?

    (A) 1   (B) 2   (C) 3

    (D) 5   (E) $7^9 + 11^{25}$

17. Evaluate $10 - 5[2^3 + 27 \div 3 - 2(8 - 10)]$

    (A) -95 (B) 105   (C) 65

    (D) -55 (E) -85

18. Fifteen percent of what number is 60?

    (A) 9   (B) 51   (C) 69

    (D) 200   (E) 400

19. Which is the largest fraction: $1/5$, $2/9$, $2/11$, $4/19$, $4/17$?

    (A) $1/5$ (B) $2/9$ (C) $2/11$

    (D) $4/19$ (E) $4/17$

20. How many of the scores 10, 20, 30, 35, 55 are larger than their arithmetic mean score?

    (A) None   (B) One   (C) Two

    (D) Three   (E) Four

21. Evaluate $\left(2^{1-\sqrt{3}}\right)^{1+\sqrt{3}}$

    (A) 4   (B) -4 (C) 16

    (D) $\frac{1}{2}$ (E) $\frac{1}{4}$

22. $\dfrac{2^{100} + 2^{98}}{2^{100} - 2^{98}} =$

    (A) 2^{198} (B) 2^{99} (C) 64

    (D) 4   (E) $\frac{5}{3}$

23. What is the least natural number which is a multiple of each number from 1 to 10?

    (A) 3,628,800   (B) 5040   (C) 840

    (D) 1,260   (E) 2,520

24. If in $\triangle ABC$, $AB = BC$ and angle A has measure $46°$, then angle B has measure

    (A) $46°$ (B) $92°$ (C) $88°$

    (D) $56°$ (E) $23°$

25. What is the last digit in the number 3^{2000}?

    (A) 0   (B) 1   (C) 3

    (D) 7   (E) 9

26. In the set of integers 1000, 1001, 1002, ..., 9998, 9999, how many of the numbers do not contain the digit 5?

    (A) 6,561   (B) 5,000   (C) 9,000

    (D) 4,500   (E) 5,832

27. $15,561 \div 25 + 9,439 \div 25 =$

    (A) 997   (B) 1,000   (C) 1,002

    (D) 1,005   (E) 1,005.08

28. What is the units digit for 4^{891}?

    (A) 4   (B) 6   (C) 8

    (D) 0   (E) 1

29. $\dfrac{1}{1\cdot2}+\dfrac{1}{2\cdot3}+\dfrac{1}{3\cdot4}+\ldots+\dfrac{1}{99\cdot100}=$

    (A) $^{49}/_{50}$ (B) $^{74}/_{75}$ (C) $^{98}/_{99}$

    (D) $^{99}/_{100}$ (E) $^{101}/_{100}$

30. $1 + 2 + 3 + 4 + \ldots + 99 =$

    (A) 4,700   (B) 4,750   (C) 4,850

    (D) 4,900   (E) 4,950

31. The decimal $.24\overline{24}$ expressed as a fraction is

    (A) $^8/_{33}$ (B) $^6/_{25}$ (C) $^1/_4$

    (D) $^{303}/_{1250}$ (E) $^{121}/_{500}$

32. $\dfrac{2^{-4}+2^{-1}}{2^{-3}}$

    (A) $9/2^7$ (B) $9/2^{-1}$ (C) $1/2$

    (D) 2^{-3} (E) $9/2$

33. What is the smallest positive number that leaves a remainder of 2 when the number is divided by 3, 4 or 5?

    (A) 22   (B) 42   (C) 62

    (D) 122   (E) 182

34. What part of three eights is one tenth?

    (A) $^1/_8$ (B) $^{15}/_2$ (C) $^4/_{15}$

    (D) $^3/_{40}$ (E) None of the above

35. $(^2/_3) + (^5/_9) =$

    (A) $^7/_{12}$ (B) $^{11}/_9$ (C) $^7/_3$

    (D) $^7/_9$ (E) $^{11}/_3$

36. Add $^3/_6 + {}^2/_6$

    (A) $^1/_{12}$ (B) $^5/_6$ (C) $^5/_{12}$

    (D) $^8/_9$ (E) $^9/_8$

37. Change 125.937% to a decimal

    (A) 1.25937 (B) 12.5937 (C) 125.937

    (D) 1259.37 (E) 12593.7

38. What is the ratio of 8 feet to 28 inches?

    (A) $^1/_7$ (B) $^7/_1$ (C) $^{24}/_7$

    (D) $^6/_7$ (E) $^7/_2$

39. Using order of operations, solve: $3 * 6 - 12/2 =$

    (A) -9 (B) 3 (C) 6

    (D) 12 (E) 18

40. The most economical price among the following prices is

    (A) 10 oz. for 16¢ (B) 2 oz. for 3¢

    (C) 4 oz. for 7¢ (D) 20 oz. for 34¢

    (E) 8 oz. for 13¢

41. Change $4^5/_6$ to an improper fraction.

    (A) $^5/_{24}$ (B) $^9/_6$ (C) $^{29}/_6$

    (D) $^{30}/_4$ (E) $^{120}/_6$

42. If the sum of four consecutive integers is 226, then the smallest of these numbers is

    (A) 55 (B) 56 (C) 57

    (D) 58 (E) 59

1/2 hr.

43. How much time is left on the parking meter shown on the previous page?

    (A) 8 minutes   (B) 9 minutes   (C) 10 minutes

    (D) 12 minutes   (E) 15 minutes

44. $15{,}561 \div 25 - 9{,}561 \div 25 =$

    (A) 997   (B) 240   (C) 1,002

    (D) 1,005   (E) 1,005.08

45. $4\% \cdot 4\% =$

    (A) 0.0016%   (B) 0.16%   (C) 1.6%

    (D) 16%   (E) 160%

46. Which of the following numbers is not between $.8\overline{5}$ and $.8\overline{6}$?

    (A) $.8\overline{51}$ (B) $.8\overline{59}$ (C) $.859$

    (D) $.8\overline{61}$ (E) $.861$

47. Change the fraction $^7/_8$ to a decimal.

    (A) .666   (B) .75   (C) .777

    (D) .875   (E) 1.142

48. $\sqrt{75} - 3\sqrt{48} + \sqrt{147} =$

    (A) $3\sqrt{3}$ (B) $7\sqrt{3}$ (C) 0

    (D) 3   (E) $\sqrt{3}$

49. The following ratio: 40 seconds : $1\frac{1}{2}$ minutes : $\frac{1}{6}$ hour, can be expressed in lowest terms as

    (A) $4 : 9 : 60$ (B) $4 : 9 : 6$ (C) $40 : 90 : 60$

    (D) $^2/_3 : 1^1/_2 : 10$ (E) $60 : 9 : 4$

50. Simplify $6\sqrt{7} + 4\sqrt{7} - \sqrt{5} + 5\sqrt{7}$

    (A) $10\sqrt{7}$ (B) $15\sqrt{7} - \sqrt{5}$ (C) $15\sqrt{21} - \sqrt{5}$

    (D) $15\sqrt{16}$ (E) 60

ARITHMETIC DIAGNOSTIC TEST

ANSWER KEY

1. (C)	11. (E)	21. (E)	31. (A)	41. (C)
2. (C)	12. (B)	22. (E)	32. (E)	42. (A)
3. (D)	13. (D)	23. (E)	33. (C)	43. (B)
4. (B)	14. (D)	24. (C)	34. (C)	44. (B)
5. (B)	15. (E)	25. (B)	35. (B)	45. (B)
6. (C)	16. (B)	26. (E)	36. (B)	46. (A)
7. (C)	17. (A)	27. (B)	37. (A)	47. (D)
8. (B)	18. (E)	28. (A)	38. (C)	48. (C)
9. (B)	19. (E)	29. (D)	39. (D)	49. (A)
10. (D)	20. (C)	30. (E)	40. (B)	50. (B)

DETAILED EXPLANATIONS
OF ANSWERS

1. **(C)** First, observe that three fourths is $^3/_4$ and one tenth is $^1/_{10}$. Let x be the unknown part which must be found. Then, one can write from the statement of the problem that the x part of three fourths is given by:

$$\frac{3}{4}x.$$

The equation for the problem is given by

$$\frac{3}{4}x = \frac{1}{10}.$$

Multiplying both sides of the equation by the reciprocal of $^3/_4$ one obtains the following:

$$\frac{4}{3}\frac{3}{4}x = \frac{4}{3}\frac{1}{10} \text{ or } x = \frac{4}{30} \text{ or } x = \frac{2}{15}$$

which is choice (C).

Response (D) is obtained by incorrectly finding the product of $^3/_4$ and $^1/_{10}$ to be the unknown part. Response (B) is obtained by dividing $^3/_4$ by $^1/_{10}$.

2. **(C)** Based on the information given in the first sentence of the problem one needs to first represent the unknown numbers. So let x be a number. Then, the other number is given by $3x + 2$, which is two more than 3 times the first number. So the two numbers are:

x and $3x + 2$.

Next, form an equation by adding the two numbers and setting the sum equal to 22 and then solve the equation for the two numbers.

$$x + 3x + 2 = 22$$
$$4x + 2 = 22$$
$$4x = 20$$
$$x = 5,$$

one of the numbers. The other number is given by

$$3x + 2 = 3(5) + 2 = 15 + 2 = 17,$$

the other number. Hence, answer choice (C) is correct. The other answer choices fail to satisfy the equation $x + 3x + 2 = 22$.

3. **(D)** The median is defined as the middle score or value when a sequence of numbers is arranged in either ascending or descending order. Thus, when this is done the middle score is 27. The answer choice (B) is the mode, the most frequent score. The other answer choices do not represent the median according to its definition.

4. **(B)** In order to find what percent of 260 is 13 one needs only to form the following equation:

$$x\%(260) = 13$$

$$\frac{x(260)}{100} = 13$$

$$260x = 13(100)$$

$$x = 1300/260 = 5 \text{ percent} = 5\%.$$

The other answer choices are incorrect, however. Response (A) is obtained by dividing 13 by 260 and attaching the percent symbol. Response (D) is obtained by again dividing 13 by 260, moving the decimal point one place to the right and attaching the percent symbol. Response (E) is obtained by dividing 260 by 13 and attaching the percent sign. Finally, response (C) is absurd because 50% of 260 is half of 260 which is 130 or 10 times 13.

5. **(B)**

$$4\frac{1}{3} - 1\frac{5}{6} = 4\frac{2}{6} - 1\frac{5}{6}$$

$$= 3\frac{2+6}{6} - 1\frac{5}{6}$$

$$= 3\frac{8}{6} - 1\frac{5}{6}$$

$$= 2\frac{3}{6} = 2\frac{1}{2}.$$

6. **(C)** Observe that to find the product the following multiplications should be done.

$$(\sqrt{3} + 6)(\sqrt{3} - 2) = \sqrt{3}(\sqrt{3} - 2) + 6(\sqrt{3} - 2)$$

$$= 3 - 2\sqrt{3} + 6\sqrt{3} - 12$$

$$= -9 + 4\sqrt{3}.$$

7. **(C)** The difference between the first two numbers is 4 (6 − 2); the difference between the second and third numbers is 6 (12 − 6) which is two more than the first difference; the difference between the third and fourth numbers is

8 (20 – 12) which is two more than the second difference; the difference between the fourth and fifth numbers is 10 (x – 20). Thus, the value of x is given by x – 20 = 10. Solving for x yields x = 30. So, the correct answer choice is (C). Similar analysis of each of the other choices will fail to satisfy the missing value of x such that it is a consistant distance in relation to the other numbers in the series.

8.   **(B)**

$$\frac{1}{1+\dfrac{1}{1+\dfrac{1}{1+\dfrac{1}{4}}}} = \frac{1}{1+\dfrac{1}{4+1}} = \frac{1}{1+\dfrac{4}{5}} = \frac{5}{5+4} = \frac{5}{9}.$$

9.   **(B)**   Note that $\dfrac{.1}{2} = \dfrac{.1 \times 10}{2 \times 10} = \dfrac{1}{20}$ for response (B).

For Choice (A), $\dfrac{1}{.2} = \dfrac{1 \times 10}{.2 \times 10} = \dfrac{10}{2} = 5$ which is larger than $^1/_{20}$.

For Choice (C), $\dfrac{.2}{1} = \dfrac{.2 \times 10}{1 \times 10} = \dfrac{2}{10} = \dfrac{1}{5}$ which is larger than $^1/_{20}$.

For Choice (D), $\dfrac{.2}{.1} = \dfrac{.2 \times 10}{.1 \times 10} = \dfrac{2}{1} = 2$ which is larger than $^1/_{20}$.

For Choice (E), $\dfrac{2}{.1} = \dfrac{2 \times 10}{.1 \times 10} = \dfrac{20}{1} = 20$ which is larger than $^1/_{20}$.

10.   **(D)**   To find the smallest number we will calculate each one

(A) $\dfrac{5 \cdot 10^{-3}}{3 \cdot 10^{-3}} = \dfrac{5 \cdot 10^{-3}}{3 \cdot 10^{-3}} = \dfrac{5}{3} = 1.6$

(B) $\dfrac{.3}{.2} = \dfrac{.3}{.2} = 1.5$

(C) $\dfrac{.3}{3} \cdot 10^{-3} = \dfrac{.3}{3 \cdot 10^{-3}} = \dfrac{.3 \cdot 10^3}{3} = \dfrac{3 \cdot 10^2}{3} = 100$

(D) $5 \cdot \dfrac{10^{-2}}{.1} = \dfrac{5 \cdot 10^{-2}}{.1} = \dfrac{5 \cdot 10^{-2}}{10^{-1}} = 5 \cdot 10^{-1} = .5$

(E) $\dfrac{.3}{3} \cdot 10^{-1} = \dfrac{.3}{3 \cdot 10^{-1}} = \dfrac{.3 \cdot 10}{3} = \dfrac{3}{3} = 1$

The correct answer is (D).

11. **(E)** $10^3 + 10^5 = 10^3 \cdot 1 + 10^3 \cdot 10^2$

$= 10^3 (1 + 10^2)$

$= 10^3 (101)$ or $10^3 = 1,000$ and $10^5 = 100,000$

$= 1,000 \cdot 101$ and thus $10^3 + 10^5 = 101,000$

$= 101,000.$

12. **(B)** $2^{31} \cdot 5^{27} = 2^4 \cdot 2^{27} \cdot 5^{27}$

$= 2^4 (2 \cdot 5)^{27}$

$= 2^4 \cdot 10^{27}$

Since $2^4 = 16$, the standard numeral for $2^4 \cdot 10^{27}$ is 16 followed by 27 zeros. Hence $2^{31} \cdot 5^{27}$ has 29 digits.

13. **(D)** Using the distributive property,

$475,826 \cdot 521,653 + 524,174 \cdot 521,653$

$= (475,826 + 524,174)521,653$

$= 1,000,000(521,653)$

$= 521,653,000,000.$

14. **(D)** The table below indicates the ways that change for a quarter can be made.

Dimes	Nickels	Pennies
2	1	0
2	0	5
1	3	0
1	2	5
1	1	10
1	0	15
0	5	0
0	4	5
0	3	10
0	2	15
0	1	20
0	0	25

15. **(E)** The decimal representation of $1/7$ is

$.142857142857142857...,$

and the digit in the 6th, 12th, 18th, ... 60th place is 7.

16.   **(B)**   Since 7^9 and 11^{25} are both odd numbers, their sum is even. Thus, 2 is a divisor of $7^9 + 11^{25}$. Also 2 is the smallest (least) prime.

17.   **(A)**   Remember the order of operation rules are PEMDAS, meaning parentheses, exponents, multiplication, division, addition, and subtraction. The correct solution is

$$10 - 5[8 + 9 - 2)(-2)] \Rightarrow 10 - 5(21) \Rightarrow 10 - 105 = -95.$$

Choice (B) comes from subtracting 10 and 5 before multiplying. $10 - 5 = 5$ and $5(21) = 105$.

Choice (C) comes from $17 - 4$ instead of $17 + 4$ inside the parentheses and also the mistake of subtracting $10 - 5$ first. This gives $5(13) = 65$.

Choice (D) comes from the mistake of $17 - 4$ without the additional mistake of subtracting $10 - 5$ first. This gives $10 - 5(13) = 10 - 65 = -55$.

Choice (E) comes from making $2^3 = 6$ instead of 8. This gives $10 - 5(19) = 10 - 95 = -85$.

18.   **(E)**   If X is the number, then $.15X = 60$. Therefore,

$$X = {}^{60}/_{.15} = 400.$$

19.   **(E)**   Since $^1/_5 = {}^2/_{10}$, $^2/_9$ is larger than either $^1/_5$ or $^2/_{11}$. Also $^4/_{17}$ is larger than $^4/_{19}$. Now $^2/_9 = {}^4/_{18}$ so that $^4/_{17}$ is larger than the two.

20.   **(C)**   The arithmetic mean of scores is

$$(10 + 20 + 30 + 35 + 55)/5 = 150/5 = 30.$$

Since only two scores, namely, 35 and 55 are larger than 30, the answer is (C).

21.   **(E)**

$$(1 - \sqrt{3})(1 + \sqrt{3}) = 1 - 3 = -2.$$

And $2^{-2} = \dfrac{1}{2^2} = \dfrac{1}{4}.$

Choice (A) comes from adding the exponents $1 - \sqrt{3} + 1 + \sqrt{3} = 2$, and $2^2 = 4$.

Choice (B) comes from incorrectly letting $2^{-2} = -4$.

Choice (C) comes from $2^{1+3} = 2^4 = 16$.

22.   **(E)**
$$\frac{2^{100} + 2^{98}}{2^{100} - 2^{98}} = \frac{2^{98}(2^2 + 1)}{2^{98}(2^2 - 1)}$$

$$= \frac{2^2 + 1}{2^2 - 1} = \frac{5}{3}.$$

23.   **(E)**   Notice the product below. Starting from the left, it is obvious that 2 and 3 are needed as factors. For the product to be a multiple of 4, two 2 factors are needed and that is the reason for the second 2 factor. Obviously, a factor of 5 is needed; but since 2 and 3 are already listed, the product is already a multiple of 6. A factor of 7 is needed, but only new factors of 2 and 3 are required to make the product a multiple of 8 and 9. Since 2 and 5 are already listed as factors, the product is already a multiple of 10.

$$2 \cdot 3 \cdot 2 \cdot 5 \cdot 7 \cdot 2 \cdot 3 = 2,520$$

24.   **(C)**   Since $AB = BC$, angle C has measure 46°. However, the sum of the measures of the angles of a tringle is 180° and $180 - (46 + 46) = 88$ so the measure of angle B is 88°.

25.   **(B)**   The last digit in the successive powers of 3 repeat at intervals of 4:

$$3^1 = 3, 3^5 = 243$$
$$3^2 = 9, 3^6 = 729$$
$$3^3 = 27, 3^7 = 2,187$$
$$3^4 = 81, 3^8 = 6,561.$$

The pattern is 3, 9, 7, 1, 3, 9, 7, 1, ... and since $2000 = 4(500)$, 3^{2000} has a last digit of 1.

Choice (A) comes from $3(2000) = 6000$.

Choices (C), (D), and (E), which are 3, 7, and 9, respectively are the other ending digits in the power of 3.

26.   **(E)**   For a 4-digit number, there are $9 \cdot 10 \cdot 10 \cdot 10$ possibilities because 0 may not be used for the thousands place but if the digit 5 is not allowed, then there are $8 \cdot 9 \cdot 9 \cdot 9 = 5,832$ possibilities.

Choice (A) is $9 \cdot 9 \cdot 9 \cdot 9$.

Choice (C) is $9 \cdot 10 \cdot 10 \cdot 10$.

27.   **(B)**   When $c \neq 0$

$$a \div c + b \div c = (a + b) \div c.$$

Thus

$$15,561 \div 25 + 9,439 \div 25 = (15,561 + (9,439) \div 25$$
$$= 25,000 \div 25$$
$$= 1,000.$$

28.   **(A)**   When n is odd, the units digit for 4^n is 4, and when n is even, the units digit for $4n$ is 6.

29.   **(D)**

$$\frac{1}{1\cdot 2}+\frac{1}{2\cdot 3}=\frac{1}{2}+\frac{1}{6} \qquad \frac{1}{1\cdot 2}+\frac{1}{2\cdot 3}+\frac{1}{3\cdot 4}=\frac{1}{2}+\frac{1}{6}+\frac{1}{12}$$

$$=\frac{2}{3} \qquad\qquad\qquad\qquad =\frac{3}{4}$$

$$\frac{1}{1\cdot 2}+\frac{1}{2\cdot 3}+\frac{1}{3\cdot 4}+\frac{1}{4\cdot 5}=\frac{1}{2}+\frac{1}{6}+\frac{1}{12}+\frac{1}{20}$$

$$=\frac{4}{5}$$

and $$\frac{1}{1\cdot 2}+\frac{1}{2\cdot 3}+\frac{1}{3\cdot 4}+\ldots+\frac{1}{99\cdot 100}=\frac{99}{100}$$

30.   **(E)**

$$1+2+3+\ldots+49+50+51+\ldots+97+98+99 = 49\cdot 100+50$$

$$= 4950$$

31.   **(A)**   Let $.24\overline{24}=X$. Then,

$$100X=100(.24\overline{24})=24.\overline{24}=24.24\overline{24}.$$

It follows that

$$100X-X=24.2424-.24\overline{24}=24,$$

so that $X=\frac{24}{99}=\frac{8}{33}$.

32.   **(E)**

$$\frac{2^{-4}+2^{-1}}{2^{-3}}=\frac{\dfrac{1}{2^4}+\dfrac{1}{2}}{\dfrac{1}{2^3}}=\frac{2^4\left(\dfrac{1}{2^4}+\dfrac{1}{2}\right)}{2^4\dfrac{1}{2^3}}=\frac{1+2^3}{2}=\frac{9}{2}.$$

33.   **(C)**   First find the least common multiple (LCM) of 3, 4, and 5, which is simply

$$3 \times 4 \times 5 = 60.$$

Since 3 divides 60, 4 divides 60, and 5 divides 60, then one needs only to add 2 to 60 in order to guarantee that the remainder in each case will be 2 when 3, 4, and 5, respectively, are divided into 62.

34.   **(C)**   First, observe that three eights is $^3/_8$ and one tenth is $^1/_{10}$. Let x be the unknown part which must be found. Then, one can write from the statement of the problem that the x part of three eighths is given by:

$$\frac{3}{8}x.$$

The equation for the problem is given by

$$\frac{3}{8}x = \frac{1}{10}.$$

Multiplying both sides of the equation by the reciprocal of $^3/_8$ one obtains the following:

$$\frac{8}{3}\frac{3}{8}x = \frac{8}{3}\frac{1}{10} \text{ or } x = \frac{8}{30} \text{ or } x = \frac{4}{15}$$

which is choice (C).

Response (D) is obtained by incorrectly finding the product of $^3/_4$ and $^1/_{10}$ to be the unknown part. Response (B) is obtained by dividing $^3/_4$ by $^1/_{10}$.

35.   **(B)**   A common denominator is needed to add fractions. The least common denominator in this problem is 9 since the smallest number that both 3 and 9 will divide into is 9. If the denominator of $^2/_3$ is multiplied by 3 then the numerator must also be multiplied by 3. Thus

$$(2 \times 3) / (3 \times 3) = 6/9.$$

Adding the numerators and using the common denominator,

$$(6/9) + (5/9) = (6 + 5)/9 = 11/9.$$

36.   **(B)**   To add fractions with a common denominator, add the numerators.

$$3 + 2 = 5$$

Write the sum over the common denominator. The correct answer is $^5/_6$.

37.   **(A)**   To change percent to a decimal, drop the percent sign and move the decimal point two place values to the left. The correct answer is 1.25937.

38.   **(C)**   Units of measurement must be the same to create a ratio. Multiply 8

* 12 to find the number of inches in 8 feet which is 96. The ratio of 96 to 28 is 96/28. Find a common factor of 96 and 28, which is 4. Divide 96 by 4, which is 24, and 28 by 4, which is 7. The correct answer is 24/7.

39.　　**(D)**　　In order of operations, do all multiplication and division from left to right first. Next, do all addition and subtraction from left to right.

　　　3 * 6 – 12/2　　　multiply 3 times 6, divide 12 by 2

　　　18 – 6　　　　　subtract 6 from 18

　　　12.

40.　　**(B)**　　This problem can be solved as follows:

1.　Divide each price by the number of ounces in each price to obtain the following prices per ounce for the given prices in answer choices (A) through (E):

$$(A)\frac{16}{10}\ ¢,\ (B)\frac{3}{2}¢,\ (C)\frac{7}{4}¢,\ (D)\frac{34}{20}¢,\ (E)\frac{13}{8}¢$$

2.　Change each of the prices per ounce obtained in step (1) above to an equivalent fraction having a denominator equal to the least common denominator, 40, we obtain,

$$(A)\frac{16}{10}=\frac{64}{40};\ (B)\frac{3}{2}=\frac{60}{40};(C)\frac{7}{4}=\frac{70}{40};(D)\frac{34}{20}=\frac{68}{40};\text{ and }(E)\frac{13}{8}=\frac{65}{40}.$$

Since the smallest of the resulting fractions in step (2) is $^{60}/_{40}$, it follows that the most economical price among the given prices is 2 oz. for 3¢.

41.　　**(C)**　　To change a mixed number to an improper fraction, multiply the whole number (4) by the denominator (6) of the fraction (4 times 6 is 24). Add the numerator (5) to the product (24). Write the sum (29) over the denominator of the fraction, $^{29}/_6$.

42.　　**(A)**　　If the smallest number is X, then

　　　$X + (X + 1) + (X + 2) + (X + 3) = 226,$

giving

　　　$4X + 6 = 226$

Therefore

　　　$4X = 220,$ or, $X = 55.$

43.　　**(B)**　　The meter shows that $^3/_{10}$ of the total time on the meter is left. However, this is a $^1/_2$-hour meter. Since

　　　$^3/_{10} \cdot ^1/_2 = ^3/_{20},$

this means that there is $^3/_{20}$ of an hour left on the meter, and $^3/_{20}$ of an hour is 9 minutes.

44.   **(B)**   When $c \neq 0$

$$a \div c - b \div c = (a - b) \div c.$$

Thus,

$$15,561 \div 25 - 9,561 \div 25 = (15,561 - 9,561) \div 25$$
$$= 6,000 \div 25$$
$$= 240.$$

45.   **(B)**

$$4\% \cdot 4\% = .04 \cdot .04$$
$$= .0016$$
$$= .16\%$$

46.   **(A)**   Since $.\overline{85} = .858585 \dots$ and

$.\overline{851} = .851851851 \dots ,$

$.\overline{851} < .\overline{85} < .\overline{86}$

47.   **(D)**   To change a fraction to a decimal, divide the numerator (7) by the denominator (8)

$8 \div 7.$

Add a decimal point after the 7 and necessary zeros.

48.   **(C)**   Certainly, the easiest and the most direct way to solve this problem is to perform the indicated operations.
    Performing the indicated operations yields,

$$\sqrt{75} - 3\sqrt{48} + \sqrt{147} = \sqrt{(25)(3)} - 3\sqrt{(16)(3)} + \sqrt{(49)(3)}$$
$$= 5\sqrt{3} - 3(4)\sqrt{3} + 7\sqrt{3}$$
$$= 5\sqrt{3} - 12\sqrt{3} + 7\sqrt{3}$$
$$= (5 - 12 + 7)\sqrt{3}$$
$$= (12 - 12)\sqrt{3}$$
$$= 0.\sqrt{3}$$
$$= 0$$

49.　**(A)**　Since 40 seconds is $^2/_3$ minute and $^1/_6$ hour is ten minutes, the ratio is

$^2/_3 : 1.5 : 10.$

Multiplying by 6 yields

$6(^2/_3) : 6(3/2) : 6(10)$ or $4 : 9 : 60.$

Thus the correct choice is (A).

50.　**(B)**　To combine radicals, the radicands (the value under the radical sign) must be equal. The distributive property allows you to add and subtract radicals.

$$\left(6\sqrt{7} + 4\sqrt{7}\right) - \sqrt{5} + 5\sqrt{7}$$
$$(6 + 4)\sqrt{7} - \sqrt{5} + 5\sqrt{7}$$
$$10\sqrt{7} - \sqrt{5} + 5\sqrt{7}$$
$$(10 + 5)\sqrt{7} - \sqrt{5}$$
$$15\sqrt{7} - \sqrt{5}$$

ARITHMETIC REVIEW

1. Integers and Real Numbers

Most of the numbers used in algebra belong to a set called the **real numbers** or **reals**. This set can be represented graphically by the real number line.

Given the number line below, we arbitrarily fix a point and label it with the number 0. In a similar manner, we can label any point on the line with one of the real numbers, depending on its position relative to 0. Numbers to the right of zero are positive, while those to the left are negative. Value increases from left to right, so that if a is to the right of b, it is said to be greater than b.

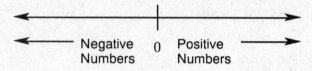

If we now divide the number line into equal segments, we can label the points on this line with real numbers. For example, the point 2 lengths to the left of zero is -2, while the point 3 lengths to the right of zero is $+3$ (the $+$ sign is usually assumed, so $+3$ is written simply as 3). The number line now looks like this:

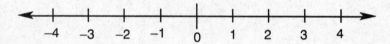

These boundary points represent the subset of the reals known as the **integers**. The set of integers is made up of both the positive and negative whole numbers: $\{\ldots -4, -3, -2, -1, 0, 1, 2, 3, 4, \ldots\}$. Some subsets of integers are:

Natural Numbers or Positive Numbers — the set of integers starting with 1 and increasing: $\mathcal{N} = \{1, 2, 3, 4, \ldots\}$.

Whole Numbers — the set of integers starting with 0 and increasing: $\mathcal{W} = \{0, 1, 2, 3, \ldots\}$.

Negative Numbers — the set of integers starting with -1 and decreasing: $\mathcal{Z} = \{-1, -2, -3 \ldots\}$.

Prime Numbers — the set of positive integers greater than 1 that are divisible only by 1 and themselves: $\{2, 3, 5, 7, 11, \ldots\}$.

Even Integers — the set of integers divisible by 2: $\{\ldots, -4, -2, 0, 2, 4, 6, \ldots\}$.

Odd Integers — the set of integers not divisible by 2: $\{\ldots, -3, -1, 1, 3, 5, 7, \ldots\}$.

PROBLEM

Classify each of the following numbers into as many different sets as possible. Example: real, integer ...

(1) 0   (2) 9   (3) $\sqrt{6}$

(4) $^1/_2$ (5) $^2/_3$ (6) 1.5

SOLUTION

(1) Zero is a real number and an integer.

(2) 9 is a real, natural number, and an integer.

(3) $\sqrt{6}$ is a real number.

(4) $^1/_2$ is a real number.

(5) $^2/_3$ is a real number.

(6) 1.5 is a real number.

ABSOLUTE VALUE

The **absolute value** of a number is represented by two vertical lines around the number, and is equal to the given number, regardless of sign.

The absolute value of a real number A is defined as follows:

$$|A| = \begin{cases} A \text{ if } A \geq 0 \\ -A \text{ if } A < 0 \end{cases}$$

EXAMPLE

$|5| = 5, |-8| = -(-8) = 8.$

Absolute values follow the given rules:

(A) $|-A| = |A|$

(B) $|A| \geq 0$, equality holding only if $A = 0$

(C) $\left|\dfrac{A}{B}\right| = \dfrac{|A|}{|B|}, B \neq 0$

(D) $|AB| = |A| \times |B|$

(E) $|A|^2 = A^2$

Absolute value can also be expressed on the real number line as the distance of the point represented by the real number from the point labeled 0.

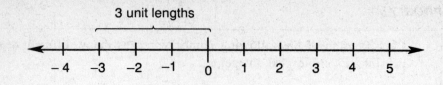

So $|-3| = 3$ because -3 is 3 units to the left of 0.

PROBLEM

Classify each of the following statements as true or false. If it is false, explain why.

(1) $|-120| > 1$

(2) $|4-12| = |4|-|12|$

(3) $|4-9| = 9-4$

(4) $|12-3| = 12-3$

(5) $|-12a| = 12|a|$

SOLUTION

(1)   True

(2)   False, $|4-12| = |4|-|12|$

$$|-8| = 4-12$$

$$8 \neq -8$$

In general, $|a+b| \neq |a|+|b|$

(3)   True

(4)   True

(5)   True

PROBLEM

Calculate the value of each of the following expressions:

(1) $||2-5|+6-14|$

(2) $|-5|\cdot|4|+\dfrac{|-12|}{4}$

SOLUTION

Before solving this problem, one must remember the order of operations: parenthesis, multiplication and division, addition and subtraction.

(1) $||-3|+6-14| = |3+6-14| = |9-14| = |-5| = 5$

(2) $(5 \times 4) + {}^{12}/_4 = 20+3 = 23$

PROBLEM

Find the absolute value for each of the following:

(1) zero

(3) $-\pi$

(2) 4

(4) a, where a is a real number

SOLUTION

(1) $|0| = 0$

(2) $|4| = 4$

(3) $|-\pi| = \pi$

(4) for $a > 0 \; |a| = a$

for $a = 0 \; |a| = 0$

for $a < 0 \; |a| = -a$

i.e., $|a| = \begin{cases} a \text{ if } a > 0 \\ 0 \text{ if } a = 0 \\ -a \text{ if } a < 0 \end{cases}$

POSITIVE AND NEGATIVE NUMBERS

A) **To add two numbers with like signs,** add their absolute values and write the sum with the common sign. So,

$$6 + 2 = 8, (-6) + (-2) = -8$$

B) **To add two numbers with unlike signs,** find the difference between their absolute values, and write the result with the sign of the number with the greater absolute value. So,

$$(-4) + 6 = 2, 15 + (-19) = -4$$

C) **To subtract a number b from another number a,** change the sign of b and add to a. Examples:

$$10 - (3) = 10 + (-3) = 7 \tag{1}$$

$$2 - (-6) = 2 + 6 = 8 \tag{2}$$

$$(-5) - (-2) = -5 + (+2) = -3 \tag{3}$$

D) **To multiply (or divide) two numbers having like signs,** multiply (or divide) their absolute values and write the result with a positive sign. Examples:

$$(5)(3) = 15 \tag{1}$$

$$-6/-3 = 2 \tag{2}$$

E) **To multiply (or divide) two numbers having unlike signs,** multiply (or divide) their absolute values and write the result with a negative sign. Examples:

$$(-2)(8) = -16 \tag{1}$$

$$9/-3 = -3 \tag{2}$$

According to the law of signs for real numbers, the square of a positive or negative number is always positive. This means that it is impossible to take the square root of a negative number in the real number system.

Drill 1: Integers and Real Numbers

Addition

1. Simplify $4 + (-7) + 2 + (-5)$.

(A) -6 (B) -4 (C) 0   (D) 6   (E) 18

2. Simplify $144 + (-317) + 213$.

(A) -357 (B) -40 (C) 40   (D) 357   (E) 674

3. Simplify $|4 + (-3)| + |-2|$.

(A) -2 (B) -1 (C) 1   (D) 3   (E) 9

4. What integer makes the equation $-13 + 12 + 7 + ? = 10$ a true statement?

(A) -22 (B) -10 (C) 4   (D) 6   (E) 10

5. Simplify $4 + 17 + (-29) + 13 + (-22) + (-3)$.

(A) -44 (B) -20 (C) 23   (D) 34   (E) 78

Subtraction

6. Simplify $319 - 428$.

(A) -111 (B) -109 (C) -99 (D) 109   (E) 747

7. Simplify $91,203 - 37,904 + 1,073$.

(A) 54,372   (B) 64,701   (C) 128,034   (D) 129,107   (E) 130,180

8.   Simplify $|43 - 62| - |-17 - 3|$.

(A) -39 (B) -19 (C) -1 (D) 1   (E) 39

9.   Simplify $-(-4-7) + (-2)$.

(A) -22 (B) -13 (C) -9 (D) 7   (E) 9

10. In the Great Smoky Mountains National Park, Mt. Le Conte rises from 1,292 feet above sea level to 6,593 feet above sea level. How tall is Mt. Le Conte?

(A) 4,009 ft   (B) 5,301 ft   (C) 5,699 ft   (D) 6,464 ft   (E) 7,885 ft

Multiplication

11. Simplify $-3(-18)(-1)$.

(A) -108 (B) -54 (C) -48 (D) 48   (E) 54

12. Simplify $|-42| * |7|$.

(A) -294 (B) -49 (C) -35 (D) 284   (E) 294

13. Simplify $-6 * 5(-10)(-4)0 * 2$.

(A) $-2,400$ (B) -240 (C) 0   (D) 280   (E) 2,700

14. Simplify $-|-6 * 8|$.

(A) -48 (B) -42 (C) 2   (D) 42   (E) 48

15. A city in Georgia had a record low temparature of $-3°F$ one winter. During the same year, a city in Michigan experienced a record low that was nine times the record low set in Georgia. What was the record low in Michigan that year?

(A) $-31°F$ (B) $-27°F$ (C) $-21°F$ (D) $-12°F$ (E) $-6°F$

Division

16. Simplify $-24 + 8$.

(A) -4 (B) -3 (C) -2 (D) 3   (E) 4

17. Simplify $(-180) + (-12)$.

(A) -30 (B) -15 (C) 1.5   (D) 15   (E) 216

18. Simplify $|-76| + |-4|$.

(A) -21 (B) -19 (C) 13   (D) 19   (E) 21.5

19. Simplify $| 216 \div (- 6) |$.

(A) $- 36$ (B) $- 12$ (C) 36   (D) 38   (E) 43

20. At the end of the year, a small firm has $2,996 in its account for bonuses. If the entire amount is equally divided among the 14 employees, how much does each one receive?

(A) $107   (B) $114   (C) $170   (D) $210   (E) $214

Order of Operations

21. Simplify $\dfrac{4 + 8 * 2}{5 - 1}$

(A) 4   (B) 5   (C) 6   (D) 8   (E) 12

22. $96 \div 3 \div 4 \div 2 =$

(A) 65   (B) 64   (C) 16   (D) 8   (E) 4

23. $3 + 4 * 2 - 6 \div 3 =$

(A) $- 1$ (B) 5/3   (C) 8/3   (D) 9   (E) 12

24. $[(4 + 8) * 3] \div 9 =$

(A) 4   (B) 8   (C) 12   (D) 24   (E) 36

25. $18 + 3 * 4 \div 3 =$

(A) 3   (B) 5   (C) 10   (D) 22   (E) 28

26. $(29 - 17 + 4) \div 4 + |-2| =$

(A) $2^2/_3$ (B) 4   (C) $4^2/_3$ (D) 6   (E) 15

27. $(- 3) * 5 - 20 \div 4 =$

(A) $- 75$ (B) $- 20$ (C) $- 10$ (D) $- 8^3/_4$ (E) 20

28. $\dfrac{11 * 2 + 2}{16 - 2 * 2} =$

(A) 11/16   (B) 1   (C) 2   (D) 3 2/3   (E) 4

29. $|- 8 - 4| \div 3 * 6 + (- 4) =$

(A) 20   (B) 26   (C) 32   (D) 62   (E) 212

30. $32 \div 2 + 4 - 15 \div 3 =$

(A) 0   (B) 7   (C) 15   (D) 23   (E) 63

2. Fractions

The fraction, a/b, where the **numerator** is a and the **denominator** is b, implies that a is being divided by b. The denominator of a fraction can never be zero since a number divided by zero is not defined. If the numerator is greater than the denominator, the fraction is called an **improper fraction**. A **mixed number** is the sum of a whole number and a fraction, i.e., $4^3/_8 = 4 + {}^3/_8$.

Operations with Fractions

A)   **To change a mixed number to an improper fraction,** simply multiply the whole number by the denominator of the fraction and add the numerator. This product becomes the numerator of the result and the denominator remains the same. E.g.,

$$5\frac{2}{3} = \frac{(5\cdot 3)+2}{3} = \frac{15+2}{3} = \frac{17}{3}$$

To change an improper fraction to a mixed number, simply divide the numerator by the denominator. The remainder becomes the numerator of the fractional part of the mixed number, and the denominator remains the same. E.g.,

$$\frac{35}{4} = 35 \div 4 = 8\frac{3}{4}$$

To check your work, change your result back to an improper fraction to see if it matches the original fraction.

B)   **To find the sum of two fractions having a common denominator,** simply add together the numerators of the given fractions and put this sum over the common denominator.

$$\frac{11}{3} + \frac{5}{3} = \frac{11+5}{3} = \frac{16}{3}$$

Similarly for subtraction,

$$\frac{11}{3} - \frac{5}{3} = \frac{11-5}{3} = \frac{6}{3} = 2$$

C)   **To find the sum of the two fractions having different denominators,** it is necessary to find the **lowest common denominator,** (LCD) of the different denominators using a process called **factoring.**

To **factor** a number means to find two numbers that when multiplied together have a product equal to the original number. These two numbers are then said to be **factors** of the original number. E.g., the factors of 6 are

(1) 1 and 6 since $1 \times 6 = 6$.

(2) 2 and 3 since $2 \times 3 = 6$.

Every number is the product of itself and 1. A **prime factor** is a number that does not have any factors besides itself and 1. This is important when finding the LCD of two fractions having different denominators.

To find the LCD of $^{11}/_6$ and $^5/_{16}$, we must first find the prime factors of each of the two denominators.

$$6 = 2 \times 3$$

$$16 = 2 \times 2 \times 2 \times 2$$

$$LCD = 2 \times 2 \times 2 \times 2 \times 3 = 48$$

Note that we do not need to repeat the 2 that appears in both the factors of 6 and 16.

Once we have determined the LCD of the denominators, each of the fractions must be converted into equivalent fractions having the LCD as a denominator.

Rewrite 11/6 and 5/16 to have 48 as their denominators.

$$6 \times ? = 48 \qquad\qquad 16 \times ? = 48$$

$$6 \times 8 = 48 \qquad\qquad 16 \times 3 = 48$$

If the numerator and denominator of each fraction is multiplied (or divided) by the same number, the value of the fraction will not change. This is because a fraction b/b, b being any number, is equal to the multiplicative identity, 1.

Therefore,

$$\frac{11}{6} \cdot \frac{8}{8} = \frac{88}{48} \qquad\qquad \frac{5}{16} \cdot \frac{3}{3} = \frac{15}{48}$$

We may now find

$$\frac{11}{6} + \frac{5}{16} = \frac{88}{48} + \frac{15}{48} = \frac{103}{48}$$

Similarly for subtraction,

$$\frac{11}{6} - \frac{5}{16} = \frac{88}{48} - \frac{15}{48} = \frac{73}{48}$$

D) **To find the product of two or more fractions,** simply multiply the numerators of the given fractions to find the numerator of the product and multiply the denominators of the given fractions to find the denominator of the product. E.g.,

$$\frac{2}{3} \cdot \frac{1}{5} \cdot \frac{4}{7} = \frac{2 \times 1 \times 4}{3 \times 5 \times 7} = \frac{8}{105}$$

E) To find the quotient of two fractions, simply invert the divisor and multiply. E.g.,

$$\frac{8}{9} \div \frac{1}{3} = \frac{8}{9} \times \frac{3}{1} = \frac{24}{9} = \frac{8}{3}$$

F) **To simplify a fraction** is to convert it into a form in which the numerator and denominator have no common factor other than 1, E.g.,

$$\frac{12}{18} = \frac{12 \div 6}{18 \div 6} = \frac{2}{3}$$

G) A **complex fraction** is a fraction whose numerator and/or denominator is made up of fractions. To simplify the fraction, find the LCD of all the fractions. Multiply both the numerator and denominator by this number and simplify.

PROBLEM

> If $a = 4$ and $b = 7$, find the value of $\dfrac{a + \frac{a}{b}}{a - \frac{a}{b}}$

SOLUTION

By substitution,

$$\frac{a + \frac{a}{b}}{a - \frac{a}{b}} = \frac{4 + \frac{4}{7}}{4 - \frac{4}{7}}$$

In order to combine the terms, we must find the LCD of 1 and 7. Since both are prime factors, the LCD $= 1 \times 7 = 7$.

Multiplying both numerator and denominator by 7, we get:

$$\frac{7(4 + \frac{4}{7})}{7(4 - \frac{4}{7})} = \frac{28 + 4}{28 - 4} = \frac{32}{24}$$

By dividing both numerator and denominator by 8, 32/24 can be reduced to 4/3.

Drill 2: Fractions

Fractions

DIRECTIONS: Add and write the answer in simplest form.

1.   5/12 + 3/12 =

(A) 5/24   (B)   1/3   (C)   8/12   (D)   2/3   (E)   1 1/3

2.   5/8 + 7/8 + 3/8 =

(A) 15/24   (B)   3/4   (C)   5/6   (D)   7/8   (E)   1 7/8

3.   131 2/15 + 28 3/15 =

(A) 159 1/6   (B)   159 1/5   (C)   159 1/3   (D)   159 1/2   (E)   159 3/5

4.   3 5/18 + 2 1/18 + 8 7/18 =

(A) 13 13/18 (B)   13 3/4   (C)   13 7/9   (D)   14 1/6   (E)   14 2/9

5.   17 9/20 + 4 3/20 + 8 11/20 =

(A) 29 23/60   (B)   29 23/20   (C)   30 3/20

(D) 30 1/5   (E)   30 3/5

Subtract Fractions with the Same Denominator

DIRECTIONS: Subtract and write the answer in simplest form.

6.   4 7/8 – 3 1/8 =

(A) 1 1/4   (B)   1 3/4   (C)   1 12/16   (D)   1 7/8   (E)   2

7.   132 5/12 – 37 3/12 =

(A) 94 1/6   (B)   95 1/12   (C)   95 1/6   (D)   105 1/6   (E)   169 2/3

8.   19 1/3 – 2 2/3 =

(A) 16 2/3   (B)   16 5/6   (C)   17 1/3   (D)   17 2/3   (E)   17 5/6

9.   8/21 – 5/21 =

(A) 1/21   (B)   1/7   (C)   3/21   (D)   2/7   (E)   3/7

10.   82 7/10 – 38 9/10 =

(A) 43 4/5   (B)   44 1/5   (C)   44 2/5   (D)   45 1/5   (E)   45 2/10

Finding the LCD

DIRECTIONS: Find the lowest common denominator of each group of fractions.

11. 2/3, 5/9, and 1/6.

(A) 9   (B) 18   (C) 27   (D) 54   (E) 162

12. 1/2, 5/6, and 3/4.

(A) 2   (B) 4   (C) 6   (D) 12   (E) 48

13. 7/16, 5/6, and 2/3.

(A) 3   (B) 6   (C) 12   (D) 24   (E) 48

14. 8/15, 2/5, and 12/25.

(A) 5   (B) 15   (C) 25   (D) 75   (E) 375

15. 2/3, 1/5, and 5/6.

(A) 15   (B) 30   (C) 48   (D) 90   (E) 120

16. 1/3, 9/42, and 4/21.

(A) 21   (B) 42   (C) 126   (D) 378   (E) 4,000

17. 4/9, 2/5, and 1/3.

(A) 15   (B) 17   (C) 27   (D) 45   (E) 135

18. 7/12, 11/36, and 1/9.

(A) 12   (B) 36   (C) 108   (D) 324   (E) 432

19. 3/7, 5/21, and 2/3.

(A) 21   (B) 42   (C) 31   (D) 63   (E) 441

20. 13/16, 5/8, and 1/4.

(A) 4   (B) 8   (C) 16   (D) 32   (E) 64

Adding Fractions with Different Denominators

DIRECTIONS: Add and write the answer in simplest form.

21. 1/3 + 5/12 =

(A) 2/5   (B) 1/2   (C) 9/12   (D) 3/4   (E) 1 1/3

22. 3 5/9 + 2 1/3 =

(A) 5 1/2   (B) 5 2/3   (C) 5 8/9   (D) 6 1/9   (E) 6 2/3

23. 12 9/16 + 17 3/4 + 8 1/8 =

(A) 37 7/16   (B) 38 7/16   (C) 38 1/2   (D) 38 2/3   (E) 39 3/16

24. 28 4/5 + 11 16/25 =

(A) 39 2/3   (B) 39 4/5   (C) 40 9/25   (D) 40 2/5   (E) 40 11/25

25. 2 1/8 + 1 3/16 + 5/12 =

(A) 3 35/48   (B) 3 3/4   (C) 3 19/24   (D) 3 13/16   (E) 4 1/12

Subtraction with Different Denominators

<u>DIRECTIONS</u>: Subtract and write the answer in simplest form.

26. 8 9/12 – 2 2/3 =

(A) 6 1/12   (B) 6 1/6   (C) 6 1/3   (D) 6 7/12   (E) 6 2/3

27. 185 11/15 – 107 2/5 =

(A) 77 2/15   (B) 78 1/5   (C) 78 3/10   (D) 78 1/3   (E) 78 9/15

28. 34 2/3 – 16 5/6 =

(A) 16   (B) 16 1/3   (C) 17 1/2   (D) 17   (E) 17 5/6

29. 3 11/48 – 2 3/16 =

(A) 47/48   (B) 1 1/48   (C) 1 1/24   (D) 1 8/48   (E) 1 7/24

30. 81 4/21 – 31 1/3 =

(A) 47 3/7   (B) 49 6/7   (C) 49 1/6   (D) 49 5/7   (E) 49 13/21

Multiplication

<u>DIRECTIONS</u>: Multiply and reduce the answer.

31. 2/3 * 4/5 =

(A) 6/8   (B) 3/4   (C) 8/15   (D) 10/12   (E) 6/5

32. 7/10 * 4/21 =

(A) 2/15   (B) 11/31   (C) 28/210   (D) 1/6   (E) 4/15

33. 5 1/3 * 3/8 =

(A) 4/11   (B) 2   (C) 8/5   (D) 5 1/8   (E) 5 17/24

34. 6 1/2 * 3 =

(A) 9 1/2   (B) 18 1/2   (C) 19 1/2   (D) 20   (E) 12 1/2

35. 3 1/4 * 2 1/3 =

(A) 5 7/12   (B) 6 2/7   (C) 6 5/7   (D) 7 7/12   (E) 7 11/12

Division

DIRECTIONS: Divide and reduce the answer.

36. 3/16 ÷ 3/4 =

(A) 9/64   (B) 1/4   (C) 6/16   (D) 9/16   (E) 3/4

37. 4/9 ÷ 2/3 =

(A) 1/3   (B) 1/2   (C) 2/3   (D) 7/11   (E) 8/9

38. 5 1/4 ÷ 7/10 =

(A) 2 4/7   (B) 3 27/40 (C) 5 19/20 (D) 7 1/2   (E) 8 1/4

39. 4 2/3 ÷ 7/9 =

(A) 2 24/27 (B) 3 2/9   (C) 4 14/27 (D) 5 12/27 (E) 6

40. 3 2/5 ÷ 1 7/10 =

(A) 2   (B) 3 4/7   (C) 4 7/25   (D) 5 1/10   (E) 5 2/7

Changing an Improper Fraction to a Mixed Number

DIRECTIONS: Write each improper fraction as a mixed number in simplest form.

41. 50/4

(A) 10 1/4   (B) 11 1/2   (C) 12 1/4   (D) 12 1/2   (E) 25

42. 17/5

(A) 3 2/5   (B) 3 3/5   (C) 3 4/5   (D) 4 1/5   (E) 4 2/5

43. 42/3

(A) 10 2/3   (B) 12   (C) 13 1/3   (D) 14   (E) 21 1/3

44.   85/6

(A)   9 1/6   (B)   10 5/6   (C)   11 1/2   (D)   12   (E)   14 1/6

45.   151/7

(A)   19 6/7   (B)   20 1/7   (C)   21 4/7   (D)   31 2/7   (E)   31 4/7

Changing a Mixed Number to an Improper Fraction

<u>DIRECTIONS</u>: Change each mixed number to an improper fraction in simplest form.

46.   2 3/5

(A)   4/5   (B)   6/5   (C)   11/5   (D)   13/5   (E)   17/5

47.   4 3/4

(A)   7/4   (B)   13/4   (C)   16/3   (D)   19/4   (E)   21/4

48.   6 7/6

(A)   13/6   (B)   43/6   (C)   19/36   (D)   42/36   (E)   48/6

49.   12 3/7

(A)   87/7   (B)   164/14   (C)   34/3   (D)   187/21   (E)   252/7

50.   21 1/2

(A)   11/2   (B)   22/2   (C)   24/2   (D)   42/2   (E)   43/2

3.   Decimals

When we divide the denominator of a fraction into its numerator, the result is a **decimal**. The decimal is based upon a fraction with a denominator of 10, 100, 1,000, ... and is written with a **decimal point**. Whole numbers are placed to the left of the decimal point where the first place to the left is the units place; the second to the left is the tens; the third to the left is the hundreds, etc. The fractions are placed on the right where the first place to the right is the tenths; the second to the right is the hundredths, etc.

EXAMPLE

$$12\frac{3}{10} = 12.3 \qquad 4\frac{17}{100} = 4.17 \qquad \frac{3}{100} = .03$$

Since a **rational number** is of the form a/b, $b \neq 0$, then all rational numbers can be expressed as decimals by dividing b into a. The result is either a **terminat-**

ing decimal, meaning that b divides a with a remainder of 0 after a certain point; or **repeating decimal**, meaning that b continues to divide a so that the decimal has a repeating pattern of integers.

EXAMPLE

(A) $^1/_2 = .5$

(B) $^1/_3 = .333...$

(C) $^{11}/_{16} = .6875$

(D) $^2/_7 = .285714285714...$

(A) and (C) are terminating decimals; (B) and (D) are repeating decimals. This explanation allows us to define **irrational numbers** as numbers whose decimal form is non-terminating and non-repeating, e.g.,

$$\sqrt{2} = 1.414...$$
$$\sqrt{3} = 1.732...$$

PROBLEM

Express $- ^{10}/_{20}$ as a decimal.

SOLUTION

$- ^{10}/_{20} = - ^{50}/_{100} = - .5$

PROBLEM

Write $^2/_7$ as a repeating decimal.

SOLUTION

To write a fraction as a repeating decimal divide the numerator by the denominator until a pattern of repeated digits appears.

$2 \div 7 = .285714285714...$

Identify the entire portion of the decimal which is repeated. The repeating decimal can then be written in the shortened form:

$^2/_7 = .\overline{285714}$

Operations with Decimals

A) **To add numbers containing decimals,** write the numbers in a column making sure the decimal points are lined up, one beneath the other. Add the numbers as usual, placing the decimal point in the sum so that it is still in line with the others. It is important not to mix the digits in the tenths place with the digits in the hundredths place, and so on.

EXAMPLES

$$2.558 + 6.391 \qquad 57.51 + 6.2$$

$$\begin{array}{r} 2.558 \\ +\ 6.391 \\ \hline 8.949 \end{array} \qquad \begin{array}{r} 57.51 \\ +\ \ 6.20 \\ \hline 63.71 \end{array}$$

Similarly with subtraction,

$$78.54 - 21.33 \qquad 7.11 - 4.2$$

$$\begin{array}{r} 78.54 \\ -\ 21.33 \\ \hline 57.21 \end{array} \qquad \begin{array}{r} 7.11 \\ -\ 4.20 \\ \hline 2.91 \end{array}$$

Note that if two numbers differ according to the amount of digits to the right of the decimal point, zeros must be added.

$$.63 - .214 \qquad 15.224 - 3.6891$$

$$\begin{array}{r} .630 \\ -\ .214 \\ \hline .416 \end{array} \qquad \begin{array}{r} 15.2240 \\ -\ 3.6891 \\ \hline 11.5349 \end{array}$$

B) **To multiply numbers with decimals**, simply multiply as usual. Then, to figure out the number of decimal places that belong in the product, find the total number of decimal places in the numbers being multiplied.

EXAMPLES

$$\begin{array}{rl} 6.555 & \text{(3 decimal places)} \\ \times\ \ \ \ 4.5 & \text{(1 decimal place)} \\ \hline 32775 & \\ 26220\ \ & \\ \hline 294975 & \\ 29.4975 & \text{(4 decimal places)} \end{array} \qquad \begin{array}{rl} 5.32 & \text{(2 decimal places)} \\ \times\ \ \ .04 & \text{(2 decimal places)} \\ \hline 2128 & \\ 000\ \ & \\ \hline 2128 & \\ .2128 & \text{(4 decimal places)} \end{array}$$

C) **To divide numbers with decimals**, you must first make the divisor a whole number by moving the decimal point the appropriate number of places to the right. The decimal point of the dividend should also be moved the same number of places. Place a decimal point in the quotient, directly in line with the decimal point in the dividend.

EXAMPLES

$$12.92 \div 3.4$$

$$\begin{array}{r} 3.8 \\ 3.4 \overline{)12.9.2} \\ -102 \\ \hline 272 \\ -272 \\ \hline 0 \end{array}$$

$$40.376 \div 7.21$$

$$\begin{array}{r} 5.6 \\ 7.21 \overline{)40.37.6} \\ -3605 \\ \hline 4326 \\ -4326 \\ \hline 0 \end{array}$$

If the question asks to find the correct answer to two decimal places, simply divide until you have three decimal places and then round off. If the third decimal place is a 5 or larger, the number in the second decimal place is increased by 1. If the third decimal place is less than 5, that number is simply dropped.

PROBLEM

Find the answer to the following to 2 decimal places:

(1)   44.3 ÷ 3   (2)   56.99 ÷ 6

SOLUTION

(1)
$$\begin{array}{r} 14.766 \\ 3 \overline{)44.300} \\ -3 \\ \hline 14 \\ -12 \\ \hline 23 \\ -21 \\ \hline 20 \\ -18 \\ \hline 20 \\ -18 \\ \hline 2 \end{array}$$

(2)
$$\begin{array}{r} 9.498 \\ 6 \overline{)56.990} \\ -54 \\ \hline 29 \\ -24 \\ \hline 59 \\ -54 \\ \hline 50 \\ -48 \\ \hline 2 \end{array}$$

14.766 can be rounded off to 14.77

9.498 can be rounded off to 9.50

D)   When comparing two numbers with decimals to see which is the larger, first look at the tenths place. The larger digit in this place represents the larger number. If the two digits are the same, however, take a look at the digits in the hundredths place, and so on.

EXAMPLES

.518 and .216

5 is larger than 2, therefore

.518 is larger than .216

.723 and .726

6 is larger than 3, therefore

.726 is larger than .723

Drill 3: Decimals

Addition

1. $1.032 + 0.987 + 3.07 =$
(A)   4.089   (B)   5.089   (C)   5.189   (D)   6.189   (E)   13.972

2. $132.03 + 97.1483 =$
(A)   98.4686   (B)   110.3513   (C)   209.1783
(D)   229.1486   (E)   229.1783

3. $7.1 + 0.62 + 4.03827 + 5.183 =$
(A)   0.2315127   (B)   16.94127   (C)   17.57127
(D)   18.561   (E)   40.4543

4. $8 + 17.43 + 9.2 =$
(A)   34.63   (B)   34.86   (C)   35.63   (D)   176.63   (E)   189.43

5. $1036.173 + 289.04 =$
(A)   382.6573   (B)   392.6573   (C)   1065.077
(D)   1325.213   (E)   3926.573

Subtraction

6. $3.972 - 2.04 =$
(A)   1.932   (B)   1.942   (C)   1.976   (D)   2.013   (E)   2.113

7. $16.047 - 13.06 =$
(A)   2.887   (B)   2.987   (C)   3.041   (D)   3.141   (E)   4.741

8. $87.4 - 56.27 =$
(A)   30.27   (B)   30.67   (C)   31.1   (D)   31.13   (E)   31.27

9. $1046.8 - 639.14 =$
(A)   303.84   (B)   313.74   (C)   407.66   (D)   489.74   (E)   535.54

10. $10,000 - 842.91 =$
(A)   157.09   (B)   942.91   (C)   5236.09   (D)   9057.91   (E)   9157.09

Multiplication

11. 1.03 * 2.6 =

(A) 2.18   (B) 2.678   (C) 2.78   (D) 3.38   (E) 3.63

12. 93 * 4.2 =

(A) 39.06   (B) 97.2   (C) 223.2   (D) 390.6   (E) 3906

13. 0.04 * 0.23 =

(A) 0.0092   (B) 0.092   (C) 0.27   (D) 0.87   (E) 0.920

14. 0.0186 * 0.03 =

(A) 0.000348 (B) 0.000558   (C) 0.0548   (D) 0.0848   (E) 0.558

15. 51.2 * 0.17 =

(A) 5.29   (B) 8.534   (C) 8.704   (D) 36.352   (E) 36.991

Division

16. 123.39 ÷ 3 =

(A) 31.12   (B) 41.13   (C) 401.13   (D) 411.3   (E) 4,113

17. 1428.6 ÷ 6 =

(A) 0.2381   (B) 2.381   (C) 23.81   (D) 238.1   (E) 2,381

18. 25.2 ÷ 0.3 =

(A) 0.84   (B) 8.04   (C) 8.4   (D) 84   (E) 840

19. 14.95 ÷ 6.5 =

(A) 2.3   (B) 20.3   (C) 23   (D) 230   (E) 2,300

20. 46.33 ÷ 1.13 =

(A) 0.41   (B) 4.1   (C) 41   (D) 410   (E) 4,100

Comparing

21. Which is the **largest** number in this set — {0.8, 0.823, 0.089, 0.807, 0.852}?

(A) 0.8   (B) 0.823   (C) 0.089   (D) 0.807   (E) 0.852

22. Which is the **smallest** number in this set − {32.98, 32.099, 32.047, 32.5, 32.304}?

(A) 32.98   (B) 32.099   (C) 32.047   (D) 32.5   (E) 32.304

23. In which set below are the numbers arranged correctly from smallest to largest?

(A) {0.98, 0.9, 0.993}   (D) {0.006, 0.061, 0.06}

(B) {0.113, 0.3, 0.31}   (E) {12.84, 12.801, 12.6}

(C) {7.04, 7.26, 7.2}

24. In which set below are the numbers arranged correctly from largest to smallest?

(A) {1.018, 1.63, 1.368}   (D) {16.34, 16.304, 16.3}

(B) {4.219, 4.29, 4.9}   (E) {12.98, 12.601, 12.86}

(C) {0.62, 0.6043, 0.643}

25. Which is the **largest** number in this set − {0.87, 0.89, 0.889, 0.8, 0.987}?

(A) 0.87   (B) 0.89   (C) 0.889   (D) 0.8   (E) 0.987

Changing a Fraction to a Decimal

26. What is 1/4 written as a decimal?

(A) 1.4   (B) 0.14   (C) 0.2   (D) 0.25   (E) 0.3

27. What is 3/5 written as a decimal?

(A) 0.3   (B) 0.35   (C) 0.6   (D) 0.65   (E) 0.8

28. What is 7/20 written as a decimal?

(A) 0.35   (B) 0.4   (C) 0.72   (D) 0.75   (E) 0.9

29. What is 2/3 written as a decimal?

(A) 0.23   (B) 0.33   (C) 0.5   (D) 0.6   (E) $0.\bar{6}$

30. What is 11/25 written as a fraction?

(A) 0.1125   (B) 0.25   (C) 0.4   (D) 0.44   (E) 0.5

4. Percentages

A **percent** is a way of expressing the relationship between part and whole, where whole is defined as 100%. A percent can be defined by a fraction with a denominator of 100. Decimals can also represent a percent. For instance,

$$56\% = 0.56 = 56/100$$

PROBLEM

Compute the value of

(1)   90% of 400   (3)   50% of 500

(2)   180% of 400   (4)   200% of 4

SOLUTION

The symbol % means per hundred, therefore $5\% = 5/100$

(1)   90% of 400 = 90/100 × 400 = 90 × 4 = 360

(2)   180% of 400 = 180/100 × 400 = 180 × 4 = 720

(3)   50% of 500 = 50/100 × 500 = 50 × 5 = 250

(4)   200% of 4 = 200/100 × 4 = 2 × 4 = 8

PROBLEM

What percent of

(1)   100 is 99.5   (2)   200 is 4

SOLUTION

(1) $99.5 = x \times 100$

$99.5 = 100x$

$.995 = x$; but this is the value of x per hundred. Therefore,

$x = 99.5\%$

(2) $4 = x \times 200$

$4 = 200x$

$.02 = x$. Again this must be changed to percent, so

$x = 2\%$

Equivalent Forms of a Number

Some problems may call for converting numbers into an equivalent or simplified form in order to make the solution more convenient.

1.   Converting a fraction to a decimal:

$^1/_2 = 0.50$

Divide the numerator by the denominator:

$$
\begin{array}{r}
.50 \\
2\overline{)1.00} \\
\underline{-10} \\
00
\end{array}
$$

2. Converting a number to a percent:

$0.50 = 50\%$

Multiply by 100:

$0.50 = (0.50 \times 100)\% = 50\%$

3. Converting a percent to a decimal:

$30\% = 0.30$

Divide by 100:

$30\% = 30/100 = 0.30$

4. Converting a decimal to a fraction:

$0.500 = \frac{1}{2}$

Convert .500 to 500/1000 and then simplify the fraction by dividing the numerator and denominator by common factors:

$$
\frac{2 \times 2 \times 5 \times 5 \times 5}{2 \times 2 \times 2 \times 5 \times 5 \times 5}
$$

and then cancel out the common numbers to get $\frac{1}{2}$.

PROBLEM

Express

(1) 1.65 as a percentage of 100

(2) 0.7 as a fraction

(3) $-\frac{10}{20}$ as a decimal

(4) $\frac{4}{2}$ as an integer

SOLUTION

(1) $(1.65/100) \times 100 = 1.65\%$

(2) $0.7 = {}^{7}/_{10}$

(3) $-{}^{10}/_{20} = -0.5$

(4) ${}^{4}/_{2} = 2$

Drill 4: Percentages

Finding Percents

1. Find 3% of 80.

(A) 0.24 (B) 2.4 (C) 24 (D) 240 (E) 2,400

2. Find 50% of 182.

(A) 9 (B) 90 (C) 91 (D) 910 (E) 9,100

3. Find 83% of 166.

(A) 0.137 (B) 1.377 (C) 13.778 (D) 137 (E) 137.78

4. Find 125% of 400.

(A) 425 (B) 500 (C) 525 (D) 600 (E) 825

5. Find 300% of 4.

(A) 12 (B) 120 (C) 1200 (D) 12,000 (E) 120,000

6. Forty-eight percent of the 1,200 students at Central High are males. How many male students are there at Central High?

(A) 57 (B) 576 (C) 580 (D) 600 (E) 648

7. For 35% of the last 40 days, there has been measurable rainfall. How many days out of the last 40 days have had measurable rainfall?

(A) 14 (B) 20 (C) 25 (D) 35 (E) 40

8. Of every 1,000 people who take a certain medicine, 0.2% develop severe side effects. How many people out of every 1,000 who take the medicine develop the side effects?

(A) 0.2 (B) 2 (C) 20 (D) 22 (E) 200

9. Of 220 applicants for a job, 75% were offered an initial interview. How many people were offered an initial interview?

(A) 75 (B) 110 (C) 120 (D) 155 (E) 165

10. Find 0.05% of 4,000.

(A) 0.05   (B) 0.5   (C) 2   (D) 20   (E) 400

Changing Percents to Fractions

11. What is 25% written as a fraction?

(A) 1/25   (B) 1/5   (C) 1/4   (D) 1/3   (E) 1/2

12. What is 33 1/3% written as a fraction?

(A) 1/4   (B) 1/3   (C) 1/2   (D) 2/3   (E) 5/9

13. What is 200% written as a fraction?

(A) 1/2   (B) 2/1   (C) 20/1   (D) 200/1   (E) 2000/1

14. What is 84% written as a fraction?

(A) 1/84   (B) 4/8   (C) 17/25   (D) 21/25   (E) 44/50

15. What is 2% written as a fraction?

(A) 1/50   (B) 1/25   (C) 1/10   (D) 1/4   (E) 1/2

Changing Fractions to Percents

16. What is 2/3 written as a percent?

(A) 23%   (B) 32%   (C) 33 1/3%   (D) 57 1/3%   (E) 66 2/3%

17. What is 3/5 written as a percent?

(A) 30%   (B) 35%   (C) 53%   (D) 60%   (E) 65%

18. What is 17/20 written as a percent?

(A) 17%   (B) 70%   (C) 75%   (D) 80%   (E) 85%

19. What is 45/50 written as a percent?

(A) 45%   (B) 50%   (C) 90%   (D) 95%   (E) 97%

20. What is 1 1/4 written as a percent?

(A) 114%   (B) 120%   (C) 125%   (D) 127%   (E) 133%

Changing Percents to Decimals

21. What is 42% written as a decimal?

(A) 0.42 (B) 4.2 (C) 42 (D) 420 (E) 422

22. What is 0.3% written as a decimal?

(A) 0.0003 (B) 0.003 (C) 0.03 (D) 0.3 (E) 3

23. What is 8% written as a decimal?

(A) 0.0008 (B) 0.008 (C) 0.08 (D) 0.80 (E) 8

24. What is 175% written as a decimal?

(A) 0.175 (B) 1.75 (C) 17.5 (D) 175 (E) 17,500

25. What is 34% written as a decimal?

(A) 0.00034 (B) 0.0034 (C) 0.034 (D) 0.34 (E) 3.4

Changing Decimals to Percents

26. What is 0.43 written as a percent?

(A) 0.0043% (B) 0.043% (C) 4.3% (D) 43% (E) 430%

27. What is 1 written as a percent?

(A) 1% (B) 10% (C) 100% (D) 111% (E) 150%

28. What is 0.08 written as a percent?

(A) 0.08% (B) 8% (C) 8.8% (D) 80% (E) 800%

29. What is 3.4 written as a percent?

(A) 0.0034% (B) 3.4% (C) 34% (D) 304% (E) 340%

30. What is 0.645 written as a percent?

(A) 64.5% (B) 65% (C) 69% (D) 70% (E) 645%

5. Radicals

The **square root** of a number is a number that when multiplied by itself results in the original number. So, the square root of 81 is 9 since 9 × 9 = 81. However, –9 is also a root of 81 since (– 9) (– 9) = 81. Every positive number will have two roots. Yet, the principal root is the positive one. Zero has only one square root, while negative numbers do not have real numbers as their roots.

A **radical sign** indicates that the root of a number or expression will be taken. The **radicand** is the number of which the root will be taken. The **index** tells how many times the root needs to be multiplied by itself to equal the radicand. E.g.,

index → radical sign → $\sqrt{}$ radicand

(1) $\sqrt[3]{64}$;

3 is the index and 64 is the radicand. Since $4 \cdot 4 \cdot 4 = 64$, $\sqrt[3]{64} = 4$

(2) $\sqrt[5]{32}$;

5 is the index and 32 is the radicand. Since $2 \cdot 2 \cdot 2 \cdot 2 \cdot 2 = 32$, $\sqrt[5]{32} = 2$

Operations with Radicals

A) **To multiply two or more radicals**, we utilize the law that states,

$$\sqrt{a} \cdot \sqrt{b} = \sqrt{ab}.$$

Simply multiply the whole numbers as usual. Then, multiply the radicands and put the product under the radical sign and simplify. E.g.,

(1) $\sqrt{12} \cdot \sqrt{5} = \sqrt{60} = 2\sqrt{15}$

(2) $3\sqrt{2} \cdot 4\sqrt{8} = 12\sqrt{16} = 48$

(3) $2\sqrt{10} \cdot 6\sqrt{5} = 12\sqrt{50} = 60\sqrt{2}$

B) **To divide radicals**, simplify both the numerator and the denominator. By multiplying the radical in the denominator by itself, you can make the denominator a rational number. The numerator, however, must also be multiplied by this radical so that the value of the expression does not change. You must choose as many factors as necessary to rationalize the denominator. E.g.,

(1) $\dfrac{\sqrt{128}}{\sqrt{2}} = \dfrac{\sqrt{64} \cdot \sqrt{2}}{\sqrt{2}} = \dfrac{8\sqrt{2}}{\sqrt{2}} = 8$

(2) $\dfrac{\sqrt{10}}{\sqrt{3}} = \dfrac{\sqrt{10} \cdot \sqrt{3}}{\sqrt{3} \cdot \sqrt{3}} = \dfrac{\sqrt{30}}{3}$

(3) $\dfrac{\sqrt{8}}{2\sqrt{3}} = \dfrac{\sqrt{8} \cdot \sqrt{3}}{2\sqrt{3} \cdot \sqrt{3}} = \dfrac{\sqrt{24}}{2 \cdot 3} = \dfrac{2\sqrt{6}}{6} = \dfrac{\sqrt{6}}{3}$

C) **To add two or more radicals,** the radicals must have the same index and the same radicand. Only where the radicals are simplified can these similarities be determined.

EXAMPLE

(1) $6\sqrt{2} + 2\sqrt{2} = (6+2)\sqrt{2} = 8\sqrt{2}$

(2) $\sqrt{27} + 5\sqrt{3} = \sqrt{9}\sqrt{3} + 5\sqrt{3} = 3\sqrt{3} + 5\sqrt{3} = 8\sqrt{3}$

(3) $7\sqrt{3} + 8\sqrt{2} + 5\sqrt{3} = 12\sqrt{3} + 8\sqrt{2}$

Similarly to subtract,

(1) $12\sqrt{3} - 7\sqrt{3} = (12-7)\sqrt{3} = 5\sqrt{3}$

(2) $\sqrt{80} - \sqrt{20} = \sqrt{16}\sqrt{5} - \sqrt{4}\sqrt{5} = 4\sqrt{5} - 2\sqrt{5} = 2\sqrt{5}$

(3) $\sqrt{50} - \sqrt{3} = 5\sqrt{2} - \sqrt{3}$

DRILL 5: Radicals

Multiplication

<u>DIRECTIONS</u>: Multiply and simplify each answer.

1. $\sqrt{6} * \sqrt{5} =$
(A) $\sqrt{11}$ (B) $\sqrt{30}$ (C) $2\sqrt{5}$ (D) $3\sqrt{10}$ (E) $2\sqrt{3}$

2. $\sqrt{3} * \sqrt{12} =$
(A) 3   (B) $\sqrt{15}$ (C) $\sqrt{36}$ (D) 6   (E) 8

3. $\sqrt{7} * \sqrt{7} =$
(A) 7   (B) 49   (C) $\sqrt{14}$ (D) $2\sqrt{7}$ (E) $2\sqrt{14}$

4. $3\sqrt{5} * 2\sqrt{5} =$
(A) $5\sqrt{5}$ (B) 25   (C) 30   (D) $5\sqrt{25}$ (E) $6\sqrt{5}$

5. $4\sqrt{6} * \sqrt{2} =$
(A) $4\sqrt{8}$ (B) $8\sqrt{2}$ (C) $5\sqrt{8}$ (D) $4\sqrt{12}$ (E) $8\sqrt{3}$

Division

DIRECTIONS: Divide and simplify the answer.

6. $\sqrt{10} \div \sqrt{2} =$

(A) $\sqrt{8}$ (B) $2\sqrt{2}$ (C) $\sqrt{5}$ (D) $2\sqrt{5}$ (E) $2\sqrt{3}$

7. $\sqrt{30} \div \sqrt{15} =$

(A) $\sqrt{2}$ (B) $\sqrt{45}$ (C) $3\sqrt{5}$ (D) $\sqrt{15}$ (E) $5\sqrt{3}$

8. $\sqrt{100} \div \sqrt{25} =$

(A) $\sqrt{4}$ (B) $5\sqrt{5}$ (C) $5\sqrt{3}$ (D) 2 (E) 4

9. $\sqrt{48} \div \sqrt{8} =$

(A) $4\sqrt{3}$ (B) $3\sqrt{2}$ (C) $\sqrt{6}$ (D) 6 (E) 12

10. $3\sqrt{12} \div \sqrt{3} =$

(A) $3\sqrt{15}$ (B) 6 (C) 9 (D) 12 (E) $3\sqrt{36}$

Addition

DIRECTIONS: Simplify each radical and add.

11. $\sqrt{7} + 3\sqrt{7} =$

(A) $3\sqrt{7}$ (B) $4\sqrt{7}$ (C) $3\sqrt{14}$ (D) $4\sqrt{14}$ (E) $3\sqrt{21}$

12. $\sqrt{5} + 6\sqrt{5} + 3\sqrt{5} =$

(A) $9\sqrt{5}$ (B) $9\sqrt{15}$ (C) $5\sqrt{10}$ (D) $10\sqrt{5}$ (E) $18\sqrt{15}$

13. $3\sqrt{32} + 2\sqrt{2} =$

(A) $5\sqrt{2}$ (B) $\sqrt{34}$ (C) $14\sqrt{2}$ (D) $5\sqrt{34}$ (E) $6\sqrt{64}$

14. $6\sqrt{15} + 8\sqrt{15} + 16\sqrt{15} =$

(A) $15\sqrt{30}$ (B) $30\sqrt{45}$ (C) $30\sqrt{30}$ (D) $15\sqrt{45}$ (E) $30\sqrt{15}$

15. $6\sqrt{5} + 2\sqrt{45} =$

(A) $12\sqrt{5}$ (B) $8\sqrt{50}$ (C) $40\sqrt{2}$ (D) $12\sqrt{50}$ (E) $8\sqrt{5}$

Subtraction

<u>DIRECTIONS</u>: Simplify each radical and subtract.

16. $8\sqrt{5} - 6\sqrt{5} =$

(A) $2\sqrt{5}$ (B) $3\sqrt{5}$ (C) $4\sqrt{5}$ (D) $14\sqrt{5}$ (E) $48\sqrt{5}$

17. $16\sqrt{33} - 5\sqrt{33} =$

(A) $3\sqrt{33}$ (B) $33\sqrt{11}$ (C) $11\sqrt{33}$ (D) $11\sqrt{0}$ (E) $\sqrt{33}$

18. $14\sqrt{2} - 19\sqrt{2} =$

(A) $5\sqrt{2}$ (B) $-5\sqrt{2}$ (C) $-33\sqrt{2}$ (D) $33\sqrt{2}$ (E) $-4\sqrt{2}$

19. $10\sqrt{2} - 3\sqrt{8} =$

(A) $6\sqrt{6}$ (B) $-2\sqrt{2}$ (C) $7\sqrt{6}$ (D) $4\sqrt{2}$ (E) $-6\sqrt{6}$

20. $4\sqrt{3} - 2\sqrt{12} =$

(A) $-2\sqrt{9}$ (B) $-6\sqrt{15}$ (C) 0 (D) $6\sqrt{15}$ (E) $2\sqrt{12}$

6. Exponents

When a number is multiplied by itself a specific number of times, it is said to be **raised to a power**. The way this is written is $a^n = b$ where a is the number or **base**, n is the **exponent** or **power** that indicates the number of times the base is to be multiplied by itself, and b is the product of this multiplication.

In the expression 3^2, 3 is the base and 2 is the exponent. This means that 3 is multiplied by itself 2 times and the product is 9.

An exponent can be either positive or negative. A negative exponent implies a fraction. Such that, if n is a positive integer

$$a^{-n} = \frac{1}{a^n}, a \neq 0. \text{ So, } 2^{-4} = \frac{1}{2^4} = \frac{1}{16}.$$

An exponent that is zero gives a result of 1, assuming that the base is not equal to zero.

$$a^0 = 1, a \neq 0.$$

An exponent can also be a fraction. If m and n are positive integers,

$$a^{\frac{m}{n}} = \sqrt[n]{a^m}$$

The numerator remains the exponent of a, but the denominator tells what root to take. For example,

$$(1) \quad 4^{\frac{3}{2}} = \sqrt[2]{4^3} = \sqrt{64} = 8 \qquad (2) \quad 3^{\frac{4}{2}} = \sqrt[2]{3^4} = \sqrt{81} = 9$$

If a fractional exponent were negative, the same operation would take place, but the result would be a fraction. For example,

$$(1) \quad 27^{-\frac{2}{3}} = \frac{1}{27^{2/3}} = \frac{1}{\sqrt[3]{27^2}} = \frac{1}{\sqrt[3]{729}} = \frac{1}{9}$$

PROBLEM

Simplify the following expressions:

$$(1) \quad -3^{-2} \qquad\qquad (3) \quad \frac{-3}{4^{-1}}$$

$$(2) \quad (-3)^{-2}$$

SOLUTION

(1) Here the exponent applies only to 3. Since

$$x^{-y} = \frac{1}{x^y}, -3^{-2} = -(3)^{-2} = -\frac{1}{3^2} = -\frac{1}{9}$$

(2) In this case the exponent applies to the negative base. Thus,

$$(-3)^{-2} = \frac{1}{(-3)^2} = \frac{1}{(-3)(-3)} = \frac{1}{9}$$

(3) $\dfrac{-3}{4^{-1}} = \dfrac{-3}{(\frac{1}{4})^1} = \dfrac{-3}{\frac{1^1}{4^1}} = \dfrac{-3}{\frac{1}{4}}$

Division by a fraction is equivalent to multiplication by that fraction's reciprocal, thus

$$\frac{-3}{\frac{1}{4}} = -3 \cdot \frac{4}{1} = -12 \quad \text{and} \quad \frac{-3}{4^{-1}} = -12$$

General Laws of Exponents

A) $\quad a^p a^q = a^{p+q}$

$$4^2 4^3 = 4^{2+3} = 1{,}024$$

B) $(a^p)^q = a^{pq}$

$(2^3)^2 = 2^6 = 64$

C) $\dfrac{a^p}{a^q} = a^{p-q}$

$\dfrac{3^6}{3^2} = 3^4 = 81$

D) $(ab)^p = a^p b^p$

$(3 \cdot 2)^2 = 3^2 \cdot 2^2 = (9)(4) = 36$

E) $\left(\dfrac{a}{b}\right)^p = \dfrac{a^p}{b^p}$, $b \neq 0$

$\left(\dfrac{4}{5}\right)^2 = \dfrac{4^2}{5^2} = \dfrac{16}{25}$

Drill 6: Exponents

Multiplication

Simplify

1. $4^6 * 4^2 =$
(A) 4^4 (B) 4^8 (C) 4^{12} (D) 16^8 (E) 16^{12}

2. $2^2 * 2^5 * 2^3 =$
(A) 2^{10} (B) 4^{10} (C) 8^{10} (D) 2^{30} (E) 8^{30}

3. $6^6 * 6^2 * 6^4 =$
(A) 18^8 (B) 18^{12} (C) 6^{12} (D) 6^{48} (E) 18^{48}

4. $a^4 b^2 * a^3 b =$
(A) ab (B) $2a^7 b^2$ (C) $2a^{12} b$ (D) $a^7 b^3$ (E) $a^7 b^2$

5. $m^8 n^3 * m^2 n * m^4 n^2 =$
(A) $3m^{16} n^6$ (B) $m^{14} n^6$ (C) $3m^{14} n^6$ (D) $3m^{14} n^5$ (E) m^2

Division

Simplify

6. $6^5 \div 6^3 =$
(A) 0 (B) 1 (C) 6 (D) 12 (E) 6^2

7. $11^8 \div 11^5 =$
(A) 1^3 (B) 11^3 (C) 11^{13} (D) 11^{40} (E) 88^5

8. $x^{10}y^8 \div x^7y^3 =$
(A) x^2y^5 (B) x^3y^4 (C) x^3y^5 (D) x^2y^4 (E) x^5y^3

9. $a^{14} \div a^9 =$
(A) 1^5 (B) a^5 (C) $2a^5$ (D) a^{23} (E) $2a^{23}$

10. $c^{17}d^{12}e^4 \div c^{12}d^8e =$
(A) $c^4d^5e^3$ (B) $c^4d^4e^3$ (C) $c^5d^8e^4$ (D) $c^5d^4e^3$ (E) $c^5d^4e^4$

Power to a Power

Simplify

11. $(3^6)^2 =$
(A) 3^4 (B) 3^8 (C) 3^{12} (D) 9^6 (E) 9^8

12. $(4^3)^5 =$
(A) 4^2 (B) 2^{15} (C) 4^8 (D) 20^3 (E) 4^{15}

13. $(a^4b^3)^2 =$
(A) $(ab)^9$ (B) a^8b^6 (C) $(ab)^{24}$ (D) a^6b^5 (E) $2a^4b^3$

14. $(r^3p^6)^3 =$
(A) r^9p^{18} (B) $(rp)^{12}$ (C) r^6p^9 (D) $3r^3p^6$ (E) $3r^9p^{18}$

15. $(m^6n^5q^3)^2 =$
(A) $2m^6n^5q^3$ (B) m^4n^3q (C) $m^8n^7q^5$
(D) $m^{12}n^{10}q^6$ (E) $2m^{12}n^{10}q^6$

7. Averages

Mean

The mean is the arithmetic average. It is the sum of the values divided by the total number of variables. For example:

$$\frac{4+3+8}{3} = 5$$

PROBLEM

Find the mean salary for four company employees who make $5/hr., $8/hr., $12/hr., and $15/hr.

SOLUTION

The mean salary is the average.

$$\frac{\$5 + \$8 + \$12 + \$15}{4} = \frac{\$40}{4} = \$10 / hr$$

PROBLEM

Find the mean length of five fish with lengths of 7.5 in, 7.75 in, 8.5 in, 8.5 in., 8.25 in.

SOLUTION

The mean length is the average length.

$$\frac{7.5 + 7.75 + 8.5 + 8.5 + 8.25}{5} = \frac{40.5}{5} = 8.1 in$$

Median

The median is the middle value in a set when there is an odd number of values. There is an equal number of values larger and smaller than the median. When the set is an even number of values, the average of the two middle values is the median. For example:

The median of (2, 3, 5, 8, 9) is 5.

The median of (2, 3, 5, 9, 10, 11) is $\frac{5+9}{2} = 7$.

Mode

The mode is the most frequently occurring value in the set of values. For example the mode of 4, 5, 8, 3, 8, 2 would be 8, since it occurs twice while the other values occur only once.

PROBLEM

For this series of observations find the mean, median, and mode.

500, 600, 800, 800, 900, 900, 900, 900, 900, 1000, 1100

SOLUTION

The mean is the value obtained by adding all the measurements and dividing by the number of measurements.

$$\frac{500 + 600 + 800 + 800 + 900 + 900 + 900 + 900 + 900 + 1000 + 1100}{11}$$

$$= \frac{9300}{11} = 845.45.$$

The median is the observation in the middle. We have 11 observations, so here the sixth, 900, is the median.

The mode is the observation that appears most frequently. That is also 900, since it has 5 appearances.

All three of these numbers are measures of central tendency. They describe the "middle" or "center" of the data.

PROBLEM

Nine rats run through a maze. The time each rat took to traverse the maze is recorded and these times are listed below.

1 min, 2.5 min, 3 min, 1.5 min, 2 min, 1.25 min, 1 min, .9 min, 30 min

Which of the three measures of central tendency would be the most appropriate in this case?

SOLUTION

We will calculate the three measures of central tendency and then compare them to determine which would be the most appropriate in describing these data.

The mean is the sum of observations divided by the number of observations. In this case

$$\frac{1 + 2.5 + 3 + 1.5 + 2 + 1.25 + 1 + .9 + 30}{9} = \frac{43.15}{9} = 4.79.$$

The median is the "middle number" in an array of the observations from the lowest to the highest.

0.9, 1.0, 1.0, 1.25, 1.5, 2.0, 2.5, 3.0, 30.0

The median is the fifth observation in this array or 1.5. There are four observations larger than 1.5 and four observations smaller than 1.5.

The mode is the most frequently occurring observation in the sample. In this data set the mode is 1.0.

mean = 4.79

median = 1.5

mode = 1.0

The mean is not appropriate here. Only one rat took more than 4.79 minutes to run the maze and this rat took 30 minutes. We see that the mean has been distorted by this one large observation.

The median or mode seems to describe this data set better and would be more appropriate to use.

Drill 7: Averages

Mean

DIRECTIONS: Find the mean of each set of numbers:

1.   18, 25, and 32.

(A) 3   (B)   25   (C)   50   (D)   75   (E)   150

2.   4/9, 2/3, and 5/6.

(A) 11/18   (B)   35/54   (C)   41/54   (D)   35/18   (E)   54/18

3.   97, 102, 116, and 137.

(A) 40   (B)   102   (C)   109   (D)   113   (E)   116

4.   12, 15, 18, 24, and 31.

(A) 18   (B)   19.3   (C)   20   (D)   25   (E)   100

5.   7, 4, 6, 3, 11, and 14.

(A) 5   (B)   6.5   (C)   7   (D)   7.5   (E)   8

Median

DIRECTIONS: Find the median value of each set of numbers.

6.   3, 8, and 6.

(A)   3   (B)   6   (C)   8   (D)   17   (E)   20

7.   19, 15, 21, 27, and 12.

(A)   19   (B)   15   (C)   21   (D)   27   (E)   94

8.   1 2/3, 1 7/8, 1 3/4, and 1 5/6.

(A)   1 30/48   (B)   1 2/3   (C)   1 3/4   (D)   1 19/24   (E)   1 21/24

9.   29, 18, 21, and 35.

(A)   29   (B)   18   (C)   21   (D)   35   (E)   25

10.   8, 15, 7, 12, 31, 3, and 28.

(A)   7   (B)   11.6   (C)   12   (D)   14.9   (E)   104

Mode

DIRECTIONS: Find the mode(s) of each set of numbers.

11.   1, 3, 7, 4, 3, and 8.

(A)   1   (B)   3   (C)   7   (D)   4   (E)   None

12.   12, 19, 25, and 42

(A)   12   (B)   19   (C)   25   (D)   42   (E)   None

13.   16, 14, 12, 16, 30, and 28.

(A)   6   (B)   14   (C)   16   (D)   19.3   (E)   None

14.   4, 3, 9, 2, 4, 5, and 2.

(A)   3 and 9   (B)   5 and 9   (C)   4 and 5   (D)   2 and 4   (E)   None

15.   87, 42, 111, 116, 39, 111, 140, 116, 97, and 111.

(A)   111   (B)   116   (C)   39   (D)   140   (E)   None

ARITHMETIC DRILLS

ANSWER KEY

Drill 1—Integers and Real Numbers

1.	(A)	9.	(E)	17.	(D)	25.	(D)
2.	(C)	10.	(B)	18.	(D)	26.	(D)
3.	(D)	11.	(B)	19.	(C)	27.	(B)
4.	(C)	12.	(E)	20.	(E)	28.	(C)
5.	(B)	13.	(C)	21.	(B)	29.	(A)
6.	(B)	14.	(A)	22.	(E)	30.	(C)
7.	(A)	15.	(B)	23.	(D)		
8.	(C)	16.	(B)	24.	(A)		

Drill 2—Fractions

1.	(D)	14.	(D)	27.	(D)	40.	(A)
2.	(E)	15.	(B)	28.	(E)	41.	(D)
3.	(C)	16.	(B)	29.	(C)	42.	(A)
4.	(A)	17.	(D)	30.	(B)	43.	(D)
5.	(C)	18.	(B)	31.	(C)	44.	(E)
6.	(B)	19.	(A)	32.	(A)	45.	(C)
7.	(C)	20.	(C)	33.	(B)	46.	(D)
8.	(A)	21.	(D)	34.	(C)	47.	(D)
9.	(B)	22.	(C)	35.	(D)	48.	(B)
10.	(A)	23.	(B)	36.	(B)	49.	(A)
11.	(B)	24.	(E)	37.	(C)	50.	(E)
12.	(D)	25.	(A)	38.	(D)		
13.	(E)	26.	(A)	39.	(E)		

Drill 3—Decimals

1.	(B)	9.	(C)	17.	(D)	25.	(E)
2.	(E)	10.	(E)	18.	(D)	26.	(D)
3.	(B)	11.	(B)	19.	(A)	27.	(C)
4.	(A)	12.	(D)	20.	(C)	28.	(A)
5.	(D)	13.	(A)	21.	(E)	29.	(E)
6.	(A)	14.	(B)	22.	(C)	30.	(D)
7.	(B)	15.	(C)	23.	(B)		
8.	(D)	16.	(B)	24.	(D)		

Drill 4—Percentages

1.	(B)	9.	(E)	17.	(D)	25.	(D)
2.	(C)	10.	(C)	18.	(E)	26.	(D)
3.	(E)	11.	(C)	19.	(C)	27.	(C)
4.	(B)	12.	(B)	20.	(C)	28.	(B)
5.	(A)	13.	(B)	21.	(A)	29.	(E)
6.	(B)	14.	(D)	22.	(B)	30.	(A)
7.	(A)	15.	(A)	23.	(C)		
8.	(B)	16.	(E)	24.	(B)		

Drill 5—Radicals

1.	(B)	6.	(C)	11.	(B)	16.	(A)
2.	(D)	7.	(A)	12.	(D)	17.	(C)
3.	(A)	8.	(D)	13.	(C)	18.	(B)
4.	(C)	9.	(C)	14.	(E)	19.	(D)
5.	(E)	10.	(B)	15.	(A)	20.	(C)

Drill 6—Exponents

1.	(B)	9.	(B)
2.	(A)	10.	(D)
3.	(C)	11.	(C)
4.	(D)	12.	(E)
5.	(B)	13.	(B)
6.	(E)	14.	(A)
7.	(B)	15.	(D)
8.	(C)		

Drill 7—Averages

1.	(B)	9.	(E)
2.	(B)	10.	(C)
3.	(D)	11.	(B)
4.	(C)	12.	(E)
5.	(D)	13.	(C)
6.	(B)	14.	(D)
7.	(A)	15.	(A)
8.	(D)		

GLOSSARY: ARITHMETIC

Absolute Value

The value of a number without regard to sign (i.e., it is always nonnegative).

Additive Identity

The number that, when added to another, results in that number. Thus the additive identity is 0.

Additive Inverse

The number that, when added to the original number, results in the additive identity, 0. The additive inverse of a number is the negative of that number.

Associative Property

The property that states (for addition) that $a + (b + c) = (a + b) + c$. This also holds for multiplication but not for subtraction or division.

Base

A number to be raised to a power.

Commutative Property

The property that states (for addition) that $a + b = b + a$. This is also true for multiplication, but not subtraction or division.

Complex Fraction

A fraction in which either the numerator, the denominator, or both are a fraction.

Composite Number

An integer that is not prime, i.e., a number that has factors besides itself and 1.

Cube Root

A number that, when multiplied by itself twice (i.e., number × number × number), results in the original number.

Decimal

A number expressed as a whole number (to the left of the decimal point) and a remainder (to the right of the decimal point). When there is no whole number to the left of the decimal point, that number is considered 0.

Decimal Point

The point that separates the whole number in a decimal from the remainder.

Denominator

The number dividing the numerator in a fraction.

Difference

The result of subtracting one number from another.

Distributive Property

The property that states (for addition and multiplication) that $a*(b+c) = a*b + a*c$. This also holds for subtraction and multiplication (i.e., $a*(b-c) = a*b - a*c$) but not for division and addition or division and subtraction. It is *not* true that $a/(b+c) = (a/b) + (a/c)$. It is true, however, that $(a+b)/c = (a/c) + (b/c)$.

Even Integer

An integer that, when divided by 2, results in an integer.

Exponent

The number of times the base is to be multiplied by itself.

Factors of a number

A set of numbers that, when multiplied together, results in the original number.

Fraction

A number expressed in the form of one number (the numerator) divided by another (the denominator).

Improper Fraction

A fraction in which the numerator exceeds the denominator.

Integer

The set of numbers $\{\ldots, -3, -2, -1, 0, 1, 2, 3, \ldots\}$.

Irrational Number

A number that is not rational, i.e., cannot be expressed as a ratio of integers.

Least Common Denominator

The smallest whole number that results in a whole number when divided by each of the numbers in a set.

Mean

The sum of a set of numbers divided by how many numbers there are in the set.

Median

The number such that half of the numbers in the given set exceed this number, and half are smaller than it (i.e., if the numbers are ordered, then the median is in the middle).

Mixed Number

The sum of a whole number and a proper fraction.

Mode

> The number that occurs most often in a set of numbers.

Multiplicative Identity

> The number that, when multiplied by another number, results in that number. Hence the multiplicative identity is 1.

Multiplicative Inverse

> The number that, when multiplied by the original number, results in the multiplicative identity, or 1. Hence the multiplicative inverse of a number is 1 divided by that number, or the reciprocal of the number.

Natural Number

> A positive integer, i.e., {1, 2, 3, ...}

Negative Number

> A number that is less than 0 or that falls to the left of 0 on the number line.

Number Line

> A line of infinite length with a 0 and positive numbers to the right of 0 and negative numbers to the left. The numbers are ordered, so each is to the left of numbers larger than it, and to the right of smaller numbers. The distances between numbers is preserved, e.g., the distance between 1 and 2 is the same as that between 6 and 7.

Numerator

> The number being divided in a fraction.

Odd Integer

> An integer that is not even, i.e., when divided by 2, the quotient is not an integer. An integer is odd if, and only if, the preceding integer is even.

Order of Operations

> The law that requires dealing first with parentheses, then powers of exponents, then multiplication or division, and finally addition or subtraction.

Percent

> A number expressed as a part of a whole (i.e., 100% = 1).

Positive Number

> A number that exceeds 0 or that falls to the right of 0 on the number line.

Power

> The exponent.

Prime Factor

> A factor of a number that is prime. That is, it has no factor besides itself and 1.

Prime Number

An integer whose only factors are itself and 1.

Product

The result of multiplying two or more numbers together.

Proper Fraction

A fraction in which the denominator exceeds the numerator.

Quotient

The result of division.

Radical Sign

The symbol that indicates to find a root of a number.

Radicand

The number whose root (possibly square or cube) is to be found.

Range

The largest of a set of numbers minus the smallest of the set.

Rational Number

A number that can be expressed as the ratio of two integers.

Real Number

Any single number (in one dimension).

Reciprocal

The multiplicative inverse.

Repeating Decimal

A decimal with a repeating pattern after the decimal point.

Square Root

A number that, when multiplied by itself, results in the original number.

Sum

The result of adding two or more numbers together.

Terminating Decimal

A decimal with a finite number of places after the decimal point.

Weighted Mean

The sum of (the original numbers multiplied by the weights) divided by (the sum of the weights).

Whole Number

A nonnegative integer, i.e., {0, 1, 2, 3, ...}.

CHAPTER 3

Algebra

➤ Diagnostic Test
➤ Algebra Review and Drills
➤ Glossary

ALGEBRA
DIAGNOSTIC TEST

1. (A) (B) (C) (D) (E)		26. (A) (B) (C) (D) (E)
2. (A) (B) (C) (D) (E)		27. (A) (B) (C) (D) (E)
3. (A) (B) (C) (D) (E)		28. (A) (B) (C) (D) (E)
4. (A) (B) (C) (D) (E)		29. (A) (B) (C) (D) (E)
5. (A) (B) (C) (D) (E)		30. (A) (B) (C) (D) (E)
6. (A) (B) (C) (D) (E)		31. (A) (B) (C) (D) (E)
7. (A) (B) (C) (D) (E)		32. (A) (B) (C) (D) (E)
8. (A) (B) (C) (D) (E)		33. (A) (B) (C) (D) (E)
9. (A) (B) (C) (D) (E)		34. (A) (B) (C) (D) (E)
10. (A) (B) (C) (D) (E)		35. (A) (B) (C) (D) (E)
11. (A) (B) (C) (D) (E)		36. (A) (B) (C) (D) (E)
12. (A) (B) (C) (D) (E)		37. (A) (B) (C) (D) (E)
13. (A) (B) (C) (D) (E)		38. (A) (B) (C) (D) (E)
14. (A) (B) (C) (D) (E)		39. (A) (B) (C) (D) (E)
15. (A) (B) (C) (D) (E)		40. (A) (B) (C) (D) (E)
16. (A) (B) (C) (D) (E)		41. (A) (B) (C) (D) (E)
17. (A) (B) (C) (D) (E)		42. (A) (B) (C) (D) (E)
18. (A) (B) (C) (D) (E)		43. (A) (B) (C) (D) (E)
19. (A) (B) (C) (D) (E)		44. (A) (B) (C) (D) (E)
20. (A) (B) (C) (D) (E)		45. (A) (B) (C) (D) (E)
21. (A) (B) (C) (D) (E)		46. (A) (B) (C) (D) (E)
22. (A) (B) (C) (D) (E)		47. (A) (B) (C) (D) (E)
23. (A) (B) (C) (D) (E)		48. (A) (B) (C) (D) (E)
24. (A) (B) (C) (D) (E)		49. (A) (B) (C) (D) (E)
25. (A) (B) (C) (D) (E)		50. (A) (B) (C) (D) (E)

ALGEBRA DIAGNOSTIC TEST

This diagnostic test is designed to help you determine your strengths and your weaknesses in algebra. Follow the directions for each part and check your answers.

Study this chapter for the following tests:
PSAT, SAT I, ACT, NTE, PPST, CBEST, GRE, GMAT, GED, and ELM

---

50 Questions

DIRECTIONS: Choose the correct answer for each of the following problems. Fill in the answer on the answer sheet.

1. The value of B in the equation $A = (h/2)(B + b)$ is:

   (A) $(2A - b)h$ (B) $2h/A - b$ (C) $2A - b$

   (D) $2A/h - b$ (E) None of the above

2. Which of the following integers is the square of an integer for every integer x?

   (A) $x^2 + x$ (B) $x^2 + 1$ (C) $x^2 + 2x$

   (D) $x^2 + 2x - 4$ (E) $x^2 + 2x + 1$

3. Each of the integers h, m and n is divisible by 3. Which of the following integers is ALWAYS divisible by 9?

   I. hm

   II. $h + m$

   III. $h + m + n$

   (A) I only   (B) II only   (C) III only

   (D) II and III only   (E) I, II, and III

4. What is the factorization of $x^2 + ax - 2x - 2a$?

   (A) $(x + 2)(x - a)$ (B) $(x - 2)(x + a)$ (C) $(x + 2)(x + a)$

   (D) $(x - 2)(x - a)$ (E) None of the above

5. What is the value of x in the equation

    $\sqrt{5x - 4} - 5 = -1$?

    (A) 2 (B) 5 (C) No value

    (D) 4 (E) -4

6. The number missing in the series, 2, 6, 12, 20, x, 42, 56 is:

    (A) 36 (B) 24 (C) 30

    (D) 38 (E) 40

7. If $T = 2\pi \sqrt{\dfrac{L}{g}}$, then L is equal to

    (A) $\dfrac{T^2}{2\pi g}$ (B) $\dfrac{T^2 g}{2\pi}$ (C) $\dfrac{T^2 g}{4\pi^2}$

    (D) $\dfrac{T^2 g}{4\pi}$ (E) $\dfrac{T^2}{4\pi^2 g}$

8. $1 + \dfrac{y}{x + 2y} - \dfrac{y}{x - 2y} =$

    (A) 0 (B) 1

    (C) $\dfrac{1}{(x - 2y)(x + 2y)}$ (D) $\dfrac{2x - y}{(x - 2y)(x + 2y)}$

    (E) $\dfrac{x^2}{(x - 2y)(x + 2y)}$

9. If $0 < a < 1$ and $b > 1$, which is the largest value?

    (A) $^a/_b$ (B) $^b/_a$ (C) $(^a/_b)^2$

    (D) $(^b/_a)^2$ (E) Cannot be determined

10. Given $\dfrac{(\alpha + x) + y}{x + y} = \dfrac{\beta + y}{y}$, $\dfrac{x}{y} = ?$

    (A) α/β (B) β/α (C) $\beta/\alpha - 1$

    (D) $\alpha/\beta - 1$ (E) 1

11. If *n* is an integer, which of the following represents an odd number?

   (A) $2n + 3$ (B) $2n$ (C) $2n + 2$

   (D) $3n$ (E) $n + 1$

12. Which of the following statements are true, if

   $$x + y + z = 10$$

   $$y \geq 5$$

   $$4 \geq z \geq 3$$

   I. $x < z$

   II. $x > y$

   III. $x + z \leq y$

   (A) I only   (B) II only   (C) III only

   (D) I and III   (E) I, II, and III

13. $\sqrt{X\sqrt{X\sqrt{X}}} = ?$

   (A) $X^{7/8}$ (B) $X^{7/4}$ (C) $X^{15/16}$

   (D) $X^{3/4}$ (E) $X^{15/8}$

14. If $v = \pi b^2 (r - {}^b/_3)$, then *r* is equal to

   (A) $\dfrac{v}{\pi b^2} + \dfrac{b}{3}$ (B) $\dfrac{v}{\pi b^2} + \dfrac{b}{3\pi}$ (C) $\dfrac{v}{\pi b^2} + 3b$

   (D) $v + \dfrac{b}{3}$ (E) $v + \dfrac{\pi b}{3}$

15. If ${}^a/_x - {}^b/_y = c$ and $xy = {}^1/_c$, then $bx = ?$

   (A) $1 - ay$ (B) ay (C) $ay + 1$

   (D) $ay - 1$ (E) $2ay$

16. If $z = x^a$, $y = x^6$ then $z^b y^a = ?$

   (A) $x^{(ab)^2}$ (B) x^{ab} (C) x^0

   (D) x^{2ab} (E) x

17. The mean (average) of the numbers 50, 60, 65, 75, x and y is 65. What is the mean of x and y?

   (A) 67   (B) 70   (C) 71

   (D) 73   (E) 75

18. If x and 10 are relatively prime natural numbers, then x could be a multiple of

   (A) 9   (B) 18   (C) 4

   (D) 25   (E) 14

19. A first square has a side of length x while the length of a side of a second square is two units greater than the length of a side of the first square. What is an expression for the sum of the areas of the two squares?

   (A) $2x^2 + 4x + 4$ (B) $x^2 + 2$ (C) $x^2 + 4$

   (D) $2x^2 + 2x + 2$ (E) $2x^2 + 3x + 4$

20. If a and b each represent a nonzero real number and if

   $$x = \frac{a}{|a|} + \frac{b}{|b|} + \frac{ab}{|ab|}$$

   the the set of all possible values for x is

   (A) $\{-3, -2, -1, 1, 2, 3\}$ (B) $\{3, -1, -2\}$

   (C) $\{3, -1, -3\}$ (D) $\{3, -1\}$

   (E) $\{3, 1, -1\}$

21. If $x - y = 9$ then $3x - 3y - 1 =$

   (A) 23   (B) 24   (C) 25

   (D) 26   (E) 28

22. $4^{x-3} = \left(\sqrt{2}\right)^x$ The value of x is

   (A) 0   (B) 5   (C) 4

   (D) $^1/_2$ (E) 3

23. Find the first term of the arithmetic progression whose third term a_3 is 7 and whose eighth term a_8 is 17.

   (A) 0   (B) 2   (C) 3

(D) 1   (E) 4

24. If $x = -2y$ and $2x - 6y = 5$ then $\dfrac{1}{x} + \dfrac{1}{y} =$

(A) $^3/_2$ (B) -3 (C) -1

(D) $-^3/_2$ (E) 3

25. If $f(x) = 2x - 5$ then $f(x + h) =$

(A) $2x + h - 5$ (B) $2h - 5$ (C) $2x + 2h - 5$

(D) $2x - 2h + 5$ (E) $2x - 5$

26. If $a + b = 3$ and $2b + c = 2$, then $2a - c =$

(A) -4 (B) -1 (C) 1

(D) 4   (E) 5

27. If $x > ^1/_5$, then

(A) x is greater than 1.   (B) x is greater than 5.

(C) $^1/_x$ is greater than 5.   (D) $^1/_x$ is less than 5.

(E) None of the above statements is true.

28. If $f(x) = x^2 + 3x + 2$, then $[f(x + a) - f(x)]/a =$

(A) $2x + a + 3$ (B) $(x + a)^2 - x^2$ (C) $a^2 + 2ax + 3a$

(D) $2x + a$ (E) $2x + 3$

29. If $x + 2y > 5$ and $x < 3$, then $y > 1$ is true

(A) never.   (B) only if $x = 0$.   (C) only if $x > 0$.

(D) only if $x < 0$.   (E) always.

30. If $x + y = 8$ and $xy = 6$, then $^1/_x + ^1/_y =$

(A) $^1/_8$ (B) $^1/_6$ (C) $^1/_4$

(D) $^4/_3$ (E) 8

31. If $x^{64} = 64$ then $x^{32} =$

(A) 8 or -8 (B) 12 or -12 (C) 16

(D) 32 or -32 (E) 48

32. If $\sqrt{x-1} = 2$ then $(x-1)^2 =$

    (A) 4   (B) 6   (C) 8

    (D) 10   (E) 16

33. If $2^x = \dfrac{16^2 \cdot 8^3}{2^{19}}$ then $x =$

    (A) -3 (B) -2 (C) 1

    (D) 2   (E) 3

34. If $2^{(6x-8)} = 16$ then $x =$

    (A) 2   (B) 4   (C) 10

    (D) 1   (E) 6

35. $\sqrt{X\sqrt{X\sqrt{X^2}}} = ?$

    (A) X (B) $X^{7/4}$ (C) $X^{15/16}$

    (D) $X^{3/4}$ (E) $X^{15/8}$

36. The quotient of $(x^2 - 5x + 3)/(x + 2)$ is:

    (A) $x - 7 + 17/(x + 2)$ (B) $x - 3 + 9/(x + 2)$

    (C) $x - 7 - 11/(x + 2)$ (D) $x - 3 - 3/(x + 2)$

    (E) $x + 3 - 3(x + 2)$

37. If x and y are two different real numbers and $xz = yz$, then what is the value of z?

    (A) $x - y$ (B) 1   (C) x/y

    (D) y/x (E) 0

38. If $2a + 2b = 1$, and $6a - 2b = 5$, which of the following statements is true?

    (A) $3a - b = 5$ (B) $a + b > 3a - b$ (C) $a + b = -2$

    (D) $a + b < 3a - b$ (E) $a + b = -1$

39. Which of the following equations can be used to find a number n, such that if you multiply it by 3 and take 2 away, the result is 5 times as great as if you divide the number by 3 and add 2?

(A) $3n - 2 = 5 + (n/3 + 2)$ (B) $3n - 2 = 5(n/3 + 2)$

(C) $3n - 2 = 5n/3 + 2$ (D) $5(3n - 2) = n/3 + 2$

(E) $5n - 2 = n/3 + 2$

40. If $3/2x = 5$, then $2/3 + x =$

(A) $10/3$ (B) 4   (C) $15/2$

(D) 8   (E) 12

41. If $x + y = 12$ sand $x^2 + y^2 = 126$ then $xy =$

(A) 9   (B) 10   (C) 11

(D) 13   (E) 16

42. If $\dfrac{7a - 5b}{b} = 7$, then $\dfrac{4a + 6b}{2a}$ equals

(A) $15/4$ (B) 4   (C) $17/4$

(D) 5   (E) 6

43. The fraction

$$\frac{7x - 11}{x^2 - 2x - 15}$$

was obtained by adding the two fractions

$$\frac{A}{x - 5} + \frac{B}{x + 3}.$$

The values of A and B are:

(A) $A = 7x, B = 11$ (B) $A = -11, B = 7x$

(C) $A = 3, B = 4$ (D) $A = 5, B = -3$

(E) $A = -5, B = 3$

44. What number must be added to 28 and 36 to give an average of 29?

(A) 23   (B) 32   (C) 21

(D) 4   (E) 5

45. Solve for x:

$$\frac{5}{x} = \frac{2}{x-1} + \frac{1}{x(x-1)}.$$

(A) -1 (B) 0 (C) 1

(D) 2 (E) 3

46. If $2X + Y = 2$ and $X + 3Y > 6$, then

(A) $Y \geq 2$ (B) $Y > 2$ (C) $Y < 2$

(D) $Y \leq 2$ (E) $Y = 2$

47. The expression $(x + y)^2 + (x - y)^2$ is equivalent to

(A) $2x^2$ (B) $4x^2$ (C) $2(x^2 + y^2)$

(D) $2x^2 + y^2$ (E) $x^2 + 2y^2$

48. If $x + y = {}^1\!/_k$ and $x - y = k$, what is the value of $x^2 - y^2$?

(A) 4 (B) 1 (C) 0

(D) k^2 (E) $\dfrac{1}{k^2}$

49. If $3^{a-b} = {}^1\!/_9$ and $3^{a+b} = 9$, then $a =$

(A) -2 (B) 0 (C) 1

(D) 2 (E) 3

50. If $\dfrac{3}{X-1} = \dfrac{2}{X+1}$, then $X =$

(A) -5 (B) -1 (C) 0

(D) 1 (E) 5

ALGEBRA DIAGNOSTIC TEST

ANSWER KEY

1. (D)	11. (A)	21. (D)	31. (A)	41. (A)
2. (E)	12. (D)	22. (C)	32. (E)	42. (A)
3. (A)	13. (A)	23. (C)	33. (B)	43. (C)
4. (B)	14. (A)	24. (C)	34. (A)	44. (A)
5. (D)	15. (D)	25. (C)	35. (A)	45. (D)
6. (C)	16. (D)	26. (D)	36. (A)	46. (B)
7. (C)	17. (B)	27. (D)	37. (E)	47. (C)
8. (E)	18. (A)	28. (A)	38. (D)	48. (B)
9. (D)	19. (A)	29. (E)	39. (B)	49. (B)
10. (D)	20. (D)	30. (D)	40. (B)	50. (A)

DETAILED EXPLANATIONS
OF ANSWERS

1.　　**(D)**　Simplify the equation by first multiplying by 2 on both sides and expand the right-hand side as follows:

$$A = (h/2)(B + b) \text{ or } 2A = 2(h/2)(B + b)$$
$$2A = h(B + b)$$
$$2A = hB + hb$$

Then, solve for B as follows:

$$hB + hb = 2A$$
$$hB = 2A - hb$$
$$B = 2A/h - hb/h$$
$$B = 2A/h - b$$

Hence answer choice (D) is correct. The other choices are incorrect because they are obtained by inappropriately applying algebra techniques.

2.　　**(E)**　If $x = 1$ then response (B) is 2, response (A) is 2, response (C) is 3, and response (D) is $- 1$. Thus, response (E) is the only response possible. Consider response (E). Notice that by factoring the expression one gets

$$x^2 + 2x + 1 = (x + 1)(x + 1) = (x + 1)^2$$

which is the square of an integer for every integer x.

3.　　**(A)**　Since h, m and n are divisible by 3, first represent each as follows: $h = 3i$, $m = 3j$, and $n = 3k$, where i, j, k are integers. Now consider the hm as follows:

$$hm = 3i(3j) = 9ij.$$

But clearly, $hm/9 = 9ij/9 = ij$. So, hm is divisible by 9.

　　Using the same technique or by a simple example it is clear that II and III are not possible, Hence, the other answer choices are not possible.

4.　　**(B)**　First, group the expression and then find the monomial factor for each group as follows:

$$(x^2 + ax) + (- 2x - 2a) = x(x + a) + (- 2)(x + a).$$

Then, the final factorization is formed by using $(x + a)$ and $(x - 2)$. So,

$$x^2 + ax - 2x - 2a = (x - 2)(x + a).$$

Notice that multiplying these two factors together will yield the original algebraic expression. So, (B) is the correct answer choice. The other answer choices are incorrect because when the factors are multiplied together in each case, the results do not yield the original algebraic expression.

5.   **(D)**   First add 5 to both sides of the equation and then square both sides as follows:

$$\sqrt{5x-4} - 5 + 5 = -1 + 5$$
$$(\sqrt{5x-4})^2 = 4^2$$
$$5x - 4 = 16$$
$$5x = 16 + 4$$
$$5x = 20$$
$$x = 4.$$

6.   **(C)**   The difference between the first two numbers is 4 (6 − 2); the difference between the second and third numbers is 6 (12 − 6) which is two more than the first difference; the difference between the third and fourth numbers is 8 (20 12) which is two more than the second difference; the difference between the fourth and fifth numbers is 10 (x − 20). Thus, the value of x is given by $x - 20 = 10$. Solving for x yields $x = 30$. So, the correct answer choice is (C). Similar analysis of each of the other choices will fail to satisfy the missing value of x such that it is a consistent distance in relation to the other numbers in the series.

7.   **(C)**   The most direct method for attacking this problem is to solve the equation

$$T = 2\pi\sqrt{\frac{L}{g}}$$

for the variable L.

8.   **(E)**   This problem can be solved easily by performing the indicated operations. The indicated operations are addition and subtraction of rational expressions with unlike denominators. When adding and/or subtracting rational expressions with unlike denominators, we must express all expressions as fractions with the same denominator, usually called the least common denominator. To find the least common denominator of a set of rational expressions,

(i)   Factor ech denominator completely and express repeated factors as powers.

(ii)   Write each different factor that appears in any denominator.

(iii)   Raise each factor in step (ii) to the highest power it occurs in any denominator.

(iv) The least common denominator is the product of all factors found in step (iii).

In this problem, denominators in factored form are:

$$1 = 1$$

$$x - 2y = (x - 2y)$$

$$x + 2y = (x + 2y)$$

Hence, all the different factors are 1, $(x - 2y)$, and $(x + 2y)$. This gives us $1(x - 2y)(x + 2y)$ as the least common denominator.

Performing the indicated operations yields:

$$1 + \frac{y}{(x - 2y)} - \frac{y}{x + 2y} =$$

$$= \frac{(x - 2y)(x + 2y)}{(x - 2y)(x + 2y)} + \frac{y(x + 2y)}{(x - 2y)(x + 2y)} - \frac{y(x - 2y)}{(x - 2y)(x + 2y)}$$

$$= \frac{x^2 - 4y^2 + xy + 2y^2 - xy + 2y^2}{(x - 2y)(x + 2y)}$$

$$= \frac{x^2}{(x - 2y)(x + 2y)}$$

9.   **(D)**   We need to find the largest value given. Given $0 < a < 1$ and $b > 1$, we know that

$$a/b < 1, \quad b/a > 1, \quad \text{so} \quad b/a > a/b, \quad \text{and} \quad (b/a)^2 > (a/b)^2.$$

Therefore, the choice is between (b/a) and $(b/a)^2$. But (b/a) $2 > (b/a)$ since $b/a > 1$. Thus the largest value is $(b/a)^2$.

10.   **(D)**   We need to find an expression for x/y as a function of α or β

$$\frac{(\alpha + x) + y}{x + y} = \frac{\beta + y}{y}$$

This is the same as

$$\frac{\alpha + (x + y)}{x + y} = \frac{\beta + y}{y}$$

Rearranging

$$\frac{\alpha}{x + y} + \frac{x + y}{x + y} = \frac{\beta}{y} + \frac{y}{y}$$

$$\frac{\alpha}{x + y} + 1 = \frac{\beta}{y} + 1$$

$$\frac{\alpha}{x+y} = \frac{\beta}{y}$$

$$\frac{\alpha}{\beta} = \frac{x+y}{y}$$

$$\frac{\alpha}{\beta} = \frac{x}{y} + \frac{y}{y}$$

$$\frac{\alpha}{\beta} = \frac{x}{y} + 1$$

$$\frac{x}{y} = \frac{\alpha}{\beta} - 1$$

11. **(A)** n is an integer means n can be an odd number or an even number. If n is odd, then $3n$ is odd (odd × odd = odd). If n is even, then $3n$ is even (odd × even = even). This simple discussion eliminates answer choice (D). Answer choice (E) is eliminated because if n is odd, then $(n + 1)$ is even, and if n is even, then $(n + 1)$ is odd.

If n is an integer (odd or even), then $2n$ is even (any integer × 2 = an even integer), and $(2n + 2)$ is even (since even + even = even). Thus, answer choices (B) and (C) are eliminated.

If n is an integer, then $2n$ is even and $2n + 3$ is odd (even + odd = odd).

12. **(D)** Rearrange the first equation

$$x = 10 - y - z$$

If we use the smallest values for y and z, we obtain the biggest one for x, that is

$$x = 10 - 5 - 3$$

$$x = 2$$

therefore

$$x < z \text{ and also } x < y.$$

Now rearrange the expression to analyze proposition III.

$$x + z = 10 - y$$

if $y = 5$ (the smallest one, $x + z = 5$

but if $y > 5$ then $x + z < 5$

therefore $x + z \le y$.

13. **(A)**

$$\sqrt{X\sqrt{X\sqrt{X}}} = \sqrt{X\sqrt{X*X^{1/2}}}$$

$$= \sqrt{X\sqrt{X^{3/2}}}$$

$$= \sqrt{X*X^{3/4}}$$

$$= \sqrt{X^{7/4}} = X^{7/8}$$

The sum of the exponents $1 + {}^3/_4 = {}^7/_4$.

14. **(A)** The most direct approach to solve this problem is to solve the equation

$$v = \pi b^2 (r - \frac{b}{3})$$

for r. Thus,

$$v = \pi b^2 (r - \frac{b}{3})$$

$$v = \pi b^2 r - \pi b^2 (\frac{b}{3})$$

$$v = \pi b^2 r - \frac{\pi b^3}{3}$$

$$v = \frac{3\pi b^2 r - \pi b^3}{3}$$

Cross multiplication yields,

$$3v = 3\pi b^2 r - \pi b^3$$

$$3v + \pi b^3 = 3\pi b^2 r$$

$$\frac{3v + \pi b^3}{3\pi b^2} = r$$

$$r = \frac{3v}{3\pi b^2} + \frac{\pi b^3}{3\pi b^2}$$

$$r = \frac{v}{\pi b^2} + \frac{b}{3}$$

Note that the right-hand side of this equation is the quantity given in answer choice (A).

Checking all the quantities given in answer choices (B), (C), (D) and (E), we find out that none of those quantities are equivalent to the quantity,

$$\frac{v}{\pi b^2} + \frac{b}{3}.$$

15. **(D)** We need to find the expression for *bx* as a function of *y*, where

$$\frac{a}{x} - \frac{b}{y} = c \quad \text{and} \quad xy = \frac{1}{c}$$

Using the first expression $^a/_x - ^b/_y = c$, we get

$$\frac{ay - bx}{xy} = c = ay - bx = cxy$$

Substituting the second expression in the right side, we have

$$ay - bx = c \cdot {}^1/_c$$
$$= ay - bx = 1$$
$$= bx = ay - 1.$$

16. **(D)** If

$$z = x^a \text{ and } y = x^b$$

then
$$z^b = (x^a)^b/b$$
$$z^b = (x^a)^b$$
$$z = x^{ab}$$

and
$$y = x^b/a$$
$$y = (x^b)a$$
$$y = x^{ba} = x^{ab}$$

so
$$z^b y^a = x^{ab} x^{ab} = x^{ab+ab}$$
$$z^b y^a = x^{2ab}$$

17. **(B)** The mean of the six numbers is 65, so

$$\frac{50 + 60 + 65 + 75 + x + y}{6} = 65$$

or $50 + 60 + 65 + 70 + x + y = 6 \cdot 65$

$$x + y = 140$$

but $\frac{x + y}{2} = 70.$

18.　**(A)**　For two natural numbers to be relatively prime, their only positive common natural number divisor is 1. Then x could not be a multiple of 18 because then x and 10 have 2 as a common divisor. By a similar argument x could not be a multiple of 4, 25 or 14. However, the odd multiples of 9 do not contain factors of 2 and 5. Thus, x could be a multiple of 9.

19.　**(A)**　The area of the first square is x^2 and the area of the second square is $(x + 2)^2$. Thus, the sum of the areas is

$$x^2 + (x + 2)^2 = x^2 + (x^2 + 4x + 4)$$

$$= 2x^2 + 4x + 4.$$

20.　**(D)**　If a is positive and b is positive then

$$x = \frac{a}{|a|} + \frac{b}{|b|} + \frac{ab}{|ab|}$$

$$= 1 + 1 + 1$$

$$= 3$$

If a is positive and b is negative then

$$x = \frac{a}{|a|} + \frac{b}{|b|} + \frac{ab}{|ab|}$$

$$= -1 + (-1) + (-1)$$

$$= -1$$

If a is negative and b is positive then

$$x = \frac{a}{|a|} + \frac{b}{|b|} + \frac{ab}{|ab|}$$

$$= 1 + 1 + (-1)$$

$$= -1$$

If a is negative and b is negative then

$$x = \frac{a}{|a|} + \frac{b}{|b|} + \frac{ab}{|ab|}$$

$$= 1 + (-1) + 1$$

$$= -1$$

21.　**(D)**　If $x - y = 9$ then

$$3(x - y) = 3(9)$$

and $\qquad 3x - 3y = 27$

and $\qquad 3x - 3y - 1 = 26.$

22. **(C)**

$4^{x-3} = (\sqrt{2})^x$ is equivalent to (since $\sqrt{2} = 2^{1/2}$)

$2^{(x-3)} = 2^{x/2}$, $2^{2x-6} = 2^{x/2}$,

since the bases are equal, we have $2x - 6 = x/2$, multiplying each term by 2 to clear the fraction gives $4x - 12 = x$, $\therefore$ $x = 4$.

23. **(C)** The formula for the nth term of an arithmetic progression with common difference d and first term a_1 is

$a_n = a_1 + (n - 1)d.$

The third term formula is

$7 = a_1 + (3 - 1)d$ or $7 = a_1 + 2d.$

The eighth term formula is

$17 = a_1 + (8 - 1)d$ or $17 = a_1 + 7d.$

Solving these two equations, by subtracting the second from the first, gives

$-10 = -5d$ or $d = 2.$

Counting back from the third term, gives

$a_2 = 7 - 2 = 5$

so that

$a_1 = 5 - 2 = 3.$

24. **(C)** Substitute $x = -2y$ for x in the equation $2x - 6y = 5$ obtaining

$-4y - 6y = 5$ or $-10y = 5$

so that $y = -\frac{1}{2}$. Therefore, $x = -2(-\frac{1}{2}) = 1$. Evaluating the expression $\frac{1}{x} + \frac{1}{y}$ for $x = 1, y = -\frac{1}{2}$ gives $1 - 2 = -1.$

25. **(C)** Evaluating a function at $x + h$ means to replace x in $2x - 5$ by the quantity $x + h$. Therefore,

$2(x + h) - 5 = 2x + 2h - 5.$

Choice (B) comes from replacing x by h only. Choice (A) comes from improper use of the distributive property:

$2(x + h) \neq 2x + h.$

26. **(D)** If

$$a + b = 3 \quad \text{and} \quad 2b + c = 2,$$

then $2(a + b) = 2(3) = 6$ so that

$$2(a + b) - (2b + c) = 6 - 2.$$

Therefore,

$$2a - c = 4.$$

27. **(D)** If $x > \frac{1}{5}$, then $x > 0$. Hence $\frac{1}{x} < 5$.

28. **(A)**

$$f(x + a) - f(x) = [(x + a)^2 + 3(x + a) + 2] - (x^2 + 3x + 2)$$
$$= (x + a)^2 - x^2 + 3a$$
$$= 2ax + a^2 + 3a.$$

Therefore,

$$[f(x + a) - f(x)]/a = (2ax + a^2 + 3a)/a$$
$$= 2x + a + 3.$$

29. **(E)** If

$$x + 2y > 5 \quad \text{and} \quad x < 3,$$

then $5 < x + 2y < 3 + 2y.$

Thus $5 - 3 < 2y, \quad \text{or} \quad y > 1.$

30. **(D)**

$$\frac{1}{x} + \frac{1}{y} = \frac{x + y}{xy} = \frac{8}{6} = \frac{4}{3}.$$

31. **(A)**

$$x^{64} = (x^{32})^2$$
$$x^{64} = 64$$
$$(x^{32})^2 = 64$$

Since the only two numbers whose square is 64 are 8 and -8, $x^{32} = 8$ or $x^{32} = -8$.

32. **(E)** Since

$$\sqrt{x - 1} = (x - 1)^{1/2}$$

and since

$$\left[(x-1)^{1/2}\right]^4 = (x-1)^2$$

$$(\sqrt{x-1})^4 = 2^4$$

$$(x-1)^2 = 16.$$

33. **(B)**

$$\frac{16^2 \cdot 8^3}{2^{19}} = \frac{(2^4)^2 \cdot (2^3)^3}{2^{19}}$$

$$= \frac{2^8 \cdot 2^9}{2^{19}}$$

$$= \frac{2^{17}}{2^{19}}$$

$$= 2^{-2}.$$

34. **(A)** $2^{(6x-8)} = 16$, 2 raised to the 4th power equals 16. Thus

$$6x - 8 = 4.$$

Add 8 to both sides

$$6x = 12.$$

Divide both sides by 6

$$x = 2.$$

35. **(A)**

$$\sqrt{X\sqrt{X\sqrt{X^2}}} = \sqrt{X\sqrt{X*X}} = \sqrt{X*X} = \sqrt{X^2} = X.$$

36. **(A)** To find the quotient and the remainder one can either use the long division procedure or the synthetic division procedure. The first procedure should be well-known so the synthetic division procedure is used below. First, take the coefficients and constant term (in order) of the dividend expression and write them as follows:

$$1 \qquad -5 \qquad 3$$

Next, write the divisor expression in the form $x - a$ and use as the divisor of the three integers above. So, $x + 2 = x - (-2)$. Hence $a = -2$. Thus, one can complete the procedure as follows:

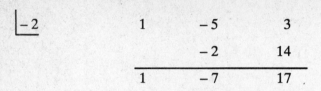

where the first coefficient is simply brought down below the line. The -2 under -5 (the second coefficient) is obtained by multiplying -2 (the divisor value) by the 1 below the line. The 14 under the constant term 3 is obtained by multiplying -2 (the divisor value) by the -7 below the line. Finally, the quotient is determined by attaching the x variable to 1 since the original dividend was a second degree expression in x and -7 becomes the constant term. The remainder is 17 which can be expressed as a fraction $17/(x + 2)$. Thus, the complete quotient is given by:

$$1x - 7 + 17/(x + 2) \text{ or } x - 7 + 17/(x + 2)$$

which is choice (A).

The other answer choices are incorrect because they fail in the synthetic division procedure.

37.   **(E)**   Observe that $xz = yz$ implies that $x = y$ if z is not zero. But x and y are two different real numbers according to the original assumption in the problem. So, the only possible way for the equality to hold is for z to have a value of 0.

38.   **(D)**   Though there are several methods to solve this problem, one method is to rewrite the equation

$$2a + 2b = 1 \quad \text{and} \quad 2(a + b) = 1.$$

Solving this equation for $(a + b)$ yields $(a + b) = \frac{1}{2}$. Similarly, rewriting the equation

$$6a - 2b = 5 \quad \text{as} \quad 2(3a - b) = 5$$

and solving for $(3a - b)$, yields $(3a - b) = \frac{5}{2}$.

Now $(a + b) = \frac{1}{2}$ and $(3a - b) = \frac{5}{2}$ eliminates answer choices (A), (C), and (E) immediately.

Since $\frac{1}{2} < \frac{5}{2}$, it follows that answer choice (B) is eliminated. However, since $\frac{1}{2} < \frac{5}{2}$, it follows that $(a + b) < (3a - b)$.

39.   **(B)**   Translating the given information into algebra yields the equation that can be used to find the required number, n.

$$3n - 2 = 5((n \div 3) + 2)$$

$$3n - 2 = 5(^n/_3 + 2)$$

This equation is the same as the equation given in answer choice (B).

Inspecting all the equations given in answer choices (A), (C), (D), and (E), we find out that none of them is equivalent to the equation

$$3n - 2 = 5(^n/_3 + 2).$$

40. **(B)**

$$\frac{3}{2}x = 5$$

$$x = \frac{(5)(2)}{3} = \frac{10}{3}$$

$$\frac{2}{3} + x = \frac{2}{3} + \frac{10}{3} = \frac{12}{3} = 4.$$

41. **(A)**

$$
\begin{aligned}
x + y &= 12 \\
(x + y)^2 &= 12^2 \\
x^2 + 2xy + y^2 &= 144 \\
x^2 + y^2 &= 126 \\
2xy &= 18 \\
xy &= 9.
\end{aligned}
$$

42. **(A)**

$$\frac{7a - 5b}{b} = 7 \qquad \frac{4a + 6b}{2a} = \frac{4a}{2a} + \frac{6b}{2a}$$

$$\frac{7a}{b} - \frac{5b}{b} = 7 \qquad\qquad = 2 + 3 \cdot \frac{b}{a}$$

$$7 \cdot \frac{a}{b} - 5 = 7 \qquad\qquad = 2 + 3 \cdot \frac{7}{12}$$

$$7\frac{a}{b} = 12 \qquad\qquad = \frac{15}{4}$$

$$\frac{a}{b} = \frac{12}{7}$$

$$\frac{b}{a} = \frac{7}{12}$$

43. **(C)**

$$\frac{A}{x - 5} + \frac{B}{x + 3} = \frac{7x - 11}{(x - 5)(x + 3)}.$$

On the left side of the equation, add fractions using the LCD in the usual manner, obtaining

$$\frac{Ax+3A+Bx-5B}{(x-5)(x+3)}, \quad Ax+3A+Bx-5B = 7x-11;$$

equating coefficients of like terms gives the system

$$A + B = 7$$

$$3A - 5B = -11.$$

Solving simultaneously gives $A = 3$ and $B = 4$. Check:

$$\frac{3}{x-5}+\frac{4}{x+3}=\frac{3x+9+4x-20}{(x-5)(x+3)}=\frac{7x-11}{(x-5)(x+3)}.$$

44. **(A)**

$$\frac{28+36+x}{3} = 29, \quad 64 + x = 3(29), \quad x = 23.$$

Choice (B) comes from adding 28 and 36 and dividing by 2. Choice (C) comes from adding and dividing by 3.

45. **(D)** If

$$\frac{5}{x}=\frac{2}{x-1}+\frac{1}{x(x-1)}$$

then $x \neq 0, x \neq 1$ and we can multiply both sides by $x(x-1)$ to get

$$5(x-1) = 2x + 1.$$

Equivalently,

$$5x - 5 = 2x + 1, \quad \text{or} \quad 3x = 6.$$

Thus $x = 2$.

46. **(B)** If $2X + Y = 2$, then

$$2X = 2 - Y, \text{ or } X = 1 - Y/2.$$

Substituting in $X + 3Y > 6$, we get

$$1 - Y/2 + 3Y > 6.$$

Thus $5Y/2 > 5$, or, $Y > 2$.

47. **(C)**

$$x^2 + 2xy + y^2 + x^2 - 2xy + y^2 = 2x^2 + 2y^2$$

$$= 2(x^2 + y^2).$$

Choice (A) is from a common mistake: Note that

$$(x + y)^2 \neq x^2 + y^2 \quad \text{and} \quad (x - y)^2 \neq x^2 - y^2.$$

Using this mistaken idea gives

$$x^2 + y^2 + x^2 - y^2 = 2x^2.$$

Choice (B) comes from putting both expressions in a parentheses:

$$(x + y + x - y)^2 = (2x)^2 = 4x^2.$$

Choice (D) comes from incorrect use of the distributive law:

$$2(x^2 + y^2) \neq 2x^2 + y^2.$$

48.   **(B)**   A very easy solution is: $x + y = {}^1/_k$, now substitute for k, its given value:

$$x + y = \frac{1}{x - y};$$

cross multiplying gives $x^2 - y^2 = 1$. The long way to do this problem (which would have more chance of error): Solve simultaneously, by adding the equations $x + y = {}^1/_k$ and $x - y = k$ getting

$$2x = k + \frac{1}{k} \quad \text{or} \quad x = \frac{1}{2}k + \frac{1}{2k}.$$

Then squaring both sides:

$$x^2 = \frac{k^2}{4} + \frac{1}{2} + \frac{1}{4k^2}.$$

Finding y from $x + y = {}^1/_k$;

$$y = \frac{1}{k} - \frac{1}{2}k - \frac{1}{2k} = \frac{k}{2} - \frac{1}{2k}.$$

Then squaring both sides:

$$y^2 = \frac{k^2}{4} - \frac{1}{2} + \frac{1}{4k^2}.$$

Therefore $x^2 - y^2 = {}^1/_2 - (- {}^1/_2) = 1$.

49.   **(B)**

$$(3^{a + b})(3^{a - b}) = 9 \cdot {}^1/_9$$

$$3^{2a} = 1$$

$$3^{2a} = 3^0 \qquad \text{(since } 3^0 = 1\text{)}$$

$$2a = 0$$

$$a = 0.$$

50. **(A)** Multiplying both sides by

$(X - 1)(X + 1)$

we get

$3(X + 1) = 2(X - 1)$,   or $3X + 3 = 2X - 2$.

Therefore, $X = -5$.

ALGEBRA REVIEW

In algebra, letters or variables are used to represent numbers. A **variable** is defined as a placeholder, which can take on any of several values at a given time. A **constant**, on the other hand, is a symbol which takes on only one value at a given time. A **term** is a constant, a variable, or a combination of constants and variables. For example: 7.76, $3x$, xyz, $5z/x$, $(0.99)x^2$ are terms. If a term is a combination of constants and variables, the constant part of the term is referred to as the **coefficient** of the variable. If a variable is written without a coefficient, the coefficient is assumed to be 1.

EXAMPLE

$3x^2$
coefficient: 3
variable: x

y^3
coefficient: 1
variable: y

An **expression** is a collection of one or more terms. If the number of terms is greater than 1, the expression is said to be the sum of the terms.

EXAMPLE

9, $9xy$, $6x + x/3$, $8yz - 2x$

An algebraic expression consisting of only one term is called a **monomial**, of two terms is called a **binomial**, of three terms is called a **trinomial**. In general, an algebraic expression consisting of two or more terms is called a **polynomial**.

1. Operations with Polynomials

A) **Addition of polynomials** is achieved by combining like terms, terms which differ only in their numerical coefficients. E.g.,

$$P(x) = (x^2 - 3x + 5) + (4x^2 + 6x - 3)$$

Note that the parentheses are used to distinguish the polynomials.

By using the commutative and associative laws, we can rewrite $P(x)$ as:

$$P(x) = (x^2 + 4x^2) + (6x - 3x) + (5 - 3)$$

Using the distributive law, $ab + ac = a(b + c)$, yields:

$$(1 + 4)x^2 + (6 - 3)x + (5 - 3) = 5x^2 + 3x + 2$$

B) **Subtraction of two polynomials** is achieved by first changing the sign of all terms in the expression which is being subtracted and then adding this result to the other expression. E.g.,

$$(5x^2 + 4y^2 + 3z^2) - (4xy + 7y^2 - 3z^2 + 1)$$

$$= 5x^2 + 4y^2 + 3z^2 - 4xy - 7y^2 + 3z^2 - 1$$

$$= (5x^2) + (4y^2 - 7y^2) + (3z^2 + 3z^2) - 4xy - 1$$

$$= (5x^2) + (-3y^2) + (6z^2) - 4xy - 1$$

C) **Multiplication of two or more polynomials** is achieved by using the laws of exponents, the rules of signs, and the commutative and associative laws of multiplication. Begin by multiplying the coefficients and then multiply the variables according to the laws of exponents. E.g.,

$$(y^2)\,(5)\,(6y^2)\,(yz)\,(2z^2)$$

$$= (1)\,(5)\,(6)\,(1)\,(2)\,(y^2)\,(y^2)\,(yz)\,(z^2)$$

$$= 60[(y^2)\,(y^2)\,(y)]\,[(z)\,(z^2)]$$

$$= 60(y^5)\,(z^3)$$

$$= 60\,y^5z^3$$

D) **Multiplication of a polynomial by a monomial** is achieved by multiplying each term of the polynomial by the monomial and combining the results. E.g.

$$(4x^2 + 3y)\,(6xz^2)$$

$$= (4x^2)\,(6xz^2) + (3y)\,(6xz^2)$$

$$= 24x^3z^2 + 18xyz^2$$

E) **Multiplication of a polynomial by a polynomial** is achieved by multiplying each of the terms of one polynomial by each of the terms of the other polynomial and combining the result. E.g.,

$$(5y + z + 1)\,(y^2 + 2y)$$

$$[(5y)\,(y^2) + (5y)\,(2y)] + [(z)\,(y^2) + (z)\,(2y)] + [(1)\,(y^2) + (1)\,(2y)]$$

$$= (5y^3 + 10y^2) + (y^2z + 2yz) + (y^2 + 2y)$$

$$= (5y^3) + (10y^2 + y^2) + (y^2z) + (2yz) + (2y)$$

$$= 5y^3 + 11y^2 + y^2z + 2yz + 2y$$

F) **Division of a monomial by a monomial** is achieved by first dividing the constant coefficients and the variable factors separately, and then multiplying these quotients. E.g.,

$$6xyz^2 \div 2y^2z$$

$$= (6/2)\,(x/1)\,(y/y^2)\,(z^2/z)$$

$$= 3xy^{-1}z$$

$$= 3xz/y$$

G) **Division of a polynomial by a polynomial** is achieved by following the given procedure called Long Division.

Step 1: The terms of both the polynomials are arranged in order of ascending or descending powers of one variable.

Step 2: The first term of the dividend is divided by the first term of the divisor which gives the first term of the quotient.

Step 3: This first term of the quotient is multiplied by the entire divisor and the result is subtracted from the dividend.

Step 4: Using the remainder obtained from Step 3 as the new dividend, Steps 2 and 3 are repeated until the remainder is zero or the degree of the remainder is less than the degree of the divisor.

Step 5: The result is written as follows:

$$\frac{\text{dividend}}{\text{divisor}} = \text{quotient} + \frac{\text{remainder}}{\text{divisor}} \qquad \text{divisor} \neq 0$$

e.g. $(2x^2 + x + 6) \div (x + 1)$

$$
\begin{array}{r}
2x - 1 \\
x + 1 \overline{\smash{\big)}\, 2x^2 + x + 6} \\
\underline{-(2x^2 + 2x)} \\
-x + 6 \\
\underline{-(-x - 1)} \\
7
\end{array}
$$

The result is $(2x^2 + x + 6) \div (x + 1) = 2x - 1 + \dfrac{7}{x + 1}$

Drill 1: Operations With Polynomials

Addition

1. $9a^2b + 3c + 2a^2b + 5c =$

(A) $19a^2bc$ (B) $11a^2b + 8c$ (C) $11a^4b^2 + 8c^2$

(D) $19a^4b^2c^2$ (E) $12a^2b + 8c^2$

2. $14m^2n^3 + 6m^2n^3 + 3m^2n^3 =$

(A) $20m^2n^3$ (B) $23m^6n^9$ (C) $23m^2n^3$

(D) $32m^6n^9$ (E) $23m^8n^{27}$

3. $3x + 2y + 16x + 3z + 6y =$

(A) $19x + 8y$ (B) $19x + 11yz$ (C) $19x + 8y + 3z$

(D) $11xy + 19xz$ (E) $30xyz$

4. $(4d^2 + 7e^3 + 12f) + (3d^2 + 6e^3 + 2f) =$

(A) $23d^2e^3f$ (B) $33d^2e^2f$ (C) $33d^4e^6f^2$

(D) $7d^2 + 13e^3 + 14f$ (E) $23d^2 + 11e^3f$

5. $3ac^2 + 2b^2c + 7ac^2 + 2ac^2 + b^2c =$

(A) $12ac^2 + 3b^2c$ (B) $14ab^2c^2$ (C) $11ac^2 + 4ab^2c$

(D) $15ab^2c^2$ (E) $15a^2b^4c^4$

Subtraction

6. $14m^2n - 6m^2n =$

(A) $20m^2n$ (B) $8m^2n$ (C) $8m$ (D) 8 (E) $8m^4n^2$

7. $3x^3y^2 - 4xz - 6x^3y^2 =$

(A) $-7x^2y^2z$ (B) $3x^3y^2 - 10x^4y^2z$ (C) $-3x^3y^2 - 4xz$

(D) $-x^2y^2z - 6x^3y^2$ (E) $-7xyz$

8. $9g^2 + 6h - 2g^2 - 5h =$

(A) $15g^2h - 7g^2h$ (B) $7g^4h^2$ (C) $11g^2 + 7h$

(D) $11g^2 - 7h^2$ (E) $7g^2 + h$

9. $7b^3 - 4c^2 - 6b^3 + 3c^2 =$

(A) $b^3 - c^2$ (B) $-11b^2 - 3c^2$ (C) $13b^3 - c$

(D) $7b - c$ (E) 0

10. $11q^2r - 4q^2r - 8q^2r =$

(A) $22q^2r$ (B) q^2r (C) $-2q^2r$

(D) $-q^2r$ (E) $2q^2r$

Multiplication

11. $5p^2t * 3p^2t =$

(A) $15p^2t$ (B) $15p^4t$ (C) $15p^4t^2$ (D) $8p^2t$ (E) $8p^4t^2$

12. $(2r + s)\,14r =$

(A) $28rs$ (B) $28r^2 + 14sr$ (C) $16r^2 + 14rs$

(D) $28r + 14sr$ (E) $17r^2s$

13. $(4m + p)\,(3m - 2p) =$

(A) $12m^2 + 5mp + 2p^2$ (B) $12m^2 - 2mp + 2p^2$ (C) $7m - p$

(D) $12m - 2p$ (E) $12m^2 - 5mp - 2p^2$

14. $(2a + b)\,(3a^2 + ab + b^2) =$

(A) $6a^3 + 5a^2b + 3ab^2 + b^3$ (B) $5a^3 + 3ab + b^3$

(C) $6a^3 + 2a^2b + 2ab^2$ (D) $3a^2 + 2a + ab + b + b^2$

(E) $6a^3 + 3a^2b + 5ab^2 + b^3$

15. $(6t^2 + 2t + 1)\,3t =$

(A) $9t^2 + 5t + 3$ (B) $18t^2 + 6t + 3$ (C) $9t^3 + 6t^2 + 3t$

(D) $18t^3 + 6t^2 + 3t$ (E) $12t^3 + 6t^2 + 3t$

Division

16. $(x^2 + x - 6) \div (x - 2) =$

(A) $x - 3$ (B) $x + 2$ (C) $x + 3$ (D) $x - 2$ (E) $2x + 2$

17. $24b^4c^3 \div 6b^2c =$

(A) $3b^2c^2$ (B) $4b^4c^3$ (C) $4b^3c^2$ (D) $4b^2c^2$ (E) $3b^4c^3$

18. $(3p^2 + pq - 2q^2) \div (p + q) =$

(A) $3p + 2q$ (B) $2q - 3p$ (C) $3p - q$

(D) $2q + 3p$ (E) $3p - 2q$

19. $(y^3 - 2y^2 - y + 2) \div (y - 2) =$

(A) $(y - 1)^2$ (B) $y^2 - 1$ (C) $(y + 2)\,(y - 1)$

(D) $(y + 1)^2$ (E) $(y + 1)\,(y - 2)$

20. $(m^2 + m - 14) \div (m + 4) =$

(A) $m - 2$ (B) $m - 3 + \dfrac{-2}{m + 4}$ (C) $m - 3 + \dfrac{4}{m + 4}$

(D) $m - 3$ (E) $m - 2 + \dfrac{-3}{m + 4}$

2. Simplifying Algebraic Expressions

To factor a polynomial completely is to find the prime factors of the polynomial with respect to a specified set of numbers.

The following concepts are important while factoring or simplifying expressions.

1. The factors of an algebraic expression consist of two or more algebraic expressions which when multiplied together produce the given algebraic expression.

2. A **prime factor** is a polynomial with no factors other than itself and 1. The **least common multiple (LCM)** for a set of numbers is the smallest quantity divisible by every number of the set. For algebraic expressions the least common numerical coefficients for each of the given expressions will be a factor.

3. The **greatest common factor (GCF)** for a set of numbers is the largest factor that is common to all members of the set. For algebraic expressions, the greatest common factor is the polynomial of highest degree and the largest numerical coefficient which is a factor of all the given expressions.

Some important formulae, useful for the factoring of polynomials, are listed below.

$$a(c + d) = ac + ad$$

$$(a + b)(a - b) = a^2 - b^2$$

$$(a + b)(a + b) = (a + b)^2 = a^2 + 2ab + b^2$$

$$(a - b)(a - b) = (a - b)^2 = a^2 - 2ab + b^2$$

$$(x + a)(x + b) = x^2 + (a + b)x + ab$$

$$(ax + b)(cx + d) = acx^2 + (ad + bc)x + bd$$

$$(a + b)(c + d) = ac + bc + ad + bd$$

$$(a + b)(a + b)(a + b) = (a + b)^3 = a^3 + 3a^2b + 3ab^2 + b^3$$

$$(a - b)(a - b)(a - b) = (a - b)^3 = a^3 - 3a^2b + 3ab^2 - b^3$$

$$(a - b)(a^2 + ab + b^2) = a^3 - b^3$$

$$(a + b)(a^2 - ab + b^2) = a^3 + b^3$$

$$(a + b + c)^2 = a^2 + b^2 + c^2 + 2ab + 2ac + 2bc$$

$$(a - b)(a^3 + a^2b + ab^2 + b^3) = a^4 - b^4$$

$$(a - b)(a^4 + a^3b + a^2b^2 + ab^3 + b^4) = a^5 - b^5$$

$$(a - b)(a^5 + a^4b + a^3b^2 + a^2b^3 + ab^4 + b^5) = a^6 - b^6$$

$$(a - b) (a^{n-1} + a^{n-2}b + a^{n-3}b^2 + \ldots + ab^{n-2} + b^{n-1}) = a^n - b^n$$

where n is any positive integer $(1, 2, 3, 4, \ldots)$.

$$(a + b) (a^{n-1} - a^{n-2}b + a^{n-3}b^2 - \ldots - ab^{n-2} + b^{n-1}) = a^n + b^n$$

where n is any positive odd integer $(1, 3, 5, 7, \ldots)$.

The procedure for factoring an algebraic expression completely is as follows:

Step 1: First find the greatest common factor if there is any. Then examine each factor remaining for greatest common factors.

Step 2: Continue factoring the factors obtained in Step 1 until all factors other than monomial factors are prime.

EXAMPLE

Factoring $4 - 16x^2$,

$$4 - 16x^2 = 4(1 - 4x^2) = 4(1 + 2x) (1 - 2x)$$

PROBLEM

Express each of the following as a single term.

(A) $3x^2 + 2x^2 - 4x^2$ (B) $5axy^2 - 7axy^2 - 3xy^2$

SOLUTION

(A) Factor x^2 in the expression.

$$3x^2 + 2x^2 - 4x^2 = (3 + 2 - 4)x^2 = 1x^2 = x^2.$$

(B) Factor xy^2 in the expression and then factor a.

$$\begin{aligned}
5axy^2 - 7axy^2 - 3xy^2 &= (5a - 7a - 3)xy^2 \\
&= [(5 - 7)a - 3]xy^2 \\
&= (-2a - 3)xy^2.
\end{aligned}$$

PROBLEM

Simplify $\dfrac{\frac{1}{x-1} - \frac{1}{x-2}}{\frac{1}{x-2} - \frac{1}{x-3}}$.

SOLUTION

Simplify the expression in the numerator by using the addition rule:

$$\frac{a}{b} + \frac{c}{d} = \frac{ad + bc}{bd}$$

Notice bd is the Least Common Denominator, LCD. We obtain

$$\frac{(x-2)-(x-1)}{(x-1)(x-2)} = \frac{-1}{(x-1)(x-2)}$$

in the numerator.

Repeat this procedure for the expression in the denominator:

$$\frac{(x-3)-(x-2)}{(x-2)(x-3)} = \frac{-1}{(x-2)(x-3)}$$

We now have

$$\frac{\frac{-1}{(x-1)(x-2)}}{\frac{-1}{(x-2)(x-3)}},$$

which is simplified by inverting the fraction in the denominator and multiplying it by the numerator and cancelling like terms

$$\frac{-1}{(x-1)(x-2)} \cdot \frac{(x-2)(x-3)}{-1} = \frac{x-3}{x-1}.$$

Drill 2: Simplifying Algebraic Expressions

1. $16b^2 - 25z^2 =$

(A) $(4b - 5z)^2$ (B) $(4b + 5z)^2$ (C) $(4b - 5z)(4b + 5z)$

(D) $(16b - 25z)^2$ (E) $(5z - 4b)(5z + 4b)$

2. $x^2 - 2x - 8 =$

(A) $(x - 4)^2$ (B) $(x - 6)(x - 2)$ (C) $(x + 4)(x - 2)$

(D) $(x - 4)(x + 2)$ (E) $(x - 4)(x - 2)$

3. $2c^2 + 5cd - 3d^2 =$

(A) $(c - 3d)(c + 2d)$ (B) $(2c - d)(c + 3d)$ (C) $(c - d)(2c + 3d)$

(D) $(2c + d)(c + 3d)$ (E) Not possible

4. $4t^3 - 20t =$

(A) $4t(t^2 - 5)$ (B) $4t^2(t - 20)$ (C) $4t(t + 4)(t - 5)$

(D) $2t(2t^2 - 10)$ (E) Not possible

5. $x^2 + xy - 2y^2 =$

(A) $(x - 2y)(x + y)$ (B) $(x - 2y)(x - y)$ (C) $(x + 2y)(x + y)$

(D) $(x + 2y)(x - y)$ (E) Not possible

6. $5b^2 + 17bd + 6d^2 =$

(A) $(5b + d)(b + 6d)$ (B) $(5b + 2d)(b + 3d)$ (C) $(5b - 2d)(b - 3d)$

(D) $(5b - 2d)(b + 3d)$ (E) Not possible

7. $x^2 + x + 1 =$

(A) $(x + 1)^2$ (B) $(x + 2)(x - 1)$ (C) $(x - 2)(x + 1)$

(D) $(x + 1)(x - 1)$ (E) Not possible

8. $3z^3 + 6z^2 =$

(A) $3(z^3 + 2z^2)$ (B) $3z^2(z + 2)$ (C) $3z(z^2 + 2z)$

(D) $z^2(3z + 6)$ (E) $3z^2(1 + 2z)$

9. $m^2p^2 + mpg - 6q^2 =$

(A) $(mp - 2q)(mp + 3q)$ (B) $mp(mp - 2q)(mp + 3q)$

(C) $mpq(1 - 6q)$ (D) $(mp + 2q)(mp + 3q)$

(E) Not possible

10. $2h^3 + 2h^2t - 4ht^2 =$

(A) $2(h^3 - t)(h + t)$ (B) $2h(h - 2t)^2$ (C) $4h(ht - t^2)$

(D) $2h(h + t) - 4ht^2$ (E) $2h(h + 2t)(h - t)$

3. Equations

An **equation** is defined as a statement that two separate expressions are equal.

A **solution** to the equation is a number that makes the equation true when it is substituted for the variable. For example, in the equation $3x = 18$, 6 is the solution since $3(6) = 18$. Depending on the equation, there can be more than one solution. Equations with the same solutions are said to be **equivalent equations**. An equation without a solution is said to have a solution set that is the **empty** or **null** set and is represented by ϕ.

Replacing an expression within an equation by an equivalent expression will result in a new equation with solutions equivalent to the original equation.

Given the equation below

$$3x + y + x + 2y = 15$$

by combining like terms, we get,

$$3x + y + x + 2y = 4x + 3y$$

Since these two expressions are equivalent, we can substitute the simpler form into the equation to get

$$4x + 3y = 15$$

Performing the same operation to both sides of an equation by the same expression will result in a new equation that is equivalent to the original equation.

A) **Addition or subtraction**

$$y + 6 = 10$$

we can add (-6) to both sides

$$y + 6 + (-6) = 10 + (-6)$$

to get $y + 0 = 10 - 6$; therefore $y = 4$.

B) **Multiplication or division**

$$3x = 6$$

$$3x/3 = 6/3$$

$$x = 2$$

$3x = 6$ is equivalent to $x = 2$.

C) **Raising to a power**

$$a = x^2y$$

$$a^2 = (x^2y)^2$$
$$a^2 = x^4y^2$$

This can be applied to negative and fractional powers as well. E.g.,

$$x^2 = 3y^4$$

If we raise both members to the -2 power, we get

$$(x^2)^{-2} = (3y^4)^{-2}$$

$$\frac{1}{(x^2)^2} = \frac{1}{(3y^4)^2}$$

$$\frac{1}{x^4} = \frac{1}{9y^8}$$

If we raise both members to the $\frac{1}{2}$ power, which is the same as taking the square root, we get:

$$(x^2)^{1/2} = (3y^4)^{1/2}$$
$$x = \sqrt{3}y^2$$

D) The **reciprocal** of both members of an equation are equivalent to the original equation. Note: The reciprocal of zero is undefined.

$$\frac{2x+y}{z} = \frac{5}{2} \qquad \frac{z}{2x+y} = \frac{2}{5}$$

PROBLEM

Solve, justifying each step. $3x - 8 = 7x + 8$.

SOLUTION

	$3x - 8 = 7x + 8$
Adding 8 to both members,	$3x - 8 + 8 = 7x + 8 + 8$
Additive inverse property,	$3x + 0 = 7x + 16$
Additive identity property,	$3x = 7x + 16$
Adding $(-7x)$ to both members,	$3x - 7x = 7x + 16 - 7x$
Commuting,	$-4x = 7x - 7x + 16$
Additive inverse property,	$-4x = 0 + 16$
Additive identity property,	$-4x = 16$
Dividing both sides by -4,	$x = {}^{16}/_{-4}$
	$x = -4$

Check: Replacing x by -4 in the original equation:

$$3x - 8 = 7x + 8$$
$$3(-4) - 8 = 7(-4) + 8$$
$$-12 - 8 = -28 + 8$$
$$-20 = -20$$

Linear Equations

A linear equation with one unknown is one that can be put into the form $ax + b = 0$, where a and b are constants, $a \neq 0$.

To solve a linear equation means to transform it in the form $x = {}^{-b}/_a$.

A) If the equation has unknowns on both sides of the equality, it is convenient to put similar terms on the same sides. E.g.,

$$4x + 3 = 2x + 9$$

$$4x + 3 - 2x = 2x + 9 - 2x$$

$$(4x - 2x) + 3 = (2x - 2x) + 9$$

$$2x + 3 = 0 + 9$$

$$2x + 3 - 3 = 0 + 9 - 3$$

$$2x = 6$$

$$^{2x}/_2 = ^6/_2$$

$$x = 3.$$

B) If the equation appears in fractional form, it is necessary to transform it, using cross multiplication, and then repeating the same procedure as in A), we obtain:

$$\frac{3x + 4}{3} \underset{\nearrow}{\overset{\searrow}{\times}} \frac{7x + 2}{5}$$

By using cross multiplication we would obtain:

$$3(7x + 2) = 5(3x + 4).$$

This is equivalent to:

$$21x + 6 = 15x + 20,$$

which can be solved as in A):

$$21x + 6 = 15x + 20$$

$$21x - 15x + 6 = 15x - 15x + 20$$

$$6x + 6 - 6 = 20 - 6$$

$$6x = 14$$

$$x = ^{14}/_6$$

$$x = ^7/_3$$

C) If there are radicals in the equation, it is necessary to square both sides and then apply A)

$$\sqrt{3x + 1} = 5$$

$$\left(\sqrt{3x + 1}\right)^2 = 5^2$$

$$3x + 1 = 25$$

$$3x + 1 - 1 = 25 - 1$$

$$3x = 24$$
$$x = {}^{24}/_3$$
$$x = 8$$

PROBLEM

Solve the equation $2(x + 3) = (3x + 5) - (x - 5)$.

SOLUTION

We transform the given equation to an equivalent equation where we can easily recognize the solution set.

$$2(x + 3) = 3x + 5 - (x - 5)$$

Distribute, $2x + 6 = 3x + 5 - x + 5$

Combine terms, $2x + 6 = 2x + 10$

Subtract $2x$ from both sides, $6 = 10$

Since $6 = 10$ is not a true statement, there is no real number which will make the original equation true. The equation is inconsistent and the solution set is ϕ, the empty set.

PROBLEM

Solve the equation $2({}^2/_3\, y + 5) + 2(y + 5) = 130$.

SOLUTION

The procedure for solving this equation is as follows:

${}^4/_3 y + 10 + 2y + 10 = 130,$	Distributive property
${}^4/_3 y + 2y + 20 = 130,$	Combining like terms
${}^4/_3 y + 2y = 110,$	Subtracting 20 from both sides
${}^4/_3 y + {}^6/_3 y = 110,$	Converting $2y$ into a fraction with denominator 3
${}^{10}/_3 y = 110,$	Combining like terms
$y = 110 \cdot {}^3/_{10} = 33,$	Dividing by ${}^{10}/_3$

Check: Replace y by 33 in the original equation,

$$2({}^2/_3(33) + 5) + 2(33 + 5) = 130$$
$$2(22 + 5) + 2(38) = 130$$
$$2(27) + 76 = 130$$

$$54 + 76 = 130$$

$$130 = 130$$

Therefore the solution to the given equation is $y = 33$.

Drill 3: Linear Equations

Solve for x:

1. $4x - 2 = 10$

(A) -1 (B) 2 (C) 3 (D) 4 (E) 6

2. $7z + 1 - z = 2z - 7$

(A) -2 (B) 0 (C) 1 (D) 2 (E) 3

3. $\frac{1}{3}b + 3 = \frac{1}{2}b$

(A) $1/2$ (B) 2 (C) $3\ 3/5$ (D) 6 (E) 18

4. $0.4p + 1 = 0.7p - 2$

(A) 0.1 (B) 2 (C) 5 (D) 10 (E) 12

5. $4(3x + 2) - 11 = 3(3x - 2)$

(A) -3 (B) -1 (C) 2 (D) 3 (E) 7

4. Two Linear Equations

Equations of the form $ax + by = c$, where a, b, c are constants and a, $b \neq 0$ are called **linear equations** with two unknown variables.

There are several ways to solve systems of linear equations in two variables:

Method 1: **Addition or subtraction** – if necessary, multiply the equations by numbers that will make the coefficients of one unknown in the resulting equations numerically equal. If the signs of equal coefficients are the same, subtract the equation, otherwise add.

The result is one equation with one unknown; we solve it and substitute the value into the other equations to find the unknown that we first eliminated.

Method 2: **Substitution** – find the value of one unknown in terms of the other, substitute this value in the other equation and solve.

Method 3: **Graph** – graph both equations. The point of intersection of the drawn lines is a simultaneous solution for the equations and its coordinates correspond to the answer that would be found analytically.

If the lines are parallel they have no simultaneous solution.

Dependent equations are equations that represent the same line, therefore every point on the line of a dependent equation represents a solution. Since there is an infinite number of points on a line there is an infinite number of simultaneous solutions, for example

$$\begin{cases} 2x + y = 8 \\ 4x + 2y = 16 \end{cases}$$

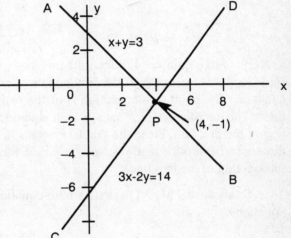

The equations above are dependent, they represent the same line, all points that satisfy either of the equations are solutions of the system.

A system of linear equations is consistent if there is only one solution for the system.

A system of linear equations is inconsistent if it does not have any solutions.

Example of a consistent system. Find the point of intersection of the graphs of the equations as shown in the previous figure

$$x + y = 3,$$

$$3x - 2y = 14$$

To solve these linear equations, solve for y in terms of x. The equations will be in the form $y = mx + b$, where m is the slope and b is the intercept on the y-axis.

$$\begin{aligned} x + y &= 3 \\ y &= 3 - x && \text{subtract } x \text{ from both sides} \\ 3x - 2y &= 14 && \text{subtract } 3x \text{ from both sides} \\ -2y &= 14 - 3x && \text{divide by } -2. \\ y &= -7 + {}^3\!/_2 x \end{aligned}$$

The graphs of the linear functions, $y = 3 - x$ and $y = -7 + {}^3\!/_2 x$ can be determined by plotting only two points. For example, for $y = 3 - x$, let $x = 0$, then $y = 3$. Let $x = 1$, then $y = 2$. The two points on this first line are $(0, 3)$ and $(1, 2)$. For $y = -7 +$

$^3/_2x$, let $x = 0$, then $y = -7$. Let $x = 1$, then $y = -5^1/_2$. The two points on this second line are $(0, -7)$ and $(1, -5^1/_2)$.

To find the point of intersection P of

$$x + y = 3 \quad \text{and} \quad 3x - 2y = 14,$$

solve them algebraically. Multiply the first equation by 2. Add these two equations to eliminate the variable y.

$$
\begin{array}{rl}
2x + 2y = & 6 \\
3x - 2y = & 14 \\
\hline
5x = & 20
\end{array}
$$

Solve for x to obtain $x = 4$. Substitute this into $y = 3 - x$ to get $y = 3 - 4 = -1$. P is $(4, -1)$. AB is the graph of the first equation, and CD is the graph of the second equation. The point of intersection P of the two graphs is the only point on both lines. The coordinates of P satisfy both equations and represent the desired solution of the problem. From the graph, P seems to be the point $(4, -1)$. These coordinates satisfy both equations, and hence are the exact coordinates of the point of intersection of the two lines.

To show that $(4, -1)$ satisfies both equations, substitute this point into both equations.

$$
\begin{array}{rclcrcl}
x + y & = & 3 & \qquad & 3x - 2y & = & 14 \\
4 + (-1) & = & 3 & \qquad & 3(4) - 2(-1) & = & 14 \\
4 - 1 & = & 3 & \qquad & 12 + 2 & = & 14 \\
3 & = & 3 & \qquad & 14 & = & 14
\end{array}
$$

Example of an inconsistent system. Solve the equations $2x + 3y = 6$ and $4x + 6y = 7$ simultaneously.

We have 2 equations in 2 unknowns,

$$2x + 3y = 6 \qquad (1)$$

and $\qquad 4x + 6y = 7 \qquad (2)$

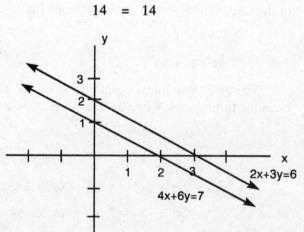

There are several methods to solve this problem. We have chosen to multiply each equation by a different number so that when the two equations are added, one of the variables drops out. Thus

multiplying equation (1) by 2: $\qquad 4x + 6y = \quad 12 \qquad\qquad (3)$

multiplying equation (2) by – 1: $-4x - 6y = -7$ (4)

adding equations (3) and (4): $0 = 5$

We obtain a peculiar result!

Actually, what we have shown in this case is that if there were a simultaneous solution to the given equations, then 0 would equal 5. But the conclusion is impossible; therefore there can be no simultaneous solution to these two equations, hence no point satisfying both.

The straight lines which are the graphs of these equations must be parallel if they never intersect, but not identical, which can be seen from the graph of these equations (see the accompanying diagram).

Example of a dependent system. Solve the equations $2x + 3y = 6$ and $y = -(2x/3) + 2$ simultaneously.

We have 2 equations in 2 unknowns.

$$2x + 3y = 6 \tag{1}$$

and $y = -(2x/3) + 2$ (2)

There are several methods of solution for this problem. Since equation (2) already gives us an expression for y, we use the method of substitution. Substituting $-(2x/3) + 2$ for y in the first equation:

$$2x + 3(-2x/3 + 2) = 6$$

Distributing, $2x - 2x + 6 = 6$

$$6 = 6$$

Apparently we have gotten nowhere! The result $6 = 6$ is true, but indicates no solution. Actually, our work shows that no matter what real number x is, if y is determined by the second equation, then the first equation will always be satisfied.

The reason for this peculiarity may be seen if we take a closer look at the equation $y = -(2x/3) + 2$. It is equivalent to $3y = -2x + 6$, or $2x + 3y = 6$.

In other words, the two equations are equivalent. Any pair of values of x and y that satisfies one satisfies the other.

It is hardly necessary to verify that in this case the graphs of the given equations are identical lines, and that there are an infinite number of simultaneous solutions of these equations.

A system of three linear equations in three unknowns is solved by eliminating one unknown from any two of the three equations and solving them. After finding two unknowns substitute them in any of the equations to find the third unknown.

PROBLEM

Solve the system

$$2x + 3y - 4z = -8 \tag{1}$$

$$x + y - 2z = -5 \tag{2}$$

$$7x - 2y + 5z = 4 \tag{3}$$

SOLUTION

We cannot eliminate any variable from two pairs of equations by a single multiplication. However, both x and z may be eliminated from equations (1) and (2) by multiplying equation 2 by -2. Then

$$2x + 3y - 4z = -8 \tag{1}$$

$$-2x - 2y + 4z = 10 \tag{4}$$

By addition, we have $y = 2$. Although we may now eliminate either x or z from another pair of equations, we can more conveniently substitute $y = 2$ in equations (2) and (3) to get two equations in two variables. Thus, making the substitution $y = 2$ in equations (2) and (3), we have

$$x - 2z = -7 \tag{5}$$

$$7x + 5z = 8 \tag{6}$$

Multiply (5) by 5 and multiply (6) by 2. Then add the two new equations. Then $x = -1$. Substitute x in either (5) or (6) to find z.

The solution of the system is $x = -1$, $y = 2$, and $z = 3$. Check by substitution.

A system of equations, as shown below, that has all constant terms $b_1, b_2, \ldots, b_n$ equal to zero is said to be a homogeneous system:

$$\begin{cases} a_{11}x_1 + a_{12}x_2 + \ldots + a_{1n}x_m = b_1 \\ a_{11}x_1 + a_{22}x_2 + \ldots + a_{2n}x_m = b_2 \\ \phantom{a_{11}x_1}\vdots \phantom{a_{12}x_2} \vdots \vdots \vdots \\ a_{n1}x_1 + a_{n2}x_2 + \ldots + a_{nm}x_m = b_n. \end{cases}$$

A homogeneous system always has at least one solution which is called the trivial solution that is $x_1 = 0, x_2 = 0, \ldots, x_m = 0$.

For any given homogeneous system of equations, in which the number of variables is greater than or equal to the number of equations, there are non-trivial solutions.

Two systems of linear equations are said to be equivalent if and only if they have the same solution set.

PROBLEM

> Solve for *x* and *y*.
>
> $$x + 2y = 8 \qquad (1)$$
>
> $$3x + 4y = 20 \qquad (2)$$

SOLUTION

Solve equation (1) for *x* in terms of *y*:

$$x = 8 - 2y \qquad (3)$$

Substitute $(8 - 2y)$ for *x* in (2):

$$3(8 - 2y) + 4y = 20 \qquad (4)$$

Solve (4) for *y* as follows:

Distribute: $24 - 6y + 4y = 20$

Combine like terms and then subtract 24 from both sides:

$$24 - 2y = 20$$
$$24 - 24 - 2y = 20 - 24$$
$$-2y = -4$$

Divide both sides by -2:

$$y = 2$$

Substitute 2 for *y* in equation (1):

$$x + 2(2) = 8$$
$$x = 4$$

Thus, our solution is $x = 4, y = 2$.

Check: Substitute $x = 4, y = 2$ in equations (1) and (2):

$$4 + 2(2) = 8$$
$$8 = 8$$
$$3(4) + 4(2) = 20$$
$$20 = 20$$

PROBLEM

> Solve algebraically:
>
> $$4x + 2y = -1 \qquad (1)$$
>
> $$5x - 3y = 7 \qquad (2)$$

SOLUTION

We arbitrarily choose to eliminate x first.

Multiply (1) by 5: $\qquad 20x + 10y = -5 \qquad\qquad\qquad\qquad\qquad$ (3)

Multiply (2) by 4: $\qquad 20x - 12y = 28 \qquad\qquad\qquad\qquad\qquad$ (4)

Subtract (3) − (4): $\qquad\qquad 22y = -33 \qquad\qquad\qquad\qquad\qquad$ (5)

Divide (5) by 22: $\qquad y = {}^{33}/_{22} = -{}^{3}/_{2},$

To find x, substitute $y = -{}^{3}/_{2}$ in either of the original equations. If we use Eq. (1), we obtain $4x + 2(-{}^{3}/_{2}) = -1$, $4x - 3 = -1$, $4x = 2$, $x = {}^{1}/_{2}$.

The solution $({}^{1}/_{2}, -{}^{3}/_{2})$ should be checked in both equations of the given system.

Replacing $({}^{1}/_{2}, -{}^{3}/_{2})$ in Eq. (1):

$$4x + 2y = -1$$

$$4({}^{1}/_{2}) + 2(-{}^{3}/_{2}) = -1$$

$$\tfrac{4}{2} - 3 = -1$$

$$2 - 3 = -1$$

$$-1 = -1$$

Replacing $({}^{1}/_{2}, -{}^{3}/_{2})$ in Eq. (2):

$$5x - 3y = 7$$

$$5({}^{1}/_{2}) - 3(-{}^{3}/_{2}) = 7$$

$$\tfrac{5}{2} + \tfrac{9}{2} = 7$$

$$\tfrac{14}{2} = 7$$

$$7 = 7$$

(Instead of eliminating x from the two given equations, we could have eliminated y by multiplying Eq. (1) by 3, multiplying Eq. (2) by 2, and then adding the two derived equations.)

Drill 4: Two Linear Equations

<u>DIRECTIONS</u>: Find the solution set for each pair of equations.

1. $\quad 3x + 4y = -2$
   $\quad\ x - 6y = -8$

(A) $(2, -1)$ (B) $(1, -2)$ (C) $(-2, -1)$

(D) $(1, 2)$ (E) $(-2, 1)$

2. $2x + y = -10$
       $-2x - 4y = 4$

(A) $(6, -2)$ (B) $(-6, 2)$ (C) $(-2, 6)$

(D) $(2, 6)$ (E) $(-6, -2)$

3. $6x + 5y = -4$
       $3x - 3y = 9$

(A) $(1, -2)$ (B) $(1, 2)$ (C) $(2, -1)$

(D) $(-2, 1)$ (E) $(-1, 2)$

4. $4x + 3y = 9$
       $2x - 2y = 8$

(A) $(-3, 1)$ (B) $(1, -3)$ (C) $(3, 1)$

(D) $(3, -1)$ (E) $(-1, 3)$

5. $x + y = 7$
       $x - y = -3$

(A) $(5, 2)$ (B) $(-5, 2)$ (C) $(2, 5)$

(D) $(-2, 5)$ (E) $(2, -5)$

6. $5x + 6y = 4$
       $3x - 2y = 1$

(A) $(3, 6)$ (B) $(1/2, 1/4)$ (C) $(-3, 6)$

(D) $(2, 4)$ (E) $(1/3, 3/2)$

7. $x - 2y = 7$
       $x + y = -2$

(A) $(-2, 7)$ (B) $(3, -1)$ (C) $(-7, 2)$

(D) $(1, -3)$ (E) $(1, -2)$

8. $4x + 3y = 3$
       $-2x + 6y = 3$

(A) $(1/2, 2/3)$ (B) $(-0.3, 0.6)$ (C) $(2/3, -1)$

(D) $(-0.2, 0.5)$ (E) $(0.3, 0.6)$

9. $4x - 2y = -14$

   $8x + y = 7$

(A) $(0, 7)$ (B) $(2, -7)$ (C) $(7, 0)$

(D) $(-7, 2)$ (E) $(0, 2)$

10. $6x - 3y = 1$

    $-9x + 5y = -1$

(A) $(1, -1)$ (B) $(2/3, 1)$ (C) $(1, 2/3)$

(D) $(-1, 1)$ (E) $(2/3, -1)$

5. Quadratic Equations

A second degree equation in x of the type $ax^2 + bx + c = 0$, $a \neq 0$, a, b and c are real numbers, is called a **quadratic equation.**

To solve a quadratic equation is to find values of x which satisfy $ax^2 + bx + c = 0$. These values of x are called **solutions**, or **roots**, of the equation.

A quadratic equation has a maximum of 2 roots. Methods of solving quadratic equations:

A) **Direct solution**: Given $x^2 - 9 = 0$.

We can solve directly by isolating the variable x:

$$x^2 = 9$$

$$x = \pm 3.$$

B) **Factoring**: Given a quadratic equation $ax^2 + bx + c = 0$, a, b, $c \neq 0$, to factor means to express it as the product $a(x - r_1)(x - r_2) = 0$, where r_1 and r_2 are the two roots.

Some helpful hints to remember are:

a) $r_1 + r_2 = -{}^b/_a$.

b) $r_1 r_2 = {}^c/_a$.

Given $x^2 - 5x + 4 = 0$.

Since $r_1 + r_2 = -{}^b/_a = -({}^{-5})/_1 = 5$, some possible solutions are $(3, 2)$, $(4, 1)$ and $(5, 0)$. Also $r_1 r_2 = {}^c/_a = {}^4/_1 = 4$; this equation is satisfied only by the second pair, so $r_1 = 4$, $r_2 = 1$ and the factored form is $(x - 4)(x - 1) = 0$.

If the coefficient of x^2 is not 1, it is necessary to divide the equation by this coefficient and then factor.

Given $2x^2 - 12x + 16 = 0$

Dividing by 2, we obtain:

$$x^2 - 6x + 8 = 0$$

Since $r_1 + r_2 = - \frac{b}{a} = 6$, possible solutions are (6, 0), (5, 1), (4, 2), (3, 3). Also $r_1 r_2 = 8$, so the only possible answer is (4, 2) and the expression $x^2 - 6x + 8 = 0$ can be factored as $(x - 4)(x - 2)$.

C) **Completing the Squares**:

If it is difficult to factor the quadratic equation using the previous method, we can complete the squares.

Given $x^2 - 12x + 8 = 0$.

We know that the two roots added up should be 12 because $r_1 + r_2 = - \frac{b}{a} = - \frac{(-12)}{1} = 12$. Possible roots are (12, 0), (11, 1), (10, 2), (9, 3), (8, 4), (7, 5), (6, 6).

But none of these satisfy $r_1 r_2 = 8$, so we cannot use (B).

To complete the square, it is necessary to isolate the constant term,

$$x^2 - 12x = -8.$$

Then take $\frac{1}{2}$ coefficient of x, square it and add to both sides

$$x^2 - 12x + \left(\frac{-12}{2}\right)^2 = -8 + \left(\frac{-12}{2}\right)^2$$

$$x^2 - 12x + 36 = -8 + 36 = 28.$$

Now we can use the previous method to factor the left side: $r_1 + r_2 = 12$, $r_1 r_2 = 36$ is satisfied by the pair (6, 6), so we have:

$$(x - 6)^2 = 28.$$

Now extract the root of both sides and solve for x.

$$(x - 6) = \pm\sqrt{28} = \pm 2\sqrt{7}$$

$$x = \pm 2\sqrt{7} + 6$$

So the roots are:

$$x = 2\sqrt{7} + 6, \quad x = -2\sqrt{7} + 6.$$

PROBLEM

Solve the equation $x^2 + 8x + 15 = 0$.

SOLUTION

Since $(x + a)(x + b) = x^2 + bx + ax + ab = x^2 + (a + b)x + ab$, we may factor the given equation, $0 = x^2 + 8x + 15$, replacing $a + b$ by 8 and ab by 15. Thus,

$$a + b = 8, \quad \text{and} \quad ab = 15.$$

We want the two numbers a and b whose sum is 8 and whose product is 15. We check all pairs of numbers whose product is 15:

(a) $1 \cdot 15 = 15$; thus $a = 1$, $b = 15$ and $ab = 15$.

  $1 + 15 = 16$, therefore we reject these values because $a + b \neq 8$.

(b) $3 \cdot 5 = 15$, thus $a = 3$, $b = 5$, and $ab = 15$.

  $3 + 5 = 8$. Therefore $a + b = 8$, and we accept these values.

Hence $x^2 + 8x + 15 = 0$ is equivalent to

$$0 = x^2 + (3 + 5)x + 3 \cdot 5 = (x + 3)(x + 5)$$

Hence, $x + 5 = 0$ or $x + 3 = 0$

since the product of these two numbers is zero, one of the numbers must be zero. Hence, $x = -5$, or $x = -3$, and the solution set is $x = \{-5, -3\}$.

The student should note that $x = -5$ or $x = -3$. We are certainly not making the statement, that $x = -5$, and $x = -3$. Also, the student should check that both these numbers do actually satisfy the given equations and hence are solutions.

Check: Replacing x by (-5) in the original equation:

$$x^2 + 8x + 15 = 0$$
$$(-5)^2 + 8(-5) + 15 = 0$$
$$25 - 40 + 15 = 0$$
$$-15 + 15 = 0$$
$$0 = 0$$

Replacing x by (-3) in the original equation:

$$x^2 + 8x + 15 = 0$$
$$(-3)^2 + 8(-3) + 15 = 0$$
$$9 - 24 + 15 = 0$$
$$-15 + 15 = 0$$
$$0 = 0.$$

PROBLEM

Solve the following equations by factoring.

(a) $2x^2 + 3x = 0$ (c) $z^2 - 2z - 3 = 0$

(b) $y^2 - 2y - 3 = y - 3$ (d) $2m^2 - 11m - 6 = 0$

SOLUTION

(a) $2x^2 + 3x = 0$. Factoring out the common factor of x from the left side of the given equation,

$$x(2x + 3) = 0.$$

Whenever a product $ab = 0$, where a and b are any two numbers, either $a = 0$ or $b = 0$. Then, either

$$x = 0 \quad \text{or} \quad 2x + 3 = 0$$
$$2x = -3$$
$$x = {}^{-3}/_2$$

Hence, the solution set to the original equation $2x^2 + 3x = 0$ is: $\{{}^{-3}/_2, 0\}$.

(b) $y^2 - 2y - 3 = y - 3$. Subtract $(y - 3)$ from both sides of the given equation:

$$y^2 - 2y - 3 - (y - 3) = y - 3 - (y - 3)$$
$$y^2 - 2y - 3 - y + 3 = y - 3 - y + 3$$
$$y^2 - 2y - 3 - y + 3 = y - 3 - y + 3$$
$$y^2 - 3y = 0.$$

Factor out a common factor of y from the left side of this equation:

$$y(y - 3) = 0.$$

Thus, $y = 0$ or $y - 3 = 0$, $y = 3$.

Therefore, the solution set to the original equation $y^2 - 2y - 3 = y - 3$ is: $\{0,3\}$.

(c) $z^2 - 2z - 3 = 0$. Factor the original equation into a product of two polynomials:

$$z^2 - 2z - 3 = (z - 3)(z + 1) = 0$$

Hence,

$$(z - 3)(z + 1) = 0; \text{ and } z - 3 = 0 \text{ or } z + 1 = 0$$
$$z = 3 \qquad z = -1$$

Therefore, the solution set to the original equation $z^2 - 2z - 3 = 0$ is: $\{-1, 3\}$.

(d) $2m^2 - 11m - 6 = 0$. Factor the original equation into a product of two polynomials:

$$2m^2 - 11m - 6 = (2m + 1)(m - 6) = 0$$

Thus,

$$2m + 1 = 0 \quad \text{or} \quad m - 6 = 0$$

$$2m = -1 \qquad m = 6$$
$$m = {}^{-1}/_2$$

Therefore, the solution set to the original equation $2m^2 - 11m - 6 = 0$ is $\{-^1/_2, 6\}$.

Drill 5: Quadratic Equations

<u>DIRECTIONS</u>: Solve for all values of x.

1. $x^2 - 2x - 8 = 0$

(A) 4 and -2 (B) 4 and 8   (C) 4

(D) -2 and 8   (E) -2

2. $x^2 + 2x - 3 = 0$

(A) -3 and 2   (B) 2 and 1   (C) 3 and 1

(D) -3 and 1   (E) -3

3. $x^2 - 7x = -10$

(A) -3 and 5   (B) 2 and 5   (C) 2

(D) -2 and -5 (E) 5

4. $x^2 - 8x + 16 = 0$

(A) 8 and 2   (B) 1 and 16   (C) 4

(D) -2 and 4   (E) 4 and -4

5. $3x^2 + 3x = 6$

(A) 3 and -6 (B) 2 and 3   (C) -3 and 2

(D) 1 and -3 (E) 1 and -2

6. $x^2 + 7x = 0$

(A) 7   (B) 0 and -7 (C) -7

(D) 0 and 7   (E) 0

7. $x^2 - 25 = 0$

(A) 5   (B) 5 and -5 (C) 15 and 10

(D) -5 and 10   (E) -5

8. $2x^2 + 4x = 16$

(A) 2 and -2 (B) 8 and -2 (C) 4 and 8

(D) 2 and -4 (E) 2 and 4

9. $6x^2 - x - 2 = 0$

(A) 2 and 3   (B) 1/2 and 1/3   (C) $-1/2$ and 2/3

(D) 2/3 and 3   (E) 2 and $-1/3$

10. $12x^2 + 5x = 3$

(A) 1/3 and $-1/4$ (B) 4 and -3 (C) 4 and 1/6

(D) 1/3 and -4 (E) $-3/4$ and 1/3

6. Absolute Value Equations

The absolute value of a, $|a|$, is defined as:

$$|a| = a \text{ when } a > 0, |a| = -a \text{ when } a < 0, |a| = 0 \text{ when } a = 0.$$

When the definition of absolute value is applied to an equation, the quantity within the absolute value symbol is considered to have two values. This value can be either positive or negative before the absolute value is taken. As a result, each absolute value equation actually contains two separate equations.

When evaluating equations containing absolute values, proceed as follows:

EXAMPLE

$|5 - 3x| = 7$ is valid if either

$$5 - 3x = 7 \qquad \text{or} \qquad 5 - 3x = -7$$
$$-3x = 2 \qquad\qquad\qquad -3x = -12$$
$$x = -2/3 \qquad\qquad\qquad x = 4$$

The solution set is therefore $x = (-2/3, 4)$.

Remember, the absolute value of a number cannot be negative. So, for the equation $|5x + 4| = -3$, there would be no solution.

EXAMPLE

Solve for x in $|2x - 6| = |4 - 5x|$

There are four possibilities here. $2x - 6$ and $4 - 5x$ can be either positive or negative. Therefore,

$$2x - 6 = 4 - 5x \qquad\qquad (1)$$
$$-(2x - 6) = 4 - 5x \qquad\qquad (2)$$
$$2x - 6 = -(4 - 5x) \qquad\qquad (3)$$
$$-(2x - 6) = -(4 - 5x) \qquad\qquad (4)$$

Equations (2) and (3) result in the same solution, as do equations (1) and (4). Therefore, it is necessary to solve only for equations (1) and (2). This gives:

$$2x - 6 = 4 - 5x \qquad \text{or} \qquad -(2x - 6) = 4 - 5x$$
$$7x = 10 \qquad\qquad\qquad -2x + 6 = 4 - 5x$$
$$3x = -2$$
$$x = 10/7 \qquad\qquad\qquad x = -2/3$$

The solution set is (10/7, – 2/3).

Drill 6: Absolute Value Equations

1. $|4x - 2| = 6$

(A) – 2 and – 1   (B) – 1 and 2   (C) 2

(D) 1/2 and – 2   (E) No solution

2. $|3 - 1/2y| = -7$

(A) – 8 and 20   (B) 8 and – 20   (C) 2 and – 5

(D) 4 and – 2   (E) No solution

3. $2|x + 7| = 12$

(A) – 13 and – 1   (B) – 6 and 6   (C) – 1 and 13

(D) 6 and – 13   (E) No solution

4. $|5x| - 7 = 3$

(A) 2 and 4   (B) 4/5 and 3   (C) – 2 and 2

(D) 2   (E) No solution

5. $\left|\dfrac{3}{4}m\right| = 9$

(A) 24 and – 16   (B) 4/27 and – 4/3   (C) 4/3 and 12

(D) – 12 and 12   (E) No solution

7. Inequalities

An inequality is a statement where the value of one quantity or expression is greater than (>), less than (<), greater than or equal to (≥), less than or equal to (≤), or not equal to (≠) that of another.

EXAMPLE

$5 > 4$.

The expression above means that the value of 5 is greater than the value of 4.

A **conditional inequality** is an inequality whose validity depends on the values of the variables in the sentence. That is, certain values of the variables will make the sentence true, and others will make it false. $3 - y > 3 + y$ is a conditional inequality for the set of real numbers, since it is true for any replacement less than zero and false for all others.

$x + 5 > x + 2$ is an **absolute inequality** for the set of real numbers, meaning that for any real value x, the expression on the left is greater than the expression on the right.

$5y < 2y + y$ is inconsistent for the set of non-negative real numbers. For any y greater than 0 the sentence is always false. A sentence is inconsistent if it is always false when its variables assume allowable values.

The solution of a given inequality in one variable x consists of all values of x for which the inequality is true.

The graph of an inequality in one variable is represented by either a ray or a line segment on the real number line.

The endpoint is not a solution if the variable is strictly less than or greater than a particular value.

EXAMPLE

$x > 2$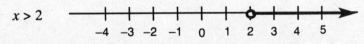

2 is not a solution and should be represented as shown.

The endpoint is a solution if the variable is either (1) less than or equal to or (2) greater than or equal to, a particular value.

EXAMPLE

$5 > x \geq 2$

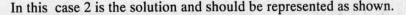

In this case 2 is the solution and should be represented as shown.

Properties of Inequalities

If x and y are real numbers then one and only one of the following statements is true.

$$x > y, x = y \text{ or } x < y.$$

This is the order property of real numbers.

If a, b and c are real numbers:

A)   If $a < b$ and $b < c$ then $a < c$.

B)   If $a > b$ and $b > c$ then $a > c$.

This is the transitive property of inequalities.

If a, b and c are real numbers and $a > b$ then $a + c > b + c$ and $a - c > b - c$. This is the **addition property of inequality**.

Two inequalities are said to have the same **sense** if their signs of inequality point in the same direction.

The sense of an inequality remains the same if both sides are multiplied or divided by the same positive real number.

EXAMPLE

$$4 > 3$$

If we multiply both sides by 5 we will obtain:

$$4 \times 5 > 3 \times 5$$

$$20 > 15$$

The sense of the inequality does not change.

The sense of an inequality becomes opposite if each side is multiplied or divided by the same negative real number.

EXAMPLE

$$4 > 3$$

If we multiply both sides by -5 we would obtain:

$$4 \times -5 < 3 \times -5$$

$$-20 < -15$$

The sense of the inequality becomes opposite.

If $a > b$ and a, b and n are positive real numbers, then:

$$a^n > b^n \text{ and } a^{-n} < b^{-n}$$

If $x > y$ and $q > p$ then $x + q > y + p$.

If $x > y > 0$ and $q > p > 0$ then $xq > yp$.

Inequalities that have the same solution set are called **equivalent inequalities**.

PROBLEM

Solve the inequality $2x + 5 > 9$.

SOLUTION

$2x + 5 + (-5) > 9 + (-5)$.	Adding -5 to both sides.
$2x + 0 > 9 + (-5)$	Additive inverse property
$2x > 9 + (-5)$	Additive identity property
$2x > 4$	Combining terms
$^1/_2(2x) > ^1/_2 \cdot 4$	Multiplying both sides by $^1/_2$.
$x > 2$	

The solution set is

$$X = \{x \mid 2x + 5 > 9\}$$
$$= \{x \mid x > 2\}$$

(that is all x, such that x is greater than 2).

PROBLEM

Solve the inequality $4x + 3 < 6x + 8$.

SOLUTION

In order to solve the inequality $4x + 3 < 6x + 8$, we must find all values of x which make it true. Thus, we wish to obtain x alone on one side of the inequality.

Add -3 to both sides:

$$\begin{array}{r} 4x + 3 < 6x + 8 \\ -3 \qquad -3 \\ \hline 4x < 6x + 5 \end{array}$$

Add $-6x$ to both sides:

$$\begin{array}{r} 4x < \quad 6x + 5 \\ -6x \qquad -6x \\ \hline -2x < \quad 5 \end{array}$$

In order to obtain x alone we must divide both sides by (-2). Recall that dividing an inequality by a negative number reverses the inequality sign, hence

$$\frac{-2x}{-2} > \frac{5}{-2}$$

Cancelling $-2/_{-2}$ we obtain, $x > -\,^5/_2$.

Thus, our solution is $\{x : x > -\,^5/_2\}$ (the set of all x such that x is greater than $-\,^5/_2$).

Drill 7: Inequalities

<u>DIRECTIONS</u>: Find the solution set for each inequality

1.　$3m + 2 < 7$

(A)　$m \geq\,^5/_3$ 　　　　(B)　$m \leq 2$ 　　　　(C)　$m < 2$

(D)　$m > 2$ 　　　　(E)　$m <\,^5/_3$

2.　$^1/_2\,x - 3 \leq 1$

(A)　$-4 \leq x \leq 8$ 　　　　(B)　$x \geq -8$ 　　　　(C)　$x \leq 8$

(D)　$2 \leq x \leq 8$ 　　　　(E)　$x \geq 8$

3.　$-3p + 1 \geq 16$

(A)　$p \geq -5$ 　　　　(B)　$p \geq \dfrac{-17}{3}$ 　　　　(C)　$p \leq \dfrac{-17}{3}$

(D)　$p \leq -5$ 　　　　(E)　$p \geq 5$

4.　$-6 <\,^2/_3\,r + 6 \leq 2$

(A)　$-6 < r \leq -3$ 　　　　(B)　$-18 < r \leq -6$ 　　　　(C)　$r \geq -6$

(D)　$-2 < r \leq\,^{-4}/_3$ 　　　　(E)　$r \leq -6$

5.　$0 < 2 - y < 6$

(A)　$-4 < y < 2$ 　　　　(B)　$-4 < y < 0$ 　　　　(C)　$-4 < y < -2$

(D)　$-2 < y < 4$ 　　　　(E)　$0 < y < 4$

8.　Ratios and Proportions

The ratio of two numbers x and y written $x : y$ is the fraction x / y where $y \neq 0$. A ratio compares x to y by dividing one by the other. Therefore, in order to compare ratios, simply compare the fractions.

A proportion is an equality of two ratios. The laws of proportion are listed below:

If $a/b = c/d$, then

(A) $\quad ad = bc$

(B) $\quad b/a = d/c$

(C) $\quad a/c = b/d$

(D) $\quad (a + b)/b = (c + d)/d$

(E) $\quad (a - b)/b = (c - d)/d$

Given a proportion $a : b = c : d$, then a and d are called extremes, b and c are called the means and d is called the fourth proportion to a, b, and c.

PROBLEM

Solve the proportion $\dfrac{x+1}{4} = \dfrac{15}{12}$.

SOLUTION

Cross multiply to determine x; that is, multiply the numerator of the first fraction by the denominator of the second, and equate this to the product of the numerator of the second and the denominator of the first.

$$(x + 1)\,12 = 4 \cdot 15$$
$$12x + 12 = 60$$
$$x = 4.$$

PROBLEM

Find the ratios of $x : y : z$ from the equations

$$7x = 4y + 8z, \quad 3z = 12x + 11y.$$

SOLUTION

By transposition we have

$$7x - 4y - 8z = 0$$
$$12x + 11y - 3z = 0.$$

To obtain the ratio of $x : y$ we convert the given system into an equation in terms of just x and y. z may be eliminated as follows: Multiply each term of the first equation by 3, and each term of the second equation by 8, and then subtract the second equation from the first. We thus obtain:

$$21x - 12y - 24z = 0$$
$$-(96x + 88y - 24z = 0)$$
$$-75x - 100y \qquad = 0$$

Dividing each term of the last equation by 25 we obtain

$$-3x - 4y = 0$$

or, $\qquad -3x = 4y.$

Dividing both sides of this equation by 4, and by -3, we have the proportion:

$$\frac{x}{4} = \frac{y}{-3}$$

We are now interested in obtaining the ratio of $y : z$. To do this we convert the given system of equations into an equation in terms of just y and z, by eliminating x as follows: Multiply each term of the first equation by 12, and each term of the second equation by 7, and then subtract the second equation from the first. We thus obtain:

$$84x - 48y - 96z = 0$$
$$-(84x + 77y - 21z = 0)$$
$$-125y - 75z = 0.$$

Dividing each term of the last equation by 25 we obtain

$$-5y - 3z = 0$$

or, $\qquad -3z = 5y.$

Dividing both sides of this equation by 5, and by -3, we have the proportion:

$$\frac{z}{5} = \frac{y}{-3}.$$

From this result and our previous result we obtain:

$$\frac{x}{4} = \frac{y}{-3} = \frac{z}{5}$$

as the desired ratios.

Drill 8: Ratios and Proportions

1. Solve for n : $\dfrac{4}{n} = \dfrac{8}{5}$

(A) 10   (B) 8   (C) 6   (D) 2.5   (E) 2

2. Solve for n: $\dfrac{2}{3} = \dfrac{n}{72}$

(A) 12   (B) 48   (C) 64   (D) 56   (E) 24

3. Solve for n: $n : 12 = 3 : 4$.

(A) 8   (B) 1   (C) 9   (D) 4   (E) 10

4. Four out of every five students at West High take a mathematics course. If the enrollment at West is 785, how many students take mathematics?

(A) 628   (B) 157   (C) 705   (D) 655   (E) 247

5. At a factory, three out of every 1,000 parts produced are defective. In a day, the factory can produce 25,000 parts. How many of these parts would be defective?

(A) 7   (B) 75   (C) 750   (D) 7,500   (E) 75,000

6. A summer league softball team won 28 out of the 32 games they played. What is the ratio of games won to games played?

(A) $4 : 5$ (B) $3 : 4$ (C) $7 : 8$ (D) $2 : 3$ (E) $1 : 8$

7. A class of 24 students contains 16 males. What is the ratio of females to males?

(A) $1 : 2$ (B) $2 : 1$ (C) $2 : 3$ (D) $3 : 1$ (E) $3 : 2$

8. A family has a monthly income of $1,250, but they spend $450 a month on rent. What is the ratio of the amount of income to the amount paid for rent?

(A) $16 : 25$ (B) $25 : 9$ (C) $25 : 16$ (D) $9 : 25$ (E) $36 : 100$

9. A student attends classes 7.5 hours a day and works a part-time job for 3.5 hours a day. She knows she must get 7 hours of sleep a night. Write the ratio of the number of free hours in this student's day to the total number of hours in a day.

(A) $1 : 3$ (B) $4 : 3$ (C) $8 : 24$ (D) $1 : 4$ (E) $5 : 12$

10. In a survey by mail, 30 out of 750 questionnaires were returned. Write the ratio of questionnaires returned to questionnaires mailed (write in simplest form).

(A) $30 : 750$ (B) $24 : 25$ (C) $3 : 75$ (D) $1 : 4$ (E) $1 : 25$

ALGEBRA DRILLS

ANSWER KEY

Drill 1—Operations With Polynomials

1.	(B)	6.	(B)	11.	(C)	16.	(C)
2.	(C)	7.	(C)	12.	(B)	17.	(D)
3.	(C)	8.	(E)	13.	(E)	18.	(E)
4.	(D)	9.	(A)	14.	(A)	19.	(B)
5.	(A)	10.	(D)	15.	(D)	20.	(B)

Drill 2—Simplifying Algebraic Expressions

1.	(C)	6.	(B)
2.	(D)	7.	(E)
3.	(B)	8.	(B)
4.	(A)	9.	(A)
5.	(D)	10.	(E)

Drill 3—Linear Equations

1.	(C)
2.	(A)
3.	(E)
4.	(D)
5.	(B)

Drill 4—Two Linear Equations

1.	(E)	6.	(B)
2.	(B)	7.	(D)
3.	(A)	8.	(E)
4.	(D)	9.	(A)
5.	(C)	10.	(B)

Drill 5—Quadratic Equations

1.	(A)	6.	(B)
2.	(D)	7.	(B)
3.	(B)	8.	(D)
4.	(C)	9.	(C)
5.	(E)	10.	(E)

Drill 6—Absolute Value Equations

1.	(B)	4.	(C)
2.	(E)	5.	(D)
3.	(A)		

Drill 7—Inequalities

1.	(E)	4.	(B)
2.	(C)	5.	(A)
3.	(D)		

Drill 8—Ratios and Proportions

1.	(D)	4.	(A)	7.	(A)	10.	(E)
2.	(B)	5.	(B)	8.	(B)		
3.	(C)	6.	(C)	9.	(D)		

GLOSSARY: ALGEBRA

Abscissa

The x (horizontal) value of a point in the Cartesian plane.

Absolute Inequality

An inequality that is true for all values of all variables.

Absolute Value

The numerical value of a number without regard to sign (i.e., it is always nonnegative).

Additive Property of Inequalities

The property that states that, if $a < b$, then $(a+c) < (b + c)$.

Algebra

The study of using letters to represent arbitrary numbers for the purpose of stating results in greater generality.

Binomial

An expression consisting of two terms.

Cartesian Coordinates

Ordered pairs of numbers assigned to points in the Cartesian plane.

Cartesian Plane

A two-dimensional grid used for graphically placing ordered pairs of reals relative to one another.

Closed Interval

An interval that contains its endpoints.

Coefficient

The number that multiplies a variable. If a variable is written alone, then the coefficient is assumed to be 1.

Completing the Squares

A method of factoring quadratic equations by adding and subtracting an appropriate quantity.

Complex Numbers

The sum of a real number and an imaginary number, i.e., $a + bi$, where a and b are real and $i^2 = -1$.

Conditional Inequality

An inequality whose validity depends on the values of one or more variables.

Constant

A variable that takes on only one fixed value.

Coordinate Axes

Two perpendicular lines (the x-axis and the y-axis) used for placing ordered pairs of reals relative to one another.

Dependent Equation

Equations with the same solution sets.

Equal Sets

Sets that contain the same members.

Equations

The statement that two expressions are equal. These expressions may depend on one or more variables.

Equivalent Equations

Equations with the same solution sets.

Equivalent Inequalities

Inequalities with the same solution sets.

Equivalent Sets

Sets that have the same number of elements.

Expression

A collection of terms joined by addition, subtraction, multiplication, or division. When all variables are given numerical values, the expression also has a numerical value.

Factoring

Finding a set of expressions whose product is the given expression. To factor the quadratic equation $ax^2 + bx + c = 0$ is to find r_1, r_2 such that $a(x - r_1)(x - r_2) = 0$.

Greatest Common Factor

The largest number that has the property that, when any of a group of numbers is divided by it, the result is an integer.

Half-Open Interval

An interval that contains one of its endpoints.

Imaginary Numbers

Numbers of the form bi, where b is real and $i^2 = -1$.

Inconsistent Inequality

An inequality that is false for all values of all variables.

Inequality

The statement that two expressions are not equal or that one exceeds the other in numerical value or that one is at least as large or small in numerical value than the other.

Least Common Multiple

The smallest number that results in an integer regardless of which of a given set of numbers it is divided by.

Linear Equation

An equation in which the exponent of each variable is 1. When plotted, the solution set forms a straight line in the Cartesian plane.

Monomial

An expression consisting of one term.

Null Set

A set with no elements or members.

Open Interval

An interval that contains neither of its endpoints.

Ordered Pair

A pair of elements of the form (x, y), in which the order is specified. Thus (x, y) in general is *not* the same as (y, x).

Ordinate

The y (vertical) value of a point in the Cartesian plane.

Origin

The intersection of the two coordinate axes. The origin corresponds to the ordered pair $(0, 0)$.

Polynomial

An expression consisting of at least two terms.

Prime Factor

A factor of an expression that is prime. That is, it has no factors other than itself and 1.

Quadrants

The four regions of the Cartesian plane, which are separated from each other by the coordinate axes. In the first quadrant, $x > 0$ and $y > 0$. In the second quadrant, $x < 0$ and $y > 0$. In the third quadrant, $x < 0$ and $y < 0$. In the fourth quadrant, $x > 0$ and $y < 0$.

Quadratic Equation

An equation of the form $ax^2 + bx + c = 0$ (the highest power is 2).

Ratio

A comparison of two numbers expressed by dividing one by the other.

Reciprocal

The number 1 divided by a given number.

Sense

The direction of an inequality. The sense is preserved if the inequality is multiplied by a positive real, but it is reversed if the inequality is multiplied by a negative real.

Solution

A set of values for the variables in an equation or inequality (one value per variable) that makes the equation or inequality true.

Solution Set

The totality of solutions to a given equation or inequality.

Term

An expression involving variables, exponents, and coefficients.

Trinomial

An expression consisting of three terms.

Universal Set

The set containing all elements under consideration.

Variable

A letter used to represent an arbitrary number.

CHAPTER 4

Geometry

➤ Diagnostic Test
➤ Geometry Review and Drills
➤ Glossary

GEOMETRY DIAGNOSTIC TEST

1. Ⓐ Ⓑ Ⓒ Ⓓ Ⓔ
2. Ⓐ Ⓑ Ⓒ Ⓓ Ⓔ
3. Ⓐ Ⓑ Ⓒ Ⓓ Ⓔ
4. Ⓐ Ⓑ Ⓒ Ⓓ Ⓔ
5. Ⓐ Ⓑ Ⓒ Ⓓ Ⓔ
6. Ⓐ Ⓑ Ⓒ Ⓓ Ⓔ
7. Ⓐ Ⓑ Ⓒ Ⓓ Ⓔ
8. Ⓐ Ⓑ Ⓒ Ⓓ Ⓔ
9. Ⓐ Ⓑ Ⓒ Ⓓ Ⓔ
10. Ⓐ Ⓑ Ⓒ Ⓓ Ⓔ
11. Ⓐ Ⓑ Ⓒ Ⓓ Ⓔ
12. Ⓐ Ⓑ Ⓒ Ⓓ Ⓔ
13. Ⓐ Ⓑ Ⓒ Ⓓ Ⓔ
14. Ⓐ Ⓑ Ⓒ Ⓓ Ⓔ
15. Ⓐ Ⓑ Ⓒ Ⓓ Ⓔ
16. Ⓐ Ⓑ Ⓒ Ⓓ Ⓔ
17. Ⓐ Ⓑ Ⓒ Ⓓ Ⓔ
18. Ⓐ Ⓑ Ⓒ Ⓓ Ⓔ
19. Ⓐ Ⓑ Ⓒ Ⓓ Ⓔ
20. Ⓐ Ⓑ Ⓒ Ⓓ Ⓔ
21. Ⓐ Ⓑ Ⓒ Ⓓ Ⓔ
22. Ⓐ Ⓑ Ⓒ Ⓓ Ⓔ
23. Ⓐ Ⓑ Ⓒ Ⓓ Ⓔ
24. Ⓐ Ⓑ Ⓒ Ⓓ Ⓔ
25. Ⓐ Ⓑ Ⓒ Ⓓ Ⓔ

26. Ⓐ Ⓑ Ⓒ Ⓓ Ⓔ
27. Ⓐ Ⓑ Ⓒ Ⓓ Ⓔ
28. Ⓐ Ⓑ Ⓒ Ⓓ Ⓔ
29. Ⓐ Ⓑ Ⓒ Ⓓ Ⓔ
30. Ⓐ Ⓑ Ⓒ Ⓓ Ⓔ
31. Ⓐ Ⓑ Ⓒ Ⓓ Ⓔ
32. Ⓐ Ⓑ Ⓒ Ⓓ Ⓔ
33. Ⓐ Ⓑ Ⓒ Ⓓ Ⓔ
34. Ⓐ Ⓑ Ⓒ Ⓓ Ⓔ
35. Ⓐ Ⓑ Ⓒ Ⓓ Ⓔ
36. Ⓐ Ⓑ Ⓒ Ⓓ Ⓔ
37. Ⓐ Ⓑ Ⓒ Ⓓ Ⓔ
38. Ⓐ Ⓑ Ⓒ Ⓓ Ⓔ
39. Ⓐ Ⓑ Ⓒ Ⓓ Ⓔ
40. Ⓐ Ⓑ Ⓒ Ⓓ Ⓔ
41. Ⓐ Ⓑ Ⓒ Ⓓ Ⓔ
42. Ⓐ Ⓑ Ⓒ Ⓓ Ⓔ
43. Ⓐ Ⓑ Ⓒ Ⓓ Ⓔ
44. Ⓐ Ⓑ Ⓒ Ⓓ Ⓔ
45. Ⓐ Ⓑ Ⓒ Ⓓ Ⓔ
46. Ⓐ Ⓑ Ⓒ Ⓓ Ⓔ
47. Ⓐ Ⓑ Ⓒ Ⓓ Ⓔ
48. Ⓐ Ⓑ Ⓒ Ⓓ Ⓔ
49. Ⓐ Ⓑ Ⓒ Ⓓ Ⓔ
50. Ⓐ Ⓑ Ⓒ Ⓓ Ⓔ

GEOMETRY DIAGNOSTIC TEST

This diagnostic test is designed to help you determine your strengths and your weaknesses in geometry. Follow the directions for each part and check your answers.

Study this chapter for the following tests:
PSAT, SAT I, ACT, NTE, PPST, CBEST, ELM, GRE, GMAT, and GED

50 Questions

DIRECTIONS: Choose the correct answer for each of the following problems. Fill in the answer on the answer sheet.

1. An old picture has dimensions 33 inches by 24 inches. What one length must be cut from each dimension so that the ratio of the shorter side to the longer side is $^2/_3$?

   (A) $4^1/_2$ inches   (B) 9 inches   (C) 6 inches

   (D) $10^1/_2$ inches   (E) 3 inches

2. The greatest area that a rectangle whose perimeter is 52 m can have is

   (A) $12\,m^2$ (B) $169\,m^2$ (C) $172\,m^2$

   (D) $168\,m^2$ (E) $52\,m^2$

3. If the triangle ABC has angle $A = 35°$ and angle $B = 85°$, then the measure of the angle x in degrees is:

   (A) 85

   (B) 90

   (C) 100

   (D) 120

   (E) 180

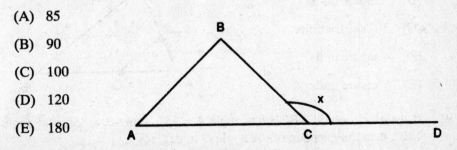

4. In the following figure, O is the center of the circle. If arc *ABC* has length 2π, what is the area of the circle?

    (A) 3 π

    (B) 6 π

    (C) 9 π

    (D) 12 π

    (E) 15 π

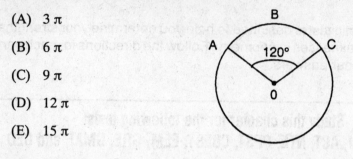

5. If the area of a rectangle is 120 and the perimeter is 44, then the length is

    (A) 30   (B) 20   (C) 15

    (D 12   (E) 10

6. What is the measure of the angle made by the minute and hour hand of a clock at 3:30?

    (A) 60°   (B) 75°   (C) 90°

    (D) 115°   (E) 120°

7. A rectangular piece of metal has an area of 35m² and a perimeter of 24 m. Which of the following are possible dimensions of the piece?

    (A) ³⁵/₂ m × 2 m   (B) 5 m × 7 m   (C) 35 m × 1 m

    (D) 6 m × 6 m   (E) 8 m × 4 m

8. The area of Δ*ADE* is 12 square units. If *B* is the midpoint of $\overline{AD}$ and *C* is the midpoint of $\overline{AE}$, what is the area of Δ*ABC*?

    (A) 2 square units

    (B) 3 square units

    (C) 3½ square units

    (D) 4 square units

    (E) 6 square units

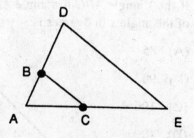

9. If the quadrilateral *ABCD* has angle *A* = 35°, angle *B* = 85°, and angle *C* = 120°, then the measure of the angle *D* in degrees is:

    (A) 85   (B) 90   (C) 100

    (D) 120   (E) 180

10. In the figure shown, two chords of the circle intersect, making the angles shown. What is the value of $x + y$?

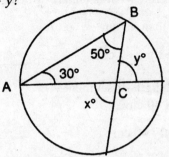

    (A) 40°

    (B) 50°

    (C) 80°

    (D) 160°

    (E) 320°

11. In the figure shown, three chords of the circle intersect making the angles shown. What is the value of θ?

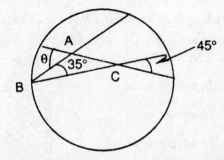

    (A) 35°

    (B) 45°

    (C) 60°

    (D) 75°

    (E) 80°

12. If a triangle of base 6 units has the same area as a circle of radius 6 units, what is the altitude of the triangle?

    (A) π   (B) 3π   (C) 6π

    (D) 12π   (E) 36π

13. A cube consists of 96 square feet. What is the volume of the cube in cubic feet?

    (A) 16   (B) 36   (C) 64

    (D) 96   (E) 216

14. If the angles of a triangle *ABC* are in the ratio of 3 : 5 : 7, then the triangle is:

    (A) acute   (B) right   (C) isosceles

    (D) obtuse   (E) equilateral

15. If the measures of the three angles of a triangle are $(3x + 15)°$, $(5x - 15)°$, and $(2x + 30)°$, what is the measure of each angle?

    (A) 75°   (B) 60°   (C) 45°

    (D) 25°   (E) 15°

16. In the figure shown below, line *l* is parallel to line *m*. If the area of triangle *ABC* is 40 cm³, what is the area of triangle *ABD*?

    (A) Less than 40 cm³

    (B) More than 40 cm³

    (C) The length of segment $\overline{AD}$ times 40 cm²

    (D) Exactly 40 cm³

    (E) Cannot be determined from the information given

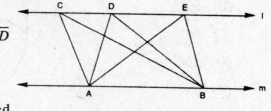

17. If the length of segment $\overline{EB}$, base of triangle *EBC*, is equal to ¹/₄ the length of segment $\overline{AB}$ ($\overline{AB}$ is the length of rectangle *ABCD*), and the area of triangle *EBC* is 12 square units, find the area of the shaded region.

    (A) 24 square units

    (B) 96 square units

    (C) 84 square units

    (D) 72 square units

    (E) 120 square units

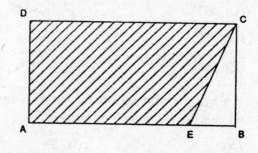

18. What is the perimeter of triangle *ABC*?

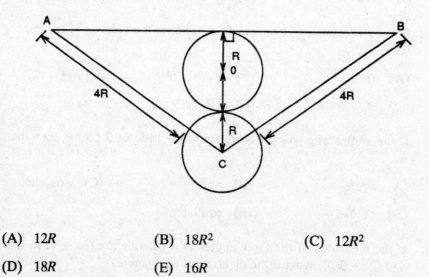

    (A) 12*R*   (B) 18*R*²   (C) 12*R*²

    (D) 18*R*   (E) 16*R*

19. Which of the following alternatives is correct?

    (A) $\alpha + \beta + \gamma = 180°$

    (B) $\gamma - \alpha + 180° = \beta$

    (C) $\alpha = \beta + \gamma$

    (D) $\gamma = \alpha + \beta$

    (E) $\alpha = 180° - \beta - \alpha$

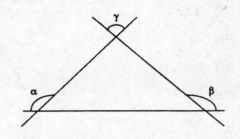

20. In the figure shown, all segments meet at right angles. Find the figure's perimeter in terms of *r* and *s*.

    (A) $r + s$

    (B) $2r + s$

    (C) $2s + r$

    (D) $r^2 + s^2$

    (E) $2r + 2s$

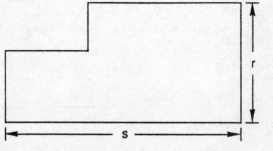

21. If lines *l*, *m*, and *n* intersect at point *P*, express $x + y$ in terms of *a*.

    (A) $180 - {}^a/_2$

    (B) ${}^a/_2 - 180$

    (C) $90 - {}^a/_2$

    (D) $a - 180$

    (E) $180 - a$

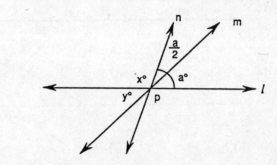

22. The measure of an inscribed angle is equal to one-half the measure of its inscribed arc. In the figure shown, triangle *ABC* is inscribed in circle *O*, and line $\overline{BD}$ is tangent to the circle at point *B*. If the measure of angle *CBD* is 70°, what is the measure of angle *BAC*?

    (A) 110°

    (B) 70°

    (C) 140°

    (D) 35°

    (E) 40°

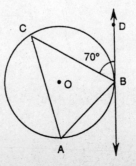

23. What is the value of *x*?

    (A) 20°

    (B) 40°

    (C) 60°

    (D) 90°

    (E) 30°

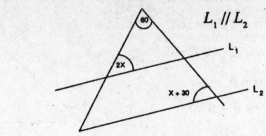

24. If the triangle *ABC* has angle *A* = 35° and angle *B* = 85°, then the measure of the angle *x* in degrees is:

    (A) 85

    (B) 90

    (C) 100

    (D) 120

    (E) 180

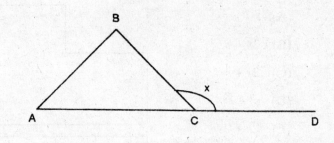

25. In the figure shown, line *r* is parallel to line *l*. Find the measure of angle *RBC*.

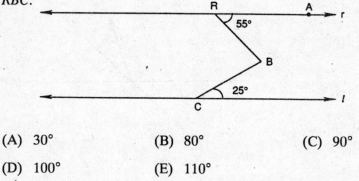

    (A) 30°   (B) 80°   (C) 90°

    (D) 100°   (E) 110°

26. In the five-pointed star shown, what is the sum of the measures of angles *A*, *B*, *C*, *D*, and *E*?

    (A) 108°

    (B) 72°

    (C) 36°

    (D) 150°

    (E) 180°

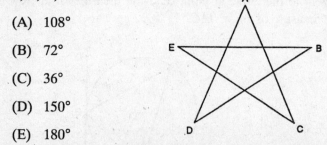

27. A room measures 13 feet by 26 feet. A rug which measures 12 feet by 18 feet is placed on the floor. What is the area of the uncovered portion of the floor?

    (A) 554 sq. ft.   (B) 216 sq. ft.   (C) 100 sq. ft.

    (D) 122 sq. ft.   (E) 338 sq. ft.

28. The area of $\triangle ADE$ is 12 square units. If B is the midpoint of $\overline{AD}$ and C is the midpoint of $\overline{AE}$, what is the area of $\triangle ABC$?

    (A) 2 square units

    (B) 3 square units

    (C) $3^1/_2$ square units

    (D) 4 square units

    (E) 6 square units

    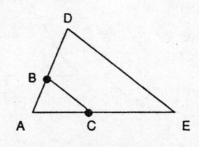

29. In $\triangle ABC$, $AB = 6$, $BC = 4$ and $AC = 3$. What kind of a triangle is it?

    (A) right and scalene   (B) obtuse and scalene

    (C) acute and scalene   (D) right and isosceles

    (E) obtuse and isosceles

30. What is the area of the shaded portion of the rectangle? The heavy dot represents the center of the semicircle.

    (A) $200 - 100\pi$ (B) $200 - 25\pi$

    (C) $30 - \dfrac{25\pi}{2}$ (D) $\dfrac{200 - 25\pi}{2}$

    (E) $\dfrac{400 - 25\pi}{2}$

31. Find the area of the isosceles trapezoid.

    (A) $250\sqrt{3}$

    (B) 150

    (C) 250

    (D) $125\sqrt{3}$

    (E) Area cannot be found.

    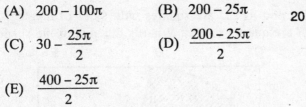

32. If the radius of a sphere is increased by a factor of 3, then the volume of the sphere is increased by a factor of

    (A) 3   (B) 6   (C) 9

    (D) 18   (E) 27

33. In the diagram shown, *ABC* is an isosceles triangle. Sides *AC* and *BC* are extended through *C* to *E* and *D* to form triangle *CDE*. The sum of the measures of angles *D* and *E* is

    (A) 150°

    (B) 105°

    (C) 90°

    (D) 60°

    (E) 30°

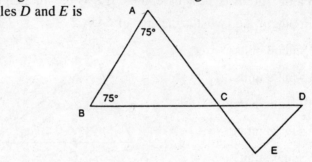

34. The box pictured has a square base with side *x* and a closed top. The surface area of the box is

    (A) $4x + h$

    (B) $4x + 4h$

    (C) hx^2

    (D) $x^2 + 4xh$

    (E) $2x^2 + 4xh$

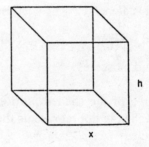

35. Quadrilaterals *ABCD* and *AFED* are squares with sides of length 10 cm. Arc *BD* and arc *DF* are quarter circles. What is the area of the shaded region?

    (A) 50 sq. cm

    (B) 100 sq. cm

    (C) 80 sq. cm

    (D) 40 sq. cm

    (E) 10 sq. cm

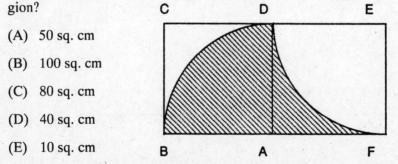

36. If the distance between two adjacent vertical or horizontal dots is 1, what is the perimeter of △*ABC*? (See figure following)

(A) 5

(B) $\sqrt{3} + \sqrt{10} + \sqrt{11}$

(C) 8

(D) 9

(E) $\sqrt{2} + \sqrt{13} + \sqrt{17}$

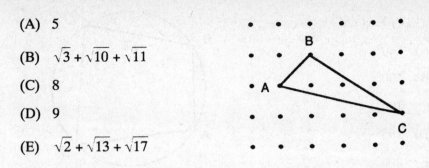

37. If the hypotenuse of a right triangle is $x + 1$ and one of the legs is x, then the other leg is

(A) $\sqrt{2x + 1}$ (B) $\sqrt{2x} + 1$ (C) $\sqrt{x^2 + (x+1)^2}$

(D) 1   (E) $2x + 1$

38. The measures of the lengths of two sides of an isosceles triangle are x and $2x + 1$. Then, the perimeter of the triangle is

(A) $4x$ (B) $4x + 1$ (C) $5x + 1$

(D) $5x + 2$ (E) None of the above

39. Find the length of the diagonal of the rectangular solid shown in the following figure.

(A) 7

(B) $2\sqrt{10}$

(C) $3\sqrt{5}$

(D) 11

(E) None of the above.

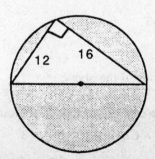

40. Find the area of the shaded portion in the following figure. The heavy dot represents the center of the circle.

(A) $100\pi - 96$

(B) $400\pi - 96$

(C) $400\pi - 192$

(D) $100\pi - 192$

(E) $256\pi - 192$

41. $m(\angle A) + m(\angle C) =$

    (A) 160°

    (B) 180°

    (C) 190°

    (D) 195°

    (E) 200°

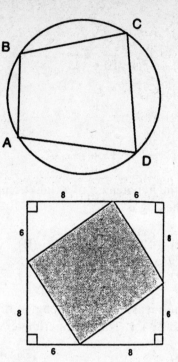

42. The area of the shaded region is:

    (A) 25 sq. units

    (B) 36 sq. units

    (C) 49 sq. units

    (D) 100 sq. units

    (E) None of the above

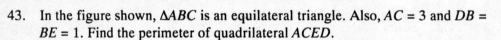

43. In the figure shown, $\triangle ABC$ is an equilateral triangle. Also, $AC = 3$ and $DB = BE = 1$. Find the perimeter of quadrilateral *ACED*.

    (A) 6

    (B) $6^1/_2$

    (C) 7

    (D) $7^1/_2$

    (E) 8

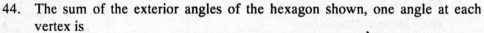

44. The sum of the exterior angles of the hexagon shown, one angle at each vertex is

    (A) 120°

    (B) 270°

    (C) 360°

    (D) 450°

    (E) None of the above

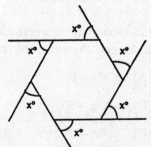

45. Find the area of the shaded region in the figure on the following page, given that $\overline{AB} = \overline{CD} = 4$ and $\overline{BC} = 8$.

(A) 40π

(B) 32π

(C) 68π

(D) 76π

(E) 36π

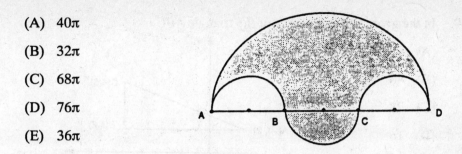

46. In the figure shown, the area of the inscribed circle is A. What is the length of a side of the square?

(A) $\sqrt{A/\pi}$

(B) $\sqrt{2A/\pi}$

(C) A/π

(D) $2\sqrt{A/\pi}$

(E) $2A/\pi$

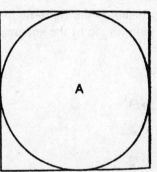

47. In the cube $ABCDEFGH$ with side $AB = 2$, what is the length of diagonal AF?

(A) 2

(B) $2\sqrt{2}$

(C) $2\sqrt{3}$

(D) 4

(E) $2\sqrt{5}$

48. Find the area of the shaded region. O is the center of the given circle, whose radius is 6. The distance $\overline{AB} = 6\sqrt{2}$.

(A) 9π

(B) 72π

(C) 18π

(D) $18\pi - 36$

(E) 36

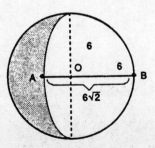

49. In the given figure, the area of the triangle *ABC* is

    (A) 65

    (B) 40

    (C) 28

    (D) 16

    (E) 14

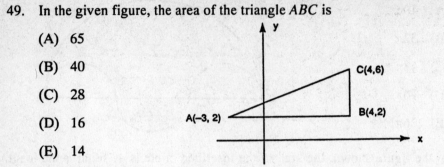

50. In the figure shown the right-angled figure is a square of length *r*, and the circular region on top of the square has radius *r*. The perimeter of the figure is

    (A) $4r + 2\pi r$

    (B) $2r + \pi r/3$

    (C) $3r + 2\pi r$

    (D) $3r + \pi r/3$

    (E) $3r + 5\pi r/3$

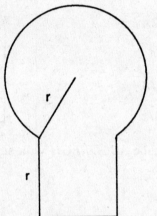

GEOMETRY DIAGNOSTIC TEST

ANSWER KEY

1. (C)	11. (E)	21. (A)	31. (D)	41. (B)
2. (B)	12. (D)	22. (B)	32. (E)	42. (D)
3. (D)	13. (C)	23. (E)	33. (A)	43. (E)
4. (C)	14. (A)	24. (D)	34. (E)	44. (C)
5. (D)	15. (B)	25. (B)	35. (B)	45. (E)
6. (B)	16. (D)	26. (E)	36. (E)	46. (D)
7. (B)	17. (B)	27. (D)	37. (A)	47. (C)
8. (B)	18. (D)	28. (B)	38. (D)	48. (E)
9. (D)	19. (B)	29. (B)	39. (A)	49. (E)
10. (D)	20. (E)	30. (E)	40. (A)	50. (E)

DETAILED EXPLANATIONS
OF ANSWERS

1. **(C)** Let x = the number of inches that must be cut from each dimension so that the ratio of the shorter side to the longer side is $^2/_3$.

Cutting off x inches from the shorter side, which is 24 inches, its length will be

$(24 - x)$ inches.

Cutting off x inches from the larger side, which is 33 inches, its length will be

$(33 - x)$ inches.

Since the ratio of the shorter side to the larger side is $^2/_3$, it follows that,

$$\frac{24 - x}{33 - x} = \frac{2}{3}$$

Solving this equation for x yields the required one length. Thus,

$$\frac{24 - x}{33 - x} = \frac{2}{3}$$

Cross-multiplication yields,

$$3(24 - x) = 2(33 - x)$$
$$72 - 3x = 66 - 2x$$
$$-3x + 2x = 66 - 72$$
$$-x = -6$$
$$x = 6.$$

2. **(B)** In order for a rectangle to encompass the greatest area all of its sides must be equal. If this is the case, its perimeter $p = 4S$; and its area $A = S^2$. We were given that its perimeter $p = 52$ m. Substituting, we get $4S = 52$ m or $S = 13$ m. Substituting into the area formula we get $A = (13 \text{ m})^2 = 169 \text{ m}^2$.

3. **(D)** The measure of the exterior angle x of triangle ABC is equal to the sum of the measures of the two remote interior angles, A and B, respectively. Thus,

angle $x = 35° + 85° = 120°$.

Another approach is to remember that the sum of the angles in triangle ABC is 35 + 85 + angle C = 180 degrees. Hence, angle C = 60 degrees. Then, since angle C

and angle x are supplementary angles it follows that angle x must be 120 degrees since angle C is 60 degrees.

4. **(C)**

$$\frac{2\pi}{120°} = \frac{2\pi r}{360°}$$

$r = 3$

Area $= \pi r^2 = 9\pi$.

5. **(D)**   If l is the length and w the width, then $lw = 120$ and $2(l + w) = 44$ so that $l + w = 22$. Now

$$(l - w)^2 = (l + w)^2 - 4lw = (22)^2 - 4(120) = 4,$$

or, $l - w = 2$. Adding $l + w = 22$ and $l - w = 2$, we get $2l = 24$, or, $l = 12$.

6. **(B)**   At 3:30 the hands of the clock will be shown below. The angle has measure $75°$.

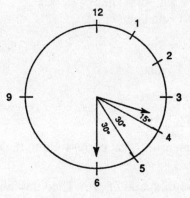

7. **(B)**   The shape given is a rectangle. Its area is equal to the length multiplied by the width.

The perimeter is twice the length plus twice the width.

Let x = length, y = width. The relevant equations are:

$$xy = 35\text{m}^2. \tag{1}$$

$$2x + 2y = 24 \text{ m}. \tag{2}$$

Rewriting equation (1):

$$y = \frac{35\text{m}^2}{x}.$$

Substituting for y in equation (2):

$$2x + 2\left(\frac{35\ m^2}{x}\right) = 24\ m.$$

Multiplying by x:

$$2x^2 + 70m^2 = 24xm.$$

Subtracting $24xm$ from both sides:

$$2x^2 - 24xm + 70m^2 = 0.$$

Dividing all terms by 2:

$$x^2 - 12xm + 35m^2 = 0.$$

This can be factored into:

$$(x - 7m)(x - 5m) = 0.$$

From this we get:

$$x - 5m = 0 \quad \text{or} \quad x - 7m = 0.$$

Two possible lengths: $x = 5m$, $x = 7m$.
   Substituting back into equation (1):

$$(5m)y = 35m^2 \Rightarrow y = 7m$$

$$(7m)y = 35m^2 \Rightarrow y = 5m$$

Thus the possible dimensions are:

$$5m \times 7m \quad \text{and} \quad 7m \times 5m.$$

$5m \times 7m$ are the only dimensions that correspond to the choices.

8.   **(B)**   Let F be the midpoint of $\overline{DE}$. Then the four small triangles are congruent and have the same area. Thus, each small triangle (including $\triangle ABC$) has $\frac{1}{4}$ the area of the large triangle and $\frac{1}{4}$ of 12 is 3.

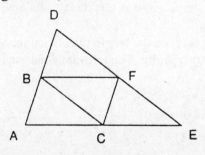

9.   **(D)**   The measure of the angle D is equal to $360°$ minus the sum of the measures of the other three angles, or

$$\text{angle } D = 360° - 35° - 85° - 120° = 120°.$$

10.   **(D)**

$$x = \angle CBA + \angle CAB$$

$$= 50° + 30°$$

$$= 80°$$

$$x = y \text{ (vertically opposite angles)}$$

Therefore, $x + y = 2(80°) = 160°$.

11.   **(E)**

$$\angle ACB = 45° \text{ (vertically opposite angles)}$$

$$\theta = \angle ABC + \angle ACB$$

$$= 35° + 45°$$

$$= 80°.$$

12.   **(D)**   To find the altitude of the triangle one must recall that the area of a triangle is given by

$$A = (1/2)bh,$$

where b denotes the base and h denotes the altitude. Also, one must recall that the area of a circle is given by

$$A = \pi r^2,$$

where r denotes the radius of the circle.

Since $b = 6$ units then

$$(1/2)(6)h = 3h = A,$$

the area of the triangle. In addition, since $r = 6$ units, then

$$A = \pi r^2 = \pi(6)^2 = 36\pi,$$

the area of the circle. But the area is the same for both figures. Thus,

$$3h = 36\pi$$

$$h = 12\pi$$

is the altitude of the triangle.

The other answer choices are incorrect and are obtained by inappropriately applying the formulas or committing errors in the calculations.

13.   **(C)**   One needs to first recall that a cube has 6 equal sized faces. Thus, the area of each face is found by dividing 6 into 96 to obtain 16 square feet. Since each face contains 16 square feet, then one can conclude that each edge of a face is 4 feet long. So, the volume of the cube, given by the formula,

$$V = (\text{length of edge})^3$$

is found to be

$$V = (4 \text{ feet})^3 = 64 \text{ cubic feet.}$$

Response (A) is found by incorrectly choosing the area of a face as the volume; response (B) is found by incorrectly squaring the 6 faces as the volume; response (E) is found by incorrectly cubing 6 as the volume; and, response (D) is found by incorrectly taking 96 as the volume of the cube.

14. **(A)** Note that the ratio (3:5:7) of the angles in the triangle ABC can be represented as three distinct angles, $3x$, $5x$, and $7x$. Since the total number of degrees in a triangle is 180 degrees, one can write and solve the equation

$$3x + 5x + 7x = 180$$
$$15x = 180$$
$$x = 12.$$

Thus, the measures of the angles in triangle ABC are:

$$3x = 3(12) = 36°, 5x = 5(12) = 60°, \text{ and } 7x = 7(12) = 84°,$$

respectively. Since each of the three angles is less than $90°$, then triangle ABC is an acute triangle.

15. **(B)** This problem can be solved easily by simply using the fact that the sum of the measures of the three interior angles of a triangle is $180°$. Thus,

$$(3x + 15) + (5x - 15) + (2x + 30) = 180$$
$$3x + 5x + 2x + 30 = 180$$
$$10x = 180 - 30$$
$$10x = 150$$
$$x = 15.$$

This gives us the measure of the

first angle	$= (3x + 15)°$	$= (3 \times 15 + 15)° = 60°$
second angle	$= (5x - 15)°$	$= (5 \times 15 - 15)° = 60°$
third angle	$= (2x + 30)°$	$= (2 \times 15 + 30)° = 60°.$

16. **(D)** Area of a triangle is equal to the product of the length of its base (any one of its sides) and the length of its altitude (the perpendicular segment drawn from the opposite vertex to the base of the triangle or to the line containing the base of the triangle).

In this problem, side $\overline{AB}$ can be taken as the base of triangle ABC, and segment $\overline{CE}$ as its altitude. Hence area of triangle ABC is equal to the

(length of $\overline{AB}$) × (length of $\overline{CE}$) = 40 cm².

In triangle ABD, side $\overline{AB}$ can be considered the base of the triangle and segment $\overline{DF}$ can be considered as its altitude. Hence,

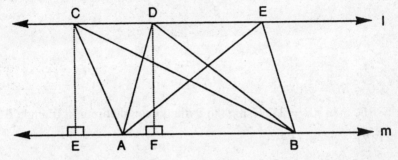

17.   **(C)**   Let (AB) represent the measure (length) of segment $\overline{AB}$, then the length of rectangle $ABCD$ is equal to (AB) and the length of its width is (BC).

Obviously, the shaded region is equal to the area of rectangle $ABCD$ minus the area of triangle EBC.

Recall that the area of a rectangle is equal to the product of the measure of its length and the measure of its width. Thus,

Area of rectangle $ABCD = (AB) (BC)$

The area of any triangle is equal to $^1/_2$ times the measure of its base, (any side of the triangle), times the measure of its altitude (the length of the perpendicular segment drawn from the vertex opposite the base to that base or to the line containing the base). That is, the area of a triangle is equal to $^1/_2bh$.

Thus,

Area of triangle $EBC = ^1/_2 (EB) (BC)$.

But $(EB) = ^1/_4(AB)$, hence,

Area of triangle $EBC = ^1/_2(^1/_4(AB))(BC)$

$= ^1/_8 (AB) (BC)$

Since the area of triangle ABC is equal to 12 square units, we have

$^1/_8 (AB) (BC) = 12$

or $(AB) (BC) = 96$.

But, $(AB) (BC)$ is the area of rectangle $ABCD$. Hence, area of rectangle $ABCD = 96$ square units.

Thus, area of shaded region = 96 – 12 = 84 square units.

18.   **(D)**   Redraw the figure. It is easy to see that

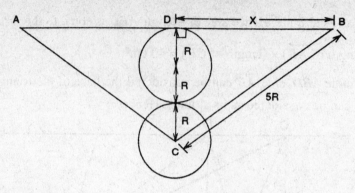

$AC = BC = 5R.$

Let $X = BD$, then $AB = 2X$. Using the Pythagorean theorem in triangle BCD

$$(3R)^2 + x^2 = (5R)^2$$

$$9R^2 + x^2 = 25R^2$$

$$x^2 = 16R^2$$

$$x = 4R$$

and the perimeter of triangle ABC will be:

$$5R + 5R + 2(4R) = 18R.$$

19. **(B)** Redraw the figure and put the interior angles in the triangle. The sum of the interior angles is 180°.

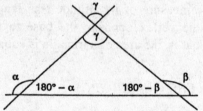

$$180° - \alpha + 180° - \beta + \gamma = 180°$$

rearranging and simplifying

$$180° - \alpha + \gamma = \beta, \quad \text{or} \quad \gamma - \alpha + 180° = \beta.$$

20. **(E)** Label the vertices of the given figure A, B, C, D, E, F and the segment $\overline{DE}$ to meet $\overline{AB}$ at G, and let $m\overline{AB}$ denote the length of segment $\overline{AB}$.

Since all the segments in the figure meet at right angles, it follows that each of the quadrilaterals $AGEF$ and $GBCD$ is a rectangle. This implies that

$$m\overline{DE} + m\overline{EG} = m\overline{CB} = r$$

But, the $m\overline{EG} = m\overline{AF}$ (since $AGEF$ is a rectangle). Hence,

$$m\overline{AF} + m\overline{ED} = r.$$

Also, $m\overline{DC} = m\overline{GB}$ (since *GBCD* is a rectangle), and the $m\overline{FE} = m\overline{AG}$ (since *AGEF* is a rectangle). Thus,

$$m\overline{DC} + m\overline{EF} = m\overline{GB} + m\overline{AG}$$
$$= m\overline{AB}$$
$$= S$$

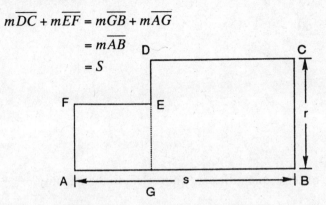

Recall that the perimeter of a closed polygon such as the figure given is equal to the sum of the measures of its segments.

Thus, the perimeter of the given figure is equal to

$$m\overline{AB} + m\overline{BC} + m\overline{CD} + m\overline{DE} + m\overline{EF} =$$
$$= m\overline{AB} + m\overline{CB} + (m\overline{DC} + m\overline{EF}) + (m\overline{ED} + m\overline{AF})$$
$$= s + r + s + r$$
$$= 2s + 2r.$$

21.　　**(A)**　　Let $m \angle A$ represent the measure of angle *A*. Since *l*, *m*, and *n* are lines intersecting at point *P*, angle *APB* is a straight angle. Recall that the measure of a straight angle is equal to 180°. That is,

$$m \angle APB = 180°.$$

Thus

$$x + y + \frac{a}{2} = 180$$

$$x + y = 180 - \frac{a}{2}$$

Now, we would like to check if any of the quantities given in the answer choices (B), (C), (D), and (E) can be equal to $x + y$. To do so, note that,

$$x + y = 180 - \frac{a}{2}$$

$$= \frac{360 - a}{2}$$

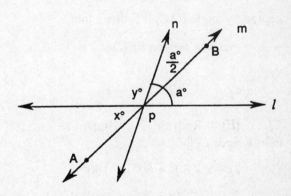

Thus, if any of the quantities given in the answer choices (B), (C), (D), and (E) are correct, that quantity must be equivalent to $\frac{360-a}{2}$. Thus,

(B) $\quad \dfrac{a}{2} - 180 = \dfrac{a-360}{2}$

(C) $\quad 90 - \dfrac{a}{2} = \dfrac{180-a}{2}$

(D) $\quad a - 180$

(E) $\quad 180 - a$

Obviously, none of these quantities are equivalent to the quantity $\frac{360-a}{2}$.

22. **(B)** Let

$m \angle A$ = the measure of angle A,

$m(\overset{\frown}{ABC})$ = the measure of arc $\overset{\frown}{ABC}$.

Since angle DBC is formed by a tangent to circle O, $\overline{BD}$ and a chord, $\overline{CB}$, intersecting at the point of tangency B, it follows that,

$$m\angle DBC = \tfrac{1}{2}m(\overset{\frown}{BEC})$$
$$70 = \tfrac{1}{2}m(\overset{\frown}{BEC})$$
$$m(\overset{\frown}{BEC}) = (70)(2)$$
$$m(\overset{\frown}{BEC}) = 140$$

Since $\angle BAC$ is an inscribed angle in the arc $\overset{\frown}{BAC}$, and since arc $\overset{\frown}{BEC}$ is intercepted by angle BAC, it follows that

$$m\angle BAC = \tfrac{1}{2}m(\overset{\frown}{BEC})$$
$$= \tfrac{1}{2}(140)$$
$$= 70°.$$

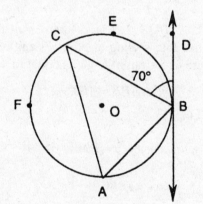

23. **(E)** Redraw the figure as below since $L_1 \parallel L_2$.

$$2x + x + 30° + 60° = 180°$$
$$3x + 90° = 180°$$
$$3x = 90°$$
$$x = 30°.$$

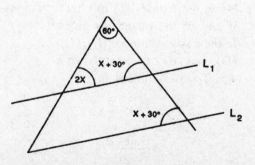

24.   **(D)**   The measure of the exterior angle x of triangle ABC is equal to the sum of the measures of the two remote interior angles, A and B, respectively. Thus,

$$\text{angle } x = 35° + 85° = 120°.$$

Another approach is to remember that the sum of the angles in triangle ABC *is* $35 + 85 + angle\ C = 180$ degrees. Hence, angle $C = 60$ degrees. Then, since angle C and angle x are supplementary angles it follows that angle x must be 120 degrees since angle C is 60 degrees.

25.   **(B)**   Extend $\overline{RB}$ to meet line l at point E, then angle ARB and angle CER are alternate interior angles. Since r is parallel to l, it follows that the measure of angle ARB is equal to the measure of angle CER. Thus, the measure of angle $CER = 55°$.

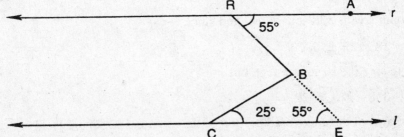

Since angle RBC is an exterior angle of triangle BEC, and the measure of an exterior angle of a triangle is equal to the sum of the measures of the two non-adjacent interior angles of the triangles, it follows that the measure of angle RBC is equal to the sum of the measures of angle BEC and angle BCE. Thus

$$\text{measure of angle } RBC = 55° + 25°$$

$$= 80°.$$

26.   **(E)**   Let $m \angle A$ represent the measure of angle A. Though there are several ways to attack this question, one way is to recall that the sum of the measures of the three interior angles of a triangle is equal to $180°$, and the measure of an exterior angle of a triangle is equal to the sum of the measures of the two non-adjacent interior angles of the triangle.

We can now start by considering triangle ACL. Of course,

$$m \angle A + m \angle C + m \angle 1 = 180°, \dots \tag{1}$$

But $\angle 1$ is an exterior angle to triangle LEF, thus,

$$m \angle 1 = m \angle E + m \angle 2.$$

Substituting this in equation (1) yields,

$$m \angle A + m \angle C + m \angle E + m \angle 2 = 180°, \dots \tag{2}$$

However, $\angle\, 2$ is an exterior angle to triangle FBD, thus,

$$m\angle 2 = m\angle B + m\angle D$$

Substituting this result in equation (2) yields,

$$m\angle A + m\angle C + m\angle E + m\angle B + m\angle D = 180°$$

Thus, the sum of the measures of angles $A, B, C, D,$ and E is equal to $180°$.

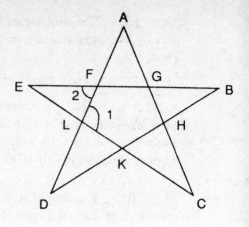

27.   **(D)**   Since

$$26 \cdot 13 = 338,$$

the room area is 338 square feet and since

$$18 \cdot 12 = 216,$$

the rug area is 216 square feet, but

$$338 - 216 = 122,$$

so the area of the uncovered portion of the room is 122 square feet.

28.   **(B)**   Let F be the midpoint of $\overline{DE}$. Then the four small triangles are congruent and have the same area. Thus, each small triangle (including $\triangle ABC$) has $^1/_4$ the area of the large triangle and $^1/_4$ of 12 is 3.

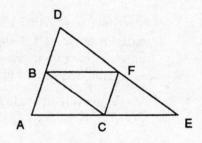

29.   **(B)**   Since all the sides are of different length, the triangle is scalene. A triangle with sides of lengths 3, 4, and 5 is a right triangle. Thus, a triangle with sides of length 3, 4, and 6 is an obtuse triangle.

30.   **(E)**

$$A = LW.$$

$$A = 20(10) = 200$$

is the area of the rectangle. The area of the semicircle is half of πr^2 where $r = 5$ or $25\pi/2$. Therefore, the shaded area is

$$200 - \frac{25\pi}{2} = \frac{400 - 25\pi}{2}.$$

Choice (D) comes from forgetting to multiply the 200 by 2 before putting both terms over the common denominator 2. Choice (A) uses 10 for the radius of the circle and does not divide the area of the circle by 2. Choice (B) does use 5 for the radius of the circle but then does not divide the area of the circle by 2.

31.   **(D)**   The height of the trapezoid must be drawn inside the figure in order to use the formula for the area of a trapezoid

$$= \frac{1}{2}h(a + b)$$

where a and b are the bases. When h is drawn, a $30° - 60° - 90°$ triangle is formed with hypotenuse given as 10 (the side of the trapezoid). The side opposite the $30°$ is 5, making the height (the side opposite the $60°$) = $5\sqrt{3}$. Base $b = 30$ as given and base $a = 30 - 10 = 20$.

$$\text{Area} = \frac{1}{2}5\sqrt{3}(20 + 20) = 25(5\sqrt{3}) = 125\sqrt{3}.$$

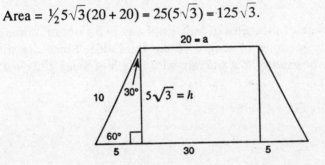

32.   **(E)**   If r is the radius of the sphere, then its volume is πr^3. If r is increased by a factor of 3, then the radius becomes $3r$ and the volume is increased to $\pi(3r)^3 = 27\pi r^3$. Thus the volume is increased by a factor of 27.

33.   **(A)**   Since the sum of measures of the interior angles of a triangle is $180°$, the measure of $\angle ACB$ is $180 - (75 + 75) = 30°$. This is also the measure of $\angle DCE$. Therefore, the sum of measures of angles D and E is $180 - 30 = 150°$.

34.   **(E)**   The surface area of the box equals the area of the base, plus area of the top, plus sum of areas of the four faces. Hence surface area of the box

$$= 2x^2 + 4xh.$$

35.   **(B)**   The shaded portion of square $ABCD$ together with the shaded portion of square $ADEF$ would cover a 10 cm by 10 cm square.

36.   **(E)**   Applying the Pythagorean theorem

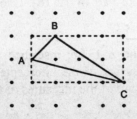

$$AB = \sqrt{1^2 + 1^2} \quad BC = \sqrt{3^2 + 2^2} \quad AC = \sqrt{1^2 + 4^2}$$
$$= \sqrt{2} \qquad\qquad = \sqrt{13} \qquad\qquad = \sqrt{17}$$

37. **(A)** By Pythagoras' theorem the square of the length of the hypotenuse is equal to the sum of the squares of the lengths of the legs. Therefore, if Y is the length of the other leg then

$$(X + 1)^2 = X^2 + Y^2,$$

or, $Y^2 = (X + 1)^2 - X^2 = 2X + 1.$

Hence, $Y = \sqrt{2X + 1}.$

38. **(D)** The sum of measures of lengths of any two sides of a triangle must be greater than the measure of length of the third side. Since the triangle is isosceles, the only possibility is a triangle with length of sides x, $2x + 1$, $2x + 1$ which has perimeter

$$x + (2x + 1) + (2x + 1) = 5x + 2.$$

39. **(A)**

$$\text{Diagonal} = \sqrt{4 + 9 + 36} = \sqrt{49} = 7.$$

Choice (B) comes from finding the diagonal of the face with 2 and 6,

$$\sqrt{4 + 36} = \sqrt{40} = 2\sqrt{10}.$$

Choice (C) comes from finding the diagonal of the other face

$$\sqrt{9 + 36} = \sqrt{45} = 3\sqrt{5}.$$

40. **(A)** The triangle is a right triangle because from geometry, an angle inscribed in a semicircle is a right angle. The hypotenuse of the triangle, which is also the diameter of the circle, is 20 (3, 4, 5 is a pythagorean triple and this triangle is 4 times 3, 4, 5). The radius of the circle is 10 and the area of the circle is $\pi r^2 = 100\pi$. The area of the triangle is

$$\tfrac{1}{2} bh = \tfrac{1}{2} 12(16) = 96$$

so shaded area is $100\pi - 96$. Choice (B) comes from using the diameter, 20 of the circle, instead of the radius. Choice (C) comes from using 20 for the circle radius and forgetting to take half of 12(16). Choice (D) comes from not taking half of 12(16).

41. **(B)** Since $\angle A$ and $\angle C$ are inscribed angles, the measure of each of these angles is half the measure of the intercepted arc. Since the two arcs comprise the entire circle, the sum of the measures of these angles is $1/2 \cdot 360°$.

42. **(D)** The four right triangles each have legs of length 6 and 8. Thus, the hypotenuse of each of those triangles is length 10 and the required area is 100 square units.

43. **(E)** In this case

$$AC = 3, AD = CE = 2 \quad \text{and} \quad DE = 1.$$

Thus the perimeter is 8.

44. **(C)** Each interior angle of a regular polygon is found by

$$\frac{(n-2)180°}{n}$$

where n = number of sides. For this hexagon, $n = 6$, each angle is

$$\frac{(6-2)180°}{6} = \frac{720°}{6} = 120°$$

∴ each exterior angle is 60°, and the sum of the exterior angles

$$= 60° \times 6 = 360°.$$

45. **(E)** Diameter $\overline{AD}$ of large circle is 16, therefore, area of semicircle is

$$\frac{\pi r^2}{2} = \frac{\pi 8^2}{2} = 32\pi.$$

Area of "cut-out" small circles is

$$2(^1/_2\pi \cdot 2^2) = 2(2\pi) = 4\pi.$$

Area of semicircle located below the diameter of large semicircle is

$$^1/_2\pi \cdot 4^2 = 8\pi.$$

Therefore, area of shaded region is

$$32\pi + 8\pi - 4\pi = 36\pi.$$

Choice (A) comes from not deleting 2 small circles, i.e., $32\pi + 8\pi$. Choice (B) comes from not taking half of area of small semicircles, i.e., $32\pi + 8\pi - 8\pi$. Choice (C) comes from not taking half of large semicircle, i.e., $64\pi + 8\pi - 4\pi$. Choice (D) comes from not taking half of both of the larger semicircles, i.e., $64\pi + 16\pi - 4\pi$.

46. **(D)** If r is the radius of a circle, then the length of a side of the square is $2r$. Since

$$A = \pi r^2, \; r = \sqrt{A/\pi} \quad \text{and} \quad 2r = 2\sqrt{A/\pi}.$$

47. **(C)** In order to find AF, we consider the right triangle AGF. By Pythagoras' theorem

$$(AF)^2 = (FG)^2 + (AG)^2 = (2)^2 + (AG)^2.$$

Also by Pythagoras' theorem

$$(AG)^2 = (AB)^2 + (BG)^2 = 2^2 = 8.$$

Hence,

$$(AF)^2 = 4 + 8 = 12 = (2\sqrt{3})^2 \text{ so that } AF = 2\sqrt{3}.$$

48. **(E)** Use the accompanying figure for the solution.

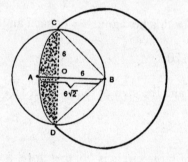

Find the area of the segment bounded by arc $\overset{\frown}{CAD}$ and subtract it from the area of the semicircle of the circle O with radius 6. In order to do this, an auxiliary circle, centered at B, is needed. Its radius is $6\sqrt{2}$. Draw

$$\overline{BC} = \overline{BD} = 6\sqrt{2}$$

as radii. Then the area of the segment = area of sector outlined by points B, C, A, D – area of triangle BCD.

$$A \text{ (sector)} = \frac{1}{2}r^2 \cdot \theta$$

where $\theta = 90° = \frac{\pi}{2}$.

Area (triangle) = $\frac{1}{2} bh$.

Area segment = area sector – area triangle

$$\frac{1}{2}(6\sqrt{2})^2 \cdot \frac{\pi}{2} - \frac{1}{2} \cdot 12 \cdot 6$$

$$18\pi - 36.$$

Area of original semicircle

$$\frac{\pi r^2}{2} = \frac{\pi \cdot 36}{2} = 18\pi$$

so that shaded area asked for is

18π $(18\pi - 36) = 36$.

Choice (A) comes from $^1/_4$ of $\pi r^2 = ^1/_4 \cdot 36\pi = 9\pi$.

Choice (B) comes from $(6\sqrt{2})^2 \pi = 72\pi$.

Choice (C) is the area of semicircle 18π.

Choice (D) is area of segment $= 18\pi - 36$.

49.   **(E)**   Since BC is parallel to the vertical axis and AB is parallel to the horizontal axis, CB is perpendicular to AB. Hence, length of BC = height of triangle

$$ABC = 6 - 2 = 4$$

and base = length of $AB = 4 - (-3) = 7$.

Therefore, area of triangle $ABC = (^1/_2)(4)(7) = 14$.

50.   **(E)**   Since the radius of the circular region is r, the angle subtended by the top side of the square at the center of the circle is $60°$. Therefore, only $60/360 = 1/6$ of the circumference of the circle is excluded from the perimeter of the figure. The perimeter is equal to

$$3r + ^5/_6(2\pi r) = 3r + 5\pi r/3.$$

GEOMETRY REVIEW

1. Points, Lines, and Angles

Geometry is built upon a series of undefined terms. These terms are those which we accept as known in order to define other undefined terms.

A) **Point**: Although we represent points on paper with small dots, a point has no size, thickness, or width.

B) **Line**: A line is a series of adjacent points which extends indefinitely. A line can be either curved or straight; however, unless otherwise stated, the term "line" refers to a straight line.

C) **Plane**: A plane is a collection of points lying on a flat surface, which extends indefinitely in all directions.

If A and B are two points on a line, then the **line segment** AB is the set of points on that line between A and B and including A and B, which are endpoints. The line segment is referred to as AB.

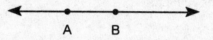

A **ray** is a series of points that lie to one side of a single endpoint.

PROBLEM

How many lines can be found that contain (a) one given point (b) two given points (c) three given points?

SOLUTION

(a)   *Given one point A*, there are an infinite number of distinct lines that contain the given point. To see this, consider line l_1 passing through point A. By rotating l_1 around A like the hands of a clock, we obtain different lines l_2, l_3, etc. Since we can rotate l_1 in infinitely many ways, there are infinitely many lines containing A.

(b)   *Given two distinct points B and C*, there is one and only one distinct line. To see this, consider all the lines containing point B; l_5, l_6, l_7 and l_8. Only l_5 contains both points B and C. Thus, there is only one line containing both points B and C. Since there is always at least one line containing two distinct points and never more than one, the line passing through the two points is said to be determined by the two points.

(c)   *Given three distinct points*, there may be one line or none. If a line exists that contains the three points, such as D, E, and F, then the points are said to be **colinear**. If no such line exists — as in the case of points G, H, and I, then the points are said to be **noncolinear**.

Intersection Lines and Angles

An **angle** is a collection of points which is the union of two rays having the same endpoint. An angle such as the one illustrated below can be referred to in any of the following ways:

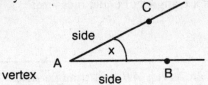

A)   by a capital letter which names its vertex, i.e., $\angle A$;

B)   by a lower-case letter or number placed inside the angle, i.e., $\angle x$;

C)   by three capital letters, where the middle letter is the vertex and the other two letters are not on the same ray, i.e., $\angle CAB$ or $\angle BAC$, both of which represent the angle illustrated in the figure.

Types of Angles

A)   **Vertical angles** are formed when two lines intersect. These angles are equal.

$\angle a = \angle b$

B)   **Adjacent angles** are two angles with a common vertex and a common side, but no common interior points. In the following figure, $\angle DAC$ and $\angle BAC$ are adjacent angles. $\angle DAB$ and $\angle BAC$ are not.

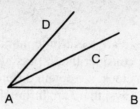

C) A **right angle** is an angle whose measure is 90°.

D) An **acute angle** is an angle whose measure is larger than 0° but less than 90°.

E) An **obtuse angle** is an angle whose measure is larger than 90° but less than 180°.

F) A **straight angle** is an angle whose measure is 180°. Such an angle is, in fact, a straight line.

G) A **reflex angle** is an angle whose measure is greater than 180° but less than 360°.

H) **Complementary angles** are two angles, the sum of the measures of which equals 90°.

I) **Supplementary angles** are two angles, the sum of the measures of which equals 180°.

J) **Congruent angles** are angles of equal measure.

PROBLEM

In the figure, we are given $\overline{AB}$ and triangle *ABC*. We are told that the measure of ∠ 1 is five times the measure of ∠ 2. Determine the measures of ∠ 1 and ∠ 2.

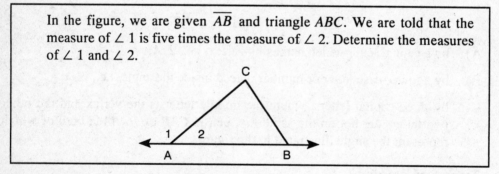

SOLUTION

Since ∠ 1 and ∠ 2 are adjacent angles whose non-common sides lie on a straight line, they are, by definition, supplementary. As supplements, their measures must sum to 180°.

If we let x = the measure of ∠2, then, $5x$ = the measure of ∠ 1.

To determine the respective angle measures, set $x + 5x = 180$ and solve for x. $6x = 180$. Therefore, $x = 30$ and $5x = 150$.

Therefore, the measure of ∠ 1 = 150 and the measure of ∠ 2 = 30.

Perpendicular Lines

Two lines are said to be **perpendicular** if they intersect and form right angles. The symbol for perpendicular (or, is therefore perpendicular to) is ⊥; $\overline{AB}$ is perpendicular to $\overline{CD}$ is written $\overline{AB} \perp \overline{CD}$.

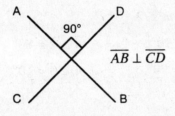

$$\overline{AB} \perp \overline{CD}$$

PROBLEM

We are given straight lines $\overline{AB}$ and $\overline{CD}$ intersecting at point P. $\overline{PR}$ ⊥ $\overline{AB}$ and the measure of ∠ APD is 170°. Find the measures of ∠ 1, ∠ 2, ∠ 3, and ∠ 4. (See figure below.)

SOLUTION

This problem will involve making use of several of the properties of supplementary and vertical angles, as well as perpendicular lines.

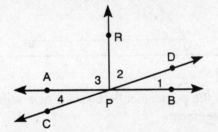

∠ APD and ∠ 1 are adjacent angles whose non-common sides lie on a straight line, $\overline{AB}$. Therefore, they are supplements and their measures sum to 180°.

$$m \angle APD + m \angle 1 = 180°.$$

We know $m \angle APD = 170°$. Therefore, by substitution, $170° + m \angle 1 = 180°$. This implies $m \angle 1 = 10°$.

∠ 1 and ∠ 4 are vertical angles because they are formed by the intersection of two straight lines, $\overline{CD}$ and $\overline{AB}$, and their sides form two pairs of opposite rays. As vertical angles, they are, by theorem, of equal measure. Since $m \angle 1 = 10°$, then $m \angle 4 = 10°$.

Since $\overline{PR} \perp \overline{AB}$, at their intersection the angles formed must be right angles. Therefore, ∠ 3 is a right angle and its measure is 90°. $m \angle 3 = 90°$.

The figure shows us that $\angle APD$ is composed of $\angle 3$ and $\angle 2$. Since the measure of the whole must be equal to the sum of the measures of its parts, $m \angle APD = m \angle 3 + m \angle 2$. We know the $m \angle APD = 170°$ and $m \angle 3 = 90°$, therefore, by substitution, we can solve for $m \angle 2$, our last unknown.

$$170° = 90° + m \angle 2$$

$$80° = m \angle 2$$

Therefore, $m \angle 1 = 10°$, $m \angle 2 = 80°$

$m \angle 3 = 90°$, $m \angle 4 = 10°$.

PROBLEM

In the accompanying figure $\overline{SM}$ is the perpendicular bisector of $\overline{QR}$, and $\overline{SN}$ is the perpendicular bisector of $\overline{QP}$. Prove that $SR = SP$.

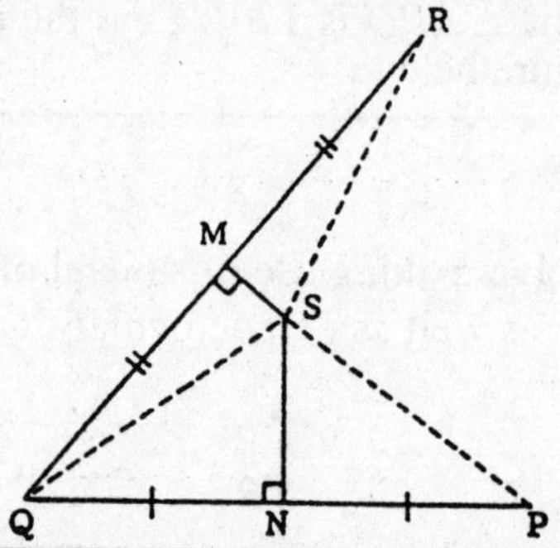

SOLUTION

Every point on the perpendicular bisector of a segment is equidistant from the endpoints of the segment.

Since point S is on the perpendicular bisector of $\overline{QR}$,

$$SR = SQ \tag{1}$$

Also, since point S is on the perpendicular bisector of $\overline{QP}$,

$$SQ = SP \tag{2}$$

By the transitive property (quantities equal to the same quantity are equal), we have:

$$SR = SP. \tag{3}$$

Parallel Lines

Two lines are called **parallel lines** if, and only if, they are in the same plane (coplanar) and do not intersect. The symbol for parallel, or is parallel to, is $||$; $\overline{AB}$ is parallel to $\overline{CD}$ is written $\overline{AB} \, || \, \overline{CD}$.

The distance between two parallel lines is the length of the perpendicular segment from any point on one line to the other line.

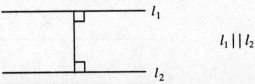

$$l_1 \parallel l_2$$

Given a line l and a point P not on line l, there is one and only one line through point P that is parallel to line l.

Two coplanar lines are either intersecting lines or parallel lines.

If two (or more) lines are perpendicular to the same line, then they are parallel to each other.

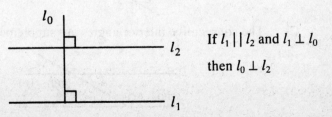

If $l_1 \perp l_0$ and $l_2 \perp l_0$.

then $l_1 \parallel l_2$

If two lines are cut by a transversal so that alternate interior angles are equal, the lines are parallel.

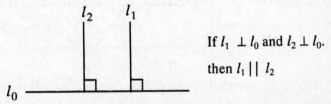

If $\angle \alpha = \angle \beta$

then $l_1 \parallel l_2$

If two lines are parallel to the same line, then they are parallel to each other.

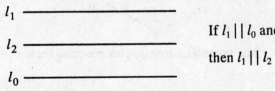

If $l_1 \parallel l_0$ and $l_2 \parallel l_0$

then $l_1 \parallel l_2$

If a line is perpendicular to one of two parallel lines, then it is perpendicular to the other line, too.

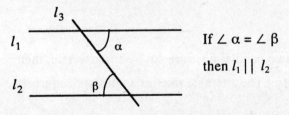

If $l_1 \parallel l_2$ and $l_1 \perp l_0$

then $l_0 \perp l_2$

If two lines being cut by a transversal form congruent corresponding angles, then the two lines are parallel.

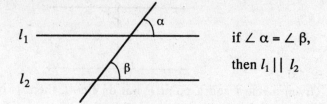

if $\angle \alpha = \angle \beta$,

then $l_1 \parallel l_2$

If two lines being cut by a transversal form interior angles on the same side of the transversal that are supplementary, then the two lines are parallel.

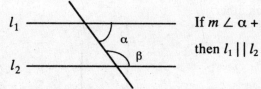

If $m \angle \alpha + m \angle \beta = 180°$

then $l_1 \parallel l_2$

If a line is parallel to one of two parallel lines, it is also parallel to the other line.

If $l_1 \parallel l_2$ and $l_0 \parallel l_1$

then $l_0 \parallel l_2$

If two parallel lines are cut by a transversal, then:

A) The alternate interior angles are congruent.

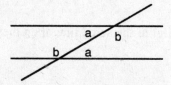

B) The corresponding angles are congruent.

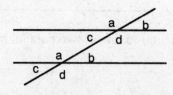

C) The consecutive interior angles are supplementary.

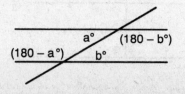

D)   The alternate exterior angles are congruent.

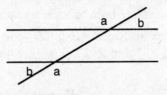

PROBLEM

Given: ∠ 2 is supplementary to ∠ 3.

Prove: $l_1 \parallel l_2$.

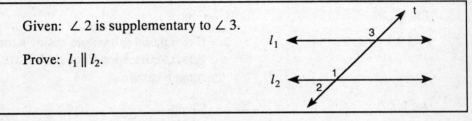

SOLUTION

Given two lines intercepted by a transversal, if a pair of corresponding angles are congruent, then the two lines are parallel. In this problem, we will show that since ∠ 1 and ∠ 2 are supplementary and ∠ 2 and ∠ 3 are supplementary, ∠ 1 and ∠ 3 are congruent. Since corresponding angles ∠ 1 and ∠ 3 are congruent, it follows $l_1 \parallel l_2$.

	Statement		Reason
1.	∠ 2 is supplementary to ∠ 3.	1.	Given.
2.	∠ 1 is supplementary to ∠ 2.	2.	Two angles that form a linear pair are supplementary.
3.	∠ 1 ≅ ∠ 3	3.	Angles supplementary to the same angle are congruent.
4.	$l_1 \parallel l_2$.	4.	Given two lines intercepted by a transversal, if a pair of corresponding angles are congruent, then the two lines are parallel.

PROBLEM

If line $\overline{AB}$ is parallel to line $\overline{CD}$ and line $\overline{EF}$ is parallel to line $\overline{GH}$, prove that $m \angle 1 = m \angle 2$.

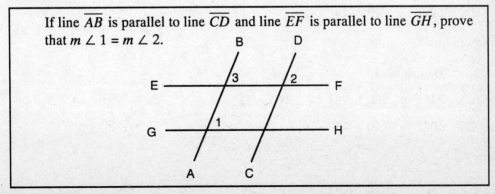

SOLUTION

To show ∠ 1 ≅ ∠ 2, we relate both to ∠ 3. Because $\overline{EF} \parallel \overline{GH}$, corresponding angles 1 and 3 are congruent. Since $\overline{AB} \parallel \overline{CD}$, corresponding angles 3 and 2 are congruent. Because both ∠ 1 and ∠ 2 are congruent to the same angle, it follows that ∠ 1 ≅ ∠ 2.

Statement	**Reason**
1. $\overline{EF} \cong \overline{GH}$	1. Given.
2. $m \angle 1 = m \angle 3$	2. If two parallel lines are cut by a transversal, corresponding angles are of equal measure.
3. $\overline{AB} \parallel \overline{CD}$	3. Given.
4. $m \angle 2 = m \angle 3$	4. If two parallel lines are cut by a transversal, corresponding angles are equal in measure.
5. $m \angle 1 = m \angle 2$	5. If two quantities are equal to the same quantity, they are equal to each other.

Drill 1: Lines and Angles

Intersection Lines

1. Find *a*.

(A) 38°   (B) 68°   (C) 78°

(D) 90°   (E) 112°

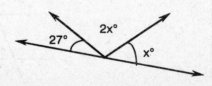

2. Find *c*.

(A) 32°   (B) 48°   (C) 58°

(D) 82°   (E) 148°

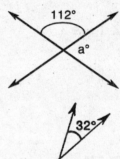

3. Determine *x*.

(A) 21°   (B) 23°   (C) 51°

(D) 102°   (E) 153°

4.   Find *x*.

(A)   8   (B)   11.75   (C)   21

(D)   23   (E)   32

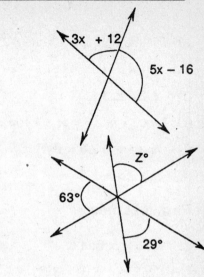

5.   Find *z*.

(A)   29°   (B)   54°   (C)   61°

(D)   88°   (E)   92°

Perpendicular Lines

6. $\overline{BA} \perp \overline{BC}$ and $m \angle DBC = 53$. Find $m \angle ABD$.

(A)   27°   (B)   33°   (C)   37°

(D)   53°   (E)   90°

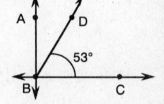

7. $m \angle 1 = 90°$. Find $m \angle 2$.

(A)   80°   (B)   90°   (C)   100°

(D)   135°   (E)   180°

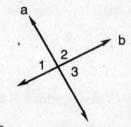

8.   If $n \perp p$, which of the following statements is true?

(A) $\angle 1 \cong \angle 2$

(B) $\angle 4 \cong \angle 5$

(C) $m\angle 4 + m \angle 5 > m \angle 1 + m \angle 2$

(D) $m \angle 3 > m \angle 2$

(E) $m \angle 4 = 90°$

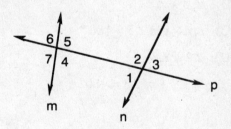

9. $\overline{CD} \perp \overline{EF}$. If $m \angle 1 = 2x$, $m \angle 2 = 30°$, and $m \angle 3 = x$, find *x*.

(A)   5°   (B)   10°   (C)   12°

(D)   20°   (E)   25°

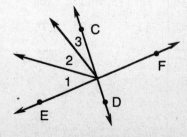

10. In the figure, $p \perp t$ and $q \perp t$. Which of the following statements is false?

(A) $\angle 1 \cong \angle 4$

(B) $\angle 2 \cong \angle 3$

(C) $m\angle 2 + m \angle 3 = m \angle 4 + m \angle 6$

(D) $m \angle 5 + m \angle 6 = 180°$

(E) $m \angle 2 > m \angle 5$

Parallel Lines

11. If $a \parallel b$, find z.

(A) 26° (B) 32° (C) 64°

(D) 86° (E) 116°

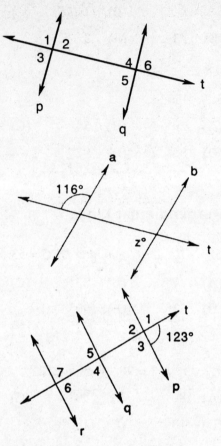

12. In the figure, $p \parallel q \parallel r$. Find $m \angle 7$.

(A) 27° (B) 33° (C) 47°

(D) 57° (E) 64°

13. If $m \parallel n$, which of the following statements is false?

(A) $\angle 2 \cong \angle 5$

(B) $\angle 3 \cong \angle 6$

(C) $m\angle 4 + m \angle 5 = 180°$

(D) $\angle 2 \cong \angle 8$

(E) $m \angle 7 + m \angle 3 = 180°$

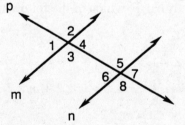

14. If $r \parallel s$, find $m \angle 2$.

(A) 17° (B) 27° (C) 43°

(D) 67° (E) 73°

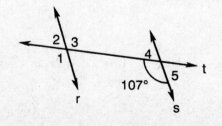

15. If *a* || *b* and *c* || d, find *m* ∠5.

(A) 55°   (B) 65°   (C) 75°

(D) 95°   (E) 125°

2. Polygons (Convex)

A **polygon** is a figure with the same number of sides as angles.

An **equilateral polygon** is a polygon all of whose sides are of equal measure.

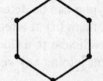

An **equiangular polygon** is a polygon all of whose angles are of equal measure.

A **regular polygon** is a polygon that is both equilateral and equiangular.

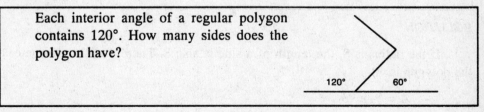

PROBLEM

Each interior angle of a regular polygon contains 120°. How many sides does the polygon have?

120°   60°

SOLUTION

At each vertex of a polygon, the exterior angle is supplementary to the interior angle, as shown in the diagram.

Since we are told that the interior angles measure 120 degrees, we can deduce that the exterior angle measures 60°.

Each exterior angle of a regular polygon of n sides measure $360°/_n$ degrees. We know that each exterior angle measures 60°, and, therefore, by setting $360°/_n$ equal to 60°, we can determine the number of sides in the polygon. The calculation is as follows:

$$360°/_n = 60°$$

$$60°n = 360°$$

$$n = 6.$$

Therefore, the regular polygon, with interior angles of 120°, has 6 sides and is called a hexagon.

The area of a regular polygon can be determined by using the **apothem** and **radius** of the polygon. The apothem (a) of a regular polygon is the segment from the center of the polygon perpendicular to a side of the polygon. The radius (r) of a regular polygon is the segment joining any vertex of a regular polygon with the center of that polygon.

(1)   All radii of a regular polygon are congruent.

(2)   The radius of a regular polygon is congruent to a side.

(3)   All apothems of a regular polygon are congruent.

The **area** of a regular polygon equals one-half the product of the length of the apothem and the perimeter.

$$\text{Area} = \frac{1}{2} a \cdot p$$

PROBLEM

Find area of the regular polygon whose radius is 8 and whose apothem is 6.

SOLUTION

If the radius is 8, the length of a side is also 8. Therefore, the perimeter of the polygon is 40.

$$A = \frac{1}{2} a \cdot p$$

$$A = \frac{1}{2}(6)(40)$$

$$A = 120.$$

PROBLEM

Find the area of a regular hexagon if one side has length 6.

SOLUTION

Since the length of a side equals 6, the radius also equals 6 and the perimeter equals 36. The base of the right triangle, formed by the radius and apothem, is half the length of a side, or 3. Using the Pythagorean theorem, you can find the length of the apothem.

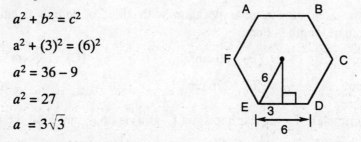

$$a^2 + b^2 = c^2$$

$$a^2 + (3)^2 = (6)^2$$

$$a^2 = 36 - 9$$

$$a^2 = 27$$

$$a = 3\sqrt{3}$$

The apothem equals $3\sqrt{3}$. Therefore, the area of the hexagon

$$= \frac{1}{2} a \cdot p$$

$$= \frac{1}{2} (3\sqrt{3})(36)$$

$$= 54\sqrt{3}$$

Drill 2: Regular Polygons

1. Find the measure of an interior angle of a regular pentagon.

(A) 55   (B) 72   (C) 90   (D) 108   (E) 540

2. Find the measure of an exterior angle of a regular octagon.

(A) 40   (B) 45   (C) 135   (D) 540   (E) 1080

3. Find the sum of the measures of the exterior angles of a regular triangle.

(A) 90   (B) 115   (C) 180   (D) 250   (E) 360

4. Find the area of a square with a perimeter of 12 cm.

(A) $9 \, cm^2$ (B) $12 \, cm^2$ (C) $48 \, cm^2$ (D) $96 \, cm^2$ (E) $144 \, cm^2$

5. A regular triangle has sides of 24 mm. If the apothem is $4\sqrt{3}$ mm, find the area of the triangle.

(A) 72 mm^2 (B) 96$\sqrt{3}$ mm^2 (C) 144 mm^2

(D) 144$\sqrt{3}$ mm^2 (E) 576 mm^2

6.   Find the area of a regular hexagon with sides of 4 cm.

(A) 12$\sqrt{3}$ cm^2 (B) 24 cm^2 (C) 24$\sqrt{3}$ cm^2

(D) 48 cm^2 (E) 48$\sqrt{3}$ cm^2

7.   Find the area of a regular decagon with sides of length 6 cm and an apothem of length 9.2 cm.

(A) 55.2 cm^2 (B) 60 cm^2 (C) 138 cm^2

(D) 138.3 cm^2 (E) 276 cm^2

8.   The perimeter of a regular heptagon (7-gon) is 36.4 cm. Find the length of each side.

(A) 4.8 cm   (B) 5.2 cm   (C) 6.7 cm   (D) 7 cm   (E) 10.4 cm

9.   The apothem of a regular quadrilateral is 4 in. Find the perimeter.

(A) 12 in   (B) 16 in   (C) 24 in   (D) 32 in   (E) 64 in

10. A regular triangle has a perimeter of 18 cm; a regular pentagon has a perimeter of 30 cm; a regular hexagon has a perimeter of 33 cm. Which figure (or figures) have sides with the longest measure?

(A) regular triangle

(B) regular triangle and regular pentagon

(C) regular pentagon

(D) regular pentagon and regular hexagon

(E) regular hexagon

3. Triangles

A closed three-sided geometric figure is called a **triangle**. The points of the intersection of the sides of a triangle are called the **vertices** of the triangle.

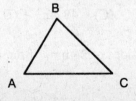

The **perimeter** of a triangle is the sum of the measures of the sides of the triangle.

A triangle with no equal sides is called a **scalene** triangle.

A triangle having at least two equal sides is called an **isosceles** triangle. The third side is called the **base** of the triangle.

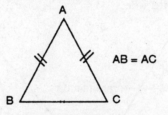

A side of a triangle is a line segment whose endpoints are the vertices of two angles of the triangle.

An interior angle of a triangle is an angle formed by two sides and includes the third side within its collection of points.

An equilateral triangle is a triangle having three equal sides. $AB = AC = BC$

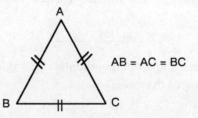

A triangle with an obtuse angle (greater than 90°) is called an **obtuse tri-angle**.

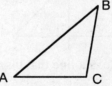

An **acute triangle** is a triangle with three acute angles (less than 90°).

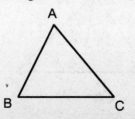

A triangle with a right angle is called a **right triangle**. The side opposite the right angle in a right triangle is called the hypotenuse of the right triangle. The other two sides are called arms or legs of the right triangle.

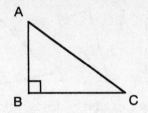

An **altitude** of a triangle is a line segment from a vertex of the triangle perpendicular to the opposite side.

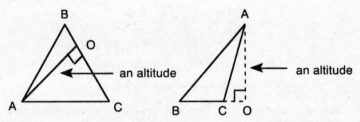

A line segment connecting a vertex of a triangle and the midpoint of the opposite side is called a **median** of the triangle.

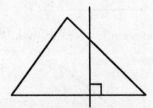

A line that bisects and is perpendicular to a side of a triangle is called a **perpendicular bisector** of that side.

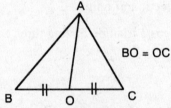

An **angle bisector** of a triangle is a line that bisects an angle and extends to the opposite side of the triangle.

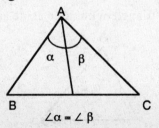

The line segment that joins the midpoints of two sides of a triangle is called a midline of the triangle.

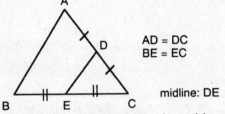

AD = DC
BE = EC

midline: DE

An exterior angle of a triangle is an angle formed outside a triangle by one side of the triangle and the extension of an adjacent side.

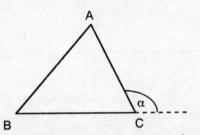

A triangle whose three interior angles have equal measure is said to be equiangular.

Three or more lines (or rays or segments) are concurrent if there exists one point common to all of them, that is, if they all intersect at the same point.

PROBLEM

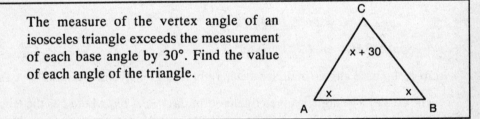

The measure of the vertex angle of an isosceles triangle exceeds the measurement of each base angle by 30°. Find the value of each angle of the triangle.

SOLUTION

We know that the sum of the values of the angles of a triangle is 180°. In an isosceles triangle, the angles opposite the congruent sides (the base angles) are, themselves, congruent and of equal value.

Therefore,

(1)   Let x = the measure of each base angle.

(2)   Then $x + 30$ = the measure of the vertex angle.

We can solve for x algebraically by keeping in mind the sum of all the measures will be 180°.

$$x + x + (x + 30) = 180$$

$$3x + 30 = 180$$
$$3x = 150$$
$$x = 50$$

Therefore, the base angles each measure 50°, and the vertex angle measures 80°.

PROBLEM

Prove that the base angles of an isosceles right triangle have measure 45°.

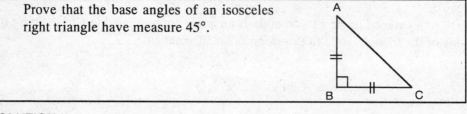

SOLUTION

As drawn in the figure, $\triangle ABC$ is an isosceles right triangle with base angles *BAC* and *BCA*. The sum of the measures of the angles of any triangle is 180°. For $\triangle ABC$, this means

$$m \angle BAC + m \angle BCA + m \angle ABC = 180° \qquad (1)$$

But $m \angle ABC = 90°$ because $\triangle ABC$ is a right triangle. Furthermore, $m \angle BCA = m \angle BAC$, since the base angles of an isosceles triangle are congruent. Using these facts in equation (1)

$$m \angle BAC + m \angle BCA + 90° = 180°$$

or $\qquad 2m \angle BAC = 2m \angle BCA = 90°$

or $\qquad m \angle BAC = m \angle BCA = 45°$.

Therefore, the base angles of an isosceles right triangle have measure 45°.

The area of a triangle is given by the formula $A = \frac{1}{2} bh$, where *b* is the length of a base, which can be any side of the triangle and *h* is the corresponding height of the triangle, which is the perpendicular line segment that is drawn from the vertex opposite the base to the base itself.

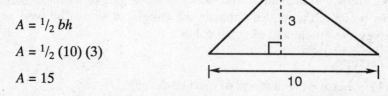

$$A = \frac{1}{2} bh$$
$$A = \frac{1}{2} (10) (3)$$
$$A = 15$$

The area of a right triangle is found by taking $\frac{1}{2}$ the product of the lengths of its two arms.

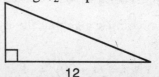

$$A = \frac{1}{2} (5) (12)$$
$$A = 30$$

Drill 3: Triangles

Angle Measures

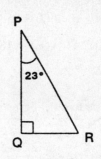

1. In △ *PQR*, ∠ *Q* is a right angle. Find *m* ∠*R*.

(A) 27°   (B) 33°   (C) 54°

(D) 67°   (E) 157°

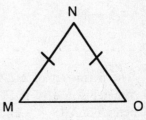

2. △ *MNO* is isosceles. If the vertex angle, ∠ *N*, has a measure of 96°, find the measure of ∠ *M*.

(A) 21°   (B) 42°   (C) 64°

(D) 84°   (E) 96°

3. Find *x*.

(A) 15°   (B) 25°   (C) 30°

(D) 45°   (E) 90°

4. Find *m* ∠1.

(A) 40   (B) 66   (C) 74

(D) 114   (E) 140

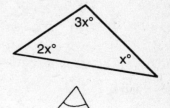

5. △ *ABC* is a right triangle with a right angle at *B*. △ *BDC* is a right triangle with right angle ∠ *BDC*. If *m* ∠*C* = 36, find *m* ∠*A*.

(A) 18   (B) 36   (C) 54

(D) 72   (E) 180

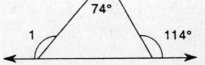

Similar Triangles

6. The two triangles shown are similar. Find *b*.

(A) 2 2/3   (B) 3   (C) 4

(D) 16   (E) 24

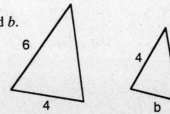

7. The two triangles shown are similar. Find $m \angle 1$.

(A) 48   (B) 53   (C) 74

(D) 127   (E) 180

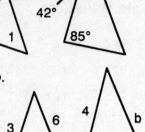

8. The two triangles shown are similar. Find a and b.

(A) 5 and 10   (B) 4 and 8

(C) 4 2/3 and 7 1/3   (D) 5 and 8

(E) 5 1/3 and 8

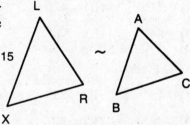

9. The perimeter of $\triangle LXR$ is 45 and the perimeter of $\triangle ABC$ is 27. If $LX = 15$, find the length of AB.

(A) 9   (B) 15   (C) 27

(D) 45   (E) 72

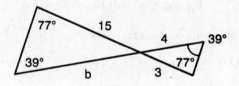

10. Find b.

(A) 9   (B) 15   (C) 20

(D) 45   (E) 60

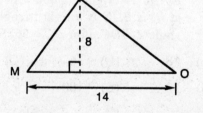

Area

11. Find the area of $\triangle MNO$.

(A) 22   (B) 49   (C) 56

(D) 84   (E) 112

12. Find the area of $\triangle PQR$.

(A) 31.5   (B) 38.5   (C) 53

(D) 77   (E) 82.5

13. Find the area of Δ *STU*.

(A) $4\sqrt{2}$ (B) $8\sqrt{2}$ (C) $12\sqrt{2}$

(D) $16\sqrt{2}$ (E) $32\sqrt{2}$

14. Find the area of Δ *ABC*.

(A) 54 cm²   (B) 81 cm²   (C) 108 cm²

(D) 135 cm²   (E) 180 cm²

15. Find the area of Δ *XYZ*.

(A) 20 cm²   (B) 50 cm²   (C) $50\sqrt{2}$ cm²

(D) 100 cm²   (E) 200 cm²

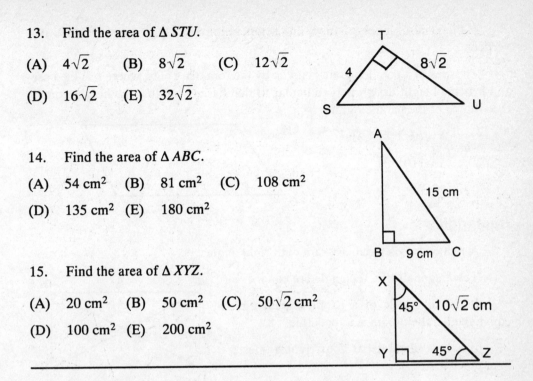

4. Quadrilaterals

A **quadrilateral** is a polygon with four sides.

Parallelograms

A **parallelogram** is a quadrilateral whose opposite sides are parallel.

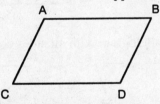

Two angles that have their vertices at the endpoints of the same side of a parallelogram are called **consecutive angles.**

The perpendicular segment connecting any point of a line containing one side of the parallelogram to the line containing the opposite side of the parallelogram is called the **altitude** of the parallelogram.

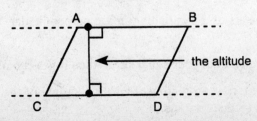

the altitude

A diagonal of a polygon is a line segment joining any two non-consecutive vertices.

The area of a parellelogram is given by the formula $A = bh$ where b is the base and h is the height drawn perpendicular to that base. Note that the height equals the altitude of the parallelogram

$A = bh$

$A = (10)(3)$

$A = 30$

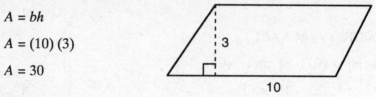

Rectangles

A rectangle is a parallelogram with right angles.

The diagonals of a rectangle are equal.

If the diagonals of a parallelogram are equal, the parallelogram is a rectangle.

If a quadrilateral has four right angles, then it is a rectangle.

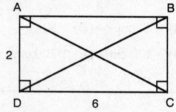

The area of a rectangle is given by the formula $A = lw$ where l is the length and w is the width.

$A = lw$

$A = (3)(10)$

$A = 30$

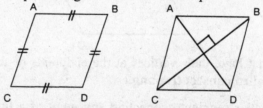

Rhombi

A rhombus is a parallelogram with all sides equal.

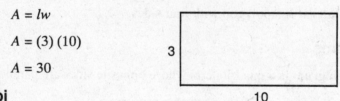

The diagonals of a rhombus are perpendicular to each other.

The diagonals of a rhombus bisect the angles of the rhombus.

If the diagonals of a parallelogram are perpendicular, the parallelogram is a rhombus.

If a quadrilateral has four equal sides, then it is a rhombus.

A parallelogram is a rhombus if either diagonal of the parallelogram bisects the angles of the vertices it joins.

Squares

A square is a rhombus with a right angle.

A square is an equilateral quadrilateral.

A square has all the properties of parallelograms, and rectangles.

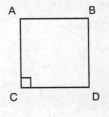

A rhombus is a square if one of its interior angles is a right angle.

In a square, the measure of either diagonal can be calculated by multiplying the length of any side by the square root of 2.

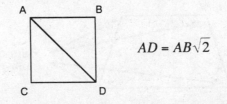

$$AD = AB\sqrt{2}$$

The area of a square is given by the formula $A = s^2$ where s is the side of the square. Since all sides of a square are equal, it does not matter which side is used.

$A = s^2$

$A = 6^2$

$A = 36$

The area of a square can also be found by taking $\frac{1}{2}$ the product of the length of the diagonal squared.

$A = \frac{1}{2}\, d^2$

$A = \frac{1}{2}\, (8)^2$

$A = 32$

Trapezoids

A **trapezoid** is a quadrilateral with two and only two sides parallel. The parallel sides of a trapezoid are called **bases**.

The **median** of a trapezoid is the line joining the midpoints of the non-parallel sides.

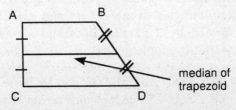

median of trapezoid

The perpendicular segment connecting any point in the line containing one base of the trapezoid to the line containing the other base is the **altitude** of the trapezoid.

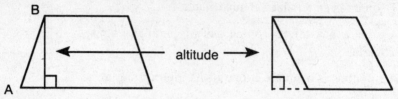

An **isosceles trapezoid** is a trapezoid whose non-parallel sides are equal. A pair of angles including only one of the parallel sides is called **a pair of base angles.**

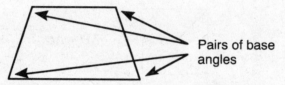

Pairs of base angles

The median of a trapezoid is parallel to the bases and equal to one-half their sum.

The base angles of an isosceles trapezoid are equal.

The diagonals of an isosceles trapezoid are equal.

The opposite angles of an isosceles trapezoid are supplementary.

PROBLEM

Prove that all pairs of consecutive angles of a parallelogram are supplementary.

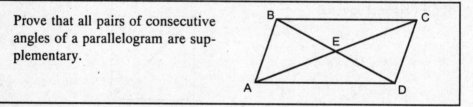

SOLUTION

We must prove that the pairs of angles ∠ *BAD* and ∠ *ADC*, ∠ *ADC* and ∠ *DCB*, ∠ *DCB* and ∠ *CBA*, and ∠ *CBA* and ∠ *BAD* are supplementary. (This means that the sum of their measures is 180°.)

Because *ABCD* is a parallelogram, $\overline{AB}$ ‖ $\overline{CD}$. Angles *BAD* and *ADC* are consecutive interior angles, as are ∠ *CBA* and ∠ *DCB*. Since the consecutive interior angles formed by 2 parallel lines and a transversal are supplementary, ∠ *BAD* and ∠ *ADC* are supplementary, as are ∠ *CBA* and ∠ *DCB*.

Similarly, $\overline{AD}$ ‖$\overline{BC}$. Angles *ADC* and *DCB* are consecutive interior angles, as are ∠ *CBA* and ∠ *BAD*. Since the consecutive interior angles formed by 2 parallel lines and a transversal are supplementary, $\angle$ CBA and $\angle$ BAD are supplementary, as are $\angle$ ADC and $\angle$ DCB.

PROBLEM

In the accompanying figure, Δ ABC is given to be an isosceles right triangle with $\angle$ ABC a right angle and $AB \cong BC$. Line segment $\overline{BD}$, which bisects $\overline{CA}$, is extended to E, so that $\overline{BD} \cong \overline{DE}$. Prove BAEC is a square.

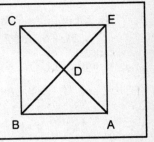

SOLUTION

A square is a rectangle in which two consecutive sides are congruent. This definition will provide the framework for the proof in this problem. We will prove that BAEC is a parallelogram that is specifically a rectangle with consecutive sides congruent, namely a square.

Statement	Reason
1. $\overline{BD} \cong \overline{DE}$	1. Given.
2. $\overline{AD} \cong \overline{DC}$	2. $\overline{BD}$ bisects $\overline{CA}$.
3. BAEC is a parallelogram	3. If diagonals of a quadrilateral bisect each other, then the quadrilateral is a parallelogram.
4. $\angle$ ABC is a right angle	4. Given.
5. BAEC is a rectangle	5. A parallelogram, one of whose angles is a right angle, is a rectangle.
6. $AB \cong BC$	6. Given.
7. BAEC is a square	7. If a rectangle has two congruent consecutive sides, then the rectangle is a square.

Drill 4: Quadrilaterals

Parallelograms, Rectangles, Rhombi, Squares, Trapezoids

1. In parallelogram *WXYZ*, *WX* = 14, *WZ* = 6, *ZY* = 3*x* + 5, and *XY* = 2*y* – 4. Find *x* and *y*.

    (A) 3 and 5   (B) 4 and 5   (C) 4 and 6

    (D) 6 and 10   (E) 6 and 14

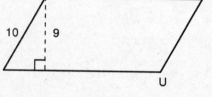

2. Quadrilateral *ABCD* is a parellelogram. If *m* ∠ *B* = 6*x* + 2 and *m* ∠ *D* = 98, find *x*.

    (A) 12   (B) 16   (C) 16 2/3

    (D) 18   (E) 20

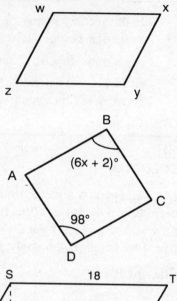

3. Find the area of parallelogram *STUV*.

    (A) 56   (B) 90   (C) 108

    (D) 162   (E) 180

4. Find the area of parallelogram *MNOP*.

    (A) 19   (B) 32   (C) $32\sqrt{3}$

    (D) 44   (E) $44\sqrt{3}$

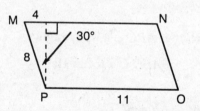

5. Find the perimeter of rectangle *PQRS*, if the area is 99 in².

    (A) 31 in   (B) 38 in   (C) 40 in

    (D) 44 in   (E) 121 in

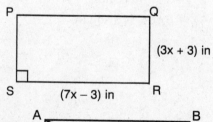

6. In rectangle *ABCD*, *AD* = 6 cm and *DC* = 8 cm. Find the length of the diagonal *AC*.

    (A) 10 cm   (B) 12 cm   (C) 20 cm

    (D) 28 cm   (E) 48 cm

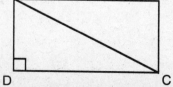

7. Find the area of rectangle *UVXY*.

(A) 17 cm²   (B) 34 cm²   (C) 35 cm²

(D) 70 cm²   (E) 140 cm²

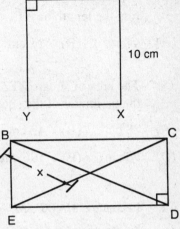

8. Find *x* in rectangle *BCDE* if the diagonal *EC* is 17 mm.

(A) 6.55 mm   (B) 8 mm   (C) 8.5 mm

(D) 17 mm   (E) 34 mm

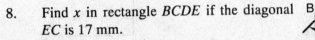

9. In rhombus *DEFG*, *DE* = 7 cm. Find the perimeter of the rhombus.

(A) 14 cm   (B) 28 cm   (C) 42 cm

(D) 49 cm   (E) 56 cm

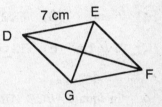

10. In rhombus *RHOM*, the diagonal $\overline{RO}$ is 8 cm and the diagonal $\overline{HM}$ is 12 cm. Find the area of the rhombus.

(A) 20 cm²   (B) 40 cm²   (C) 48 cm²

(D) 68 cm²   (E) 96 cm²

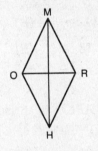

11. In rhombus *GHIJ*, *GI* = 6 cm and *HJ* = 8 cm. Find the length of *GH*.

(A) 3 cm   (B) 4 cm   (C) 5 cm

(D) $4\sqrt{3}$ cm   (E) 14 cm

12. In rhombus *CDEF*, *CD* is 13 mm and *DX* is 5 mm. Find the area of the rhombus.

(A) 31 mm²   (B) 60 mm²   (C) 78 mm²

(D) 120 mm²   (E) 260 mm²

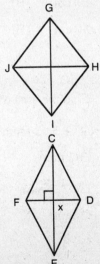

13. Quadrilateral *ATUV* is a square. If the perimeter of the square is 44 cm, find the length of $\overline{AT}$.

(A) 4 cm   (B) 11 cm   (C) 22 cm   (D) 30 cm   (E) 40 cm

14. The area of square *XYZW* is 196 cm². Find the perimeter of the square.

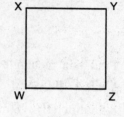

(A) 28 cm   (B) 42 cm   (C) 56 cm

(D) 98 cm   (E) 196 cm.

15. In square *MNOP*, *MN* is 6 cm. Find the length of diagonal $\overline{MO}$.

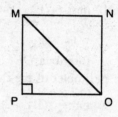

(A) 6 cm   (B) $6\sqrt{2}$ cm   (C) $6\sqrt{3}$ cm

(D) $6\sqrt{6}$ cm   (E) 12 cm

16. In square *ABCD*, *AB* = 3 cm. Find the area of the square.

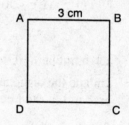

(A) 9 cm²   (B) 12 cm²   (C) 15 cm²

(D) 18 cm²   (E) 21 cm²

17. *ABCD* is an isosceles trapezoid. Find the perimeter.

(A) 21 cm   (B) 27 cm   (C) 30 cm

(D) 50 cm   (E) 54 cm

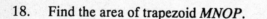

18. Find the area of trapezoid *MNOP*.

(A) $(17 + 3\sqrt{3})$ mm²

(B) 33/2 mm²

(C) $33\sqrt{3}/2$ mm²

(D) 33 mm²

(E) $33\sqrt{3}$ mm²

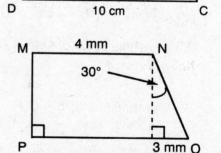

19. Trapezoid *XYZW* is isosceles. If *m* ∠*W* = 58 and *m* ∠ *Z* = 4*x* – 6, find *x*.

(A) 8   (B) 12   (C) 13

(D) 16   (E) 58

5. Circles

A **circle** is a set of points in the same plane equidistant from a fixed point called its center.

A **radius** of a circle is a line segment drawn from the center of the circle to any point on the circle.

A portion of a circle is called an **arc** of the circle.

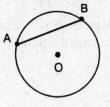

Arc

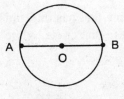

Secant

A line that intersects a circle in two points is called a **secant**.

A line segment joining two points on a circle is called a **chord** of the circle.

Chord

Diameter

A chord that passes through the center of the circle is called a **diameter** of the circle.

The line passing through the centers of two (or more) circles is called the **line of centers**.

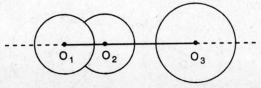

An angle whose vertex is on the circle and whose sides are chords of the circle is called an **inscribed angle**.

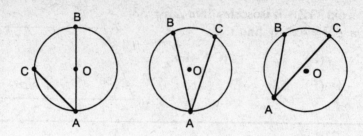

An angle whose vertex is at the center of a circle and whose sides are radii is called a **central angle.**

The measure of a minor arc is the measure of the central angle that intercepts that arc.

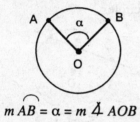

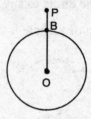

$$m\,\overset{\frown}{AB} = \alpha = m \angle AOB$$

The distance from a point P to a given circle is the distance from that point to the point where the circle intersects with a line segment with endpoints at the center of the circle and point P. The distance of point P to the diagrammed circle (above right) with center O is the line segment PB of line segment PO.

A line that has one and only one point of intersection with a circle is called a tangent to that circle, while their common point is called a **point of tangency.**

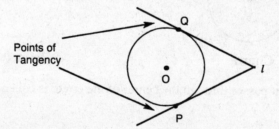

Congruent circles are circles whose radii are congruent.

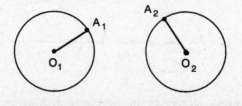

If $O_1A_1 \cong O_2A_2$, then $O_1 \cong O_2$.

The measure of a semicircle is 180°.

A **circumscribed circle** is a circle passing through all the vertices of a polygon.

Circles that have the same center and unequal radii are called **concentric circles**.

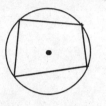

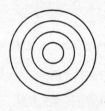

Circumscribed Circle   **Concentric Circles**

PROBLEM

A and *B* are points on circle *Q* such that
△*AQB* is equilateral. If length of side *AB* =
12, find the length of arc *AB*.

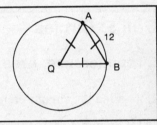

SOLUTION

To find the arc length of $\overset{\frown}{AB}$, we must find the measure of the central angle ∠ *AQB* and the measure of the radius $\overline{QA}$. ∠ *AQB* is an interior angle of the equilateral triangle △ *AQB*. Therefore, $m\angle AQB = 60°$. Similarly, in the equilateral △ *AQB*, *AQ* = *AB* = *QB* = 12. Given the radius, *r*, and the central angle, *n*, the arc length is given by $n/360 \cdot 2\pi r$. Therefore, by substitution, $60/360 \cdot 2\pi \cdot 12 = \frac{1}{6} \cdot 2\pi \cdot 12 = 4\pi$. Therefore, length of arc $\overset{\frown}{AB} = 4\pi$.

PROBLEM

In circle *O*, the measure of $\overset{\frown}{AB}$ is 80°. Find
the measure of ∠ *A*.

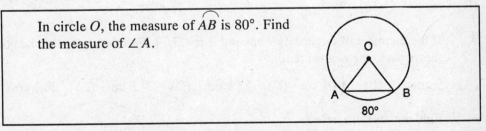

SOLUTION

The accompanying figure shows that $\overset{\frown}{AB}$ is intercepted by central angle *AOB*. By definition, we know that the measure of the central angle is the measure of its intercepted arc. In this case,

$$\overset{\frown}{mAB} = m \angle AOB = 80°.$$

Radius   and radius   are congruent and form two sides of $\triangle OAB$. By a theorem, the angles opposite these two congruent sides must, themselves, be congruent. Therefore, $m \angle A = m \angle B$.

The sum of the measures of the angles of a triangle is 180°. Therefore,

$$m \angle A + m \angle B + m \angle AOB = 180°.$$

Since $m \angle A = m \angle B$, we can write

$$m \angle A + m \angle A + 80° = 180°$$

or $2m\angle A = 100°$

or $m \angle A = 50°.$

Therefore, the measure of $\angle A$ is 50°.

Drill 5: Circles

Circumference, Area, Concentric Circles

1. Find the circumference of circle A if its radius is 3 mm.

(A) 3π mm   (B) 6π mm   (C) 9π mm   (D) 12π mm   (E) 15π mm

2. The circumference of circle H is 20π cm. Find the length of the radius.

(A) 10 cm   (B) 20 cm   (C) 10π cm   (D) 15π cm   (E) 20π cm

3. The circumference of circle A is how many millimeters larger than the circumference of circle B?

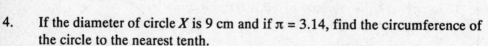

(A) 3   (B) 6   (C) 3π

(D) 6π (E) 7π

4. If the diameter of circle X is 9 cm and if $\pi = 3.14$, find the circumference of the circle to the nearest tenth.

(A) 9 cm   (B) 14.1 cm   (C) 21.1 cm   (D) 24.6 cm   (E) 28.3 cm

5. Find the area of circle I.

(A) 22 mm²   (B) 121 mm²

(C) 121π mm²   (D) 132 mm²

(E) 132π mm²

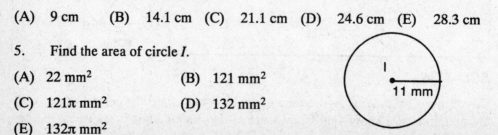

6. The diameter of circle Z is 27 mm. Find the area of the circle.

(A) 91.125 mm^2 (B) 182.25 mm^2 (C) 191.5π mm^2

(D) 182.25π mm^2 (E) 729 mm^2

7. The area of circle B is 225π cm^2. Find the length of the diameter of the circle.

(A) 15 cm   (B) 20 cm   (C) 30 cm   (D) 20π cm   (E) 25π cm

8. The area of circle X is 144π mm^2 while the area of circle Y is 81π mm^2. Write the ratio of the radius of circle X to that of circle Y.

(A) 3 : 4   (B) 4 : 3   (C) 9 : 12   (D) 27 : 12   (E) 18 : 24

9. The circumference of circle M is 18π cm. Find the area of the circle.

(A) 18π cm^2 (B) 81 cm^2 (C) 36 cm^2 (D) 36π cm^2 (E) 81π cm^2

10. In two concentric circles, the smaller circle has a radius of 3 mm while the larger circle has a radius of 5 mm. Find the area of the shaded region.

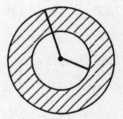

(A) 2π mm^2 (B) 8π mm^2 (C) 13π mm^2

(D) 16π mm^2 (E) 26π mm^2

11. The radius of the smaller of two concentric circles is 5 cm while the radius of the larger circle is 7 cm. Determine the area of the shaded region.

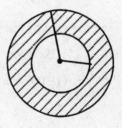

(A) 7π cm^2 (B) 24π cm^2 (C) 25π cm^2

(D) 36π cm^2 (E) 49π cm^2

12. Find the measure of arc MN if $m \angle MON$ = 62°.

(A) 16°   (B) 32°   (C) 59°

(D) 62°   (E) 124°

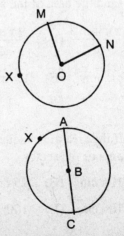

13. Find the measure of arc AXC.

(A) 150°   (B) 160°   (C) 180°

(D) 270°   (E) 360°

14. If arc *MXP* = 236°, find the measure of arc *MP*.

(A) 62°   (B) 124°   (C) 236°

(D) 270°   (E) 360°

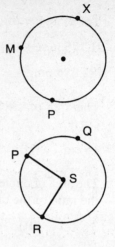

15. In circle *S*, major arc *PQR* has a measure of 298°. Find the measure of the central angle ∠ *PSR*.

(A) 62°   (B) 124°   (C) 149°

(D) 298°   (E) 360°

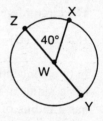

16. Find the measure of arc *XY* in circle *W*.

(A) 40°   (B) 120°   (C) 140°

(D) 180°   (E) 220°

17. Find the area of the sector shown.

(A) 4 cm²   (B) 2π cm²   (C) 16 cm²

(D) 8π cm²   (E) 16π cm²

18. Find the area of the shaded region.

(A) 10   (B) 5π   (C) 25

(D) 20π   (E) 25π

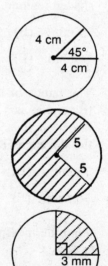

19. Find the area of the sector shown.

(A) $\dfrac{9\pi\ \text{mm}^2}{4}$ (B) $\dfrac{9\pi\ \text{mm}^2}{2}$ (C) 18 mm²

(D) 6π mm²   (E) 9π mm²

20. If the area of the square is 100 cm², find the area of the sector.

(A) 10π cm²   (B) 25 cm²   (C) 25π cm²

(D) 100 cm²   (E) 100π cm²

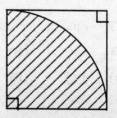

6. Solids

Solid geometry is the study of figures which consist of points not all in the same plane.

Rectangular Solids

A solid with lateral faces and bases that are rectangles is called a **rectangular solid**.

The surface area of a rectangular solid is the sum of the areas of all the faces.

The volume of a rectangular solid is equal to the product of its length, width and height.

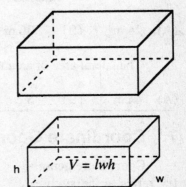

$V = lwh$

PROBLEM

What are the dimensions of a solid cube whose surface area is numerically equal to its volume?

SOLUTION

The surface area of a cube of edge length a is equal to the sum of the areas of its 6 faces. Since a cube is a regular polygon, all 6 faces are congruent. Each face of a cube is a square of edge length a. Hence, the surface area of a cube of edge length a is

$$S = 6a^2.$$

The volume of a cube of edge length a is

$$V = a^3.$$

We require that $A = V$, or that

$$6a^2 = a^3 \quad \text{or} \quad a = 6$$

Hence, if a cube has edge length 6, its surface area will be numerically equal to its volume.

Drill 6: Solids

1. Find the surface area of the rectangular prism shown.

    (A) 138 cm² (B) 336 cm² (C) 381 cm²

    (D) 426 cm² (E) 540 cm²

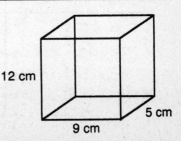

12 cm

5 cm

9 cm

2. Find the volume of the rectangular storage tank shown.

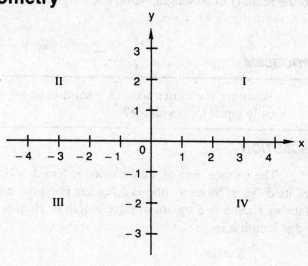

6 m

(A)   24 m³   (B)   36 m³   (C)   38 m³   (D)   42 m³   (E)   45 m³

3. The lateral area of a cube is 100 cm². Find the length of an edge of the cube.

(A)   4 cm   (B)   5 cm   (C)   10 cm   (D)   12 cm   (E)   15 cm

7. Coordinate Geometry

Coordinate geometry refers to the study of geometric figures using algebraic principles.

The graph shown is called the Cartesian coordinate plane. The graph consists of a pair of perpendicular lines called **coordinate axes**. The **vertical axis** is the y-axis and the **horizontal axis** is the x-axis. The point of intersection of these two axes is called the **origin**; it is the zero point of both axes. Furthermore, points to the right of the origin on the x-axis and above the origin on the y-axis represent positive real numbers. Points to the left of the origin on the x-axis or below the origin on the y-axis represent negative real numbers.

The four regions cut off by the coordinate axes are, in counterclockwise direction from the top right, called the first, second, third and fourth quadrant, respectively. The first

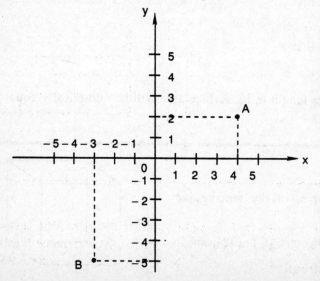

quadrant contains all points with two positive coordinates.

In the graph shown, two points are identified by the ordered pair, (x, y) of numbers. The x-coordinate is the first number and the y-coordinate is the second number.

To plot a point on the graph when given the coordinates, draw perpendicular lines from the number-line coordinates to the point where the two lines intersect.

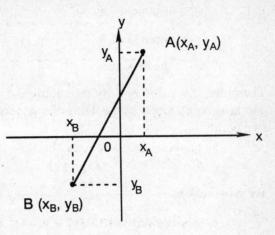

To find the coordinates of a given point on the graph, draw perpendicular lines from the point to the coordinates on the number line. The x-coordinate is written before the y-coordinate and a comma is used to separate the two.

In this case, point A has the coordinates $(4, 2)$ and the coordinates of point B are $(-3, -5)$.

For any two points A and B with coordinates (X_A, Y_A) and (X_B, Y_B), respectively, the distance between A and B is represented by:

$$AB = \sqrt{(X_A - X_B)^2 + (Y_A - Y_B)^2}$$

This is commonly known as the distance formula or the **Pythagorean Theorem**.

PROBLEM

Find the distance between the point $A(1, 3)$ and $B(5, 3)$.

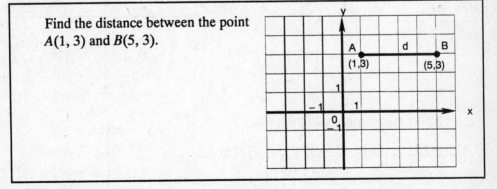

SOLUTION

In this case, where the ordinate of both points is the same, the distance between the two points is given by the absolute value of the difference between the two abscissas. In fact, this case reduces to merely counting boxes as the figure shows.

Let, x_1 = abscissa of A y_1 = ordinate of A

x_2 = abscissa of B y_2 = ordinate of B

d = the distance.

Therefore, $d = |x_1 - x_2|$. By substitution, $d = |1 - 5| = |-4| = 4$. This answer can also be obtained by applying the general formula for distance between any two points

$$d = \sqrt{(x_1 - x_2)^2 + (y_1 - y_2)^2}$$

By substitution,

$$d = \sqrt{(1-5)^2 + (3-3)^2} = \sqrt{(-4)^2 + (0)^2} = \sqrt{16} = 4.$$

The distance is 4.

To find the midpoint of a segment between the two given endpoints, use the formula,

$$MP = \left(\frac{x_1 + x_2}{2}, \frac{y_1 + y_2}{2}\right)$$

where x_1 and y_1 are the coordinates of one point; x_2 and y_2 are the coordinates of the other point.

Drill 7: Coordinate Geometry

1.   Which point shown has the coordinates $(-3, 2)$?

(A)   A   (B)   B   (C)   C

(D)   D   (E)   E

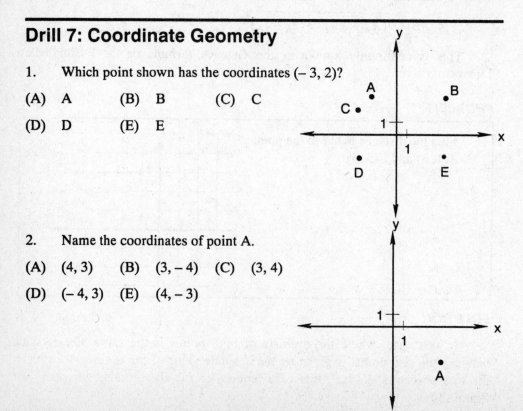

2.   Name the coordinates of point A.

(A) $(4, 3)$ (B) $(3, -4)$ (C) $(3, 4)$

(D) $(-4, 3)$ (E) $(4, -3)$

3. Which point shown has the coordinates $(2.5, -1)$?

(A) M   (B) N   (C) P

(D) Q   (E) R

4. The correct x-coordinate for point H is what number?

(A) 3   (B) 4   (C) -3

(D) -4 (E) -5

5. The correct y-coordinate for point R is what number?

(A) -7 (B) 2   (C) -2

(D) 7   (E) 8

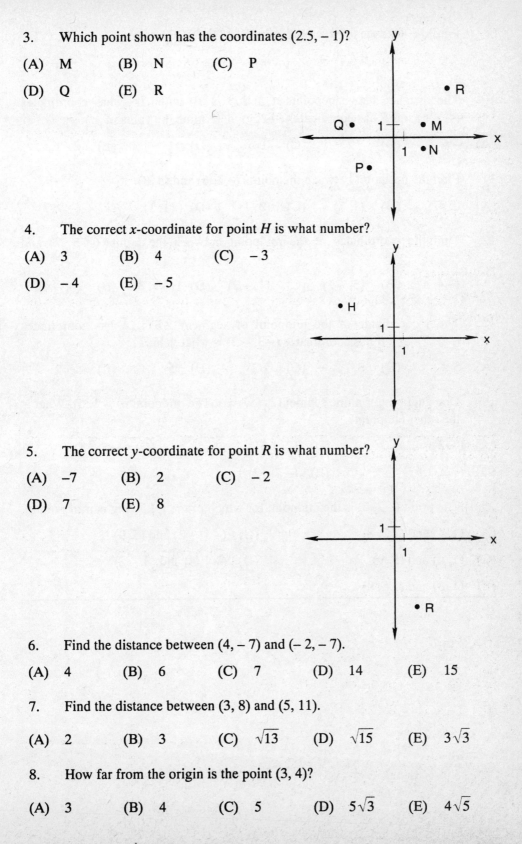

6. Find the distance between $(4, -7)$ and $(-2, -7)$.

(A) 4   (B) 6   (C) 7   (D) 14   (E) 15

7. Find the distance between $(3, 8)$ and $(5, 11)$.

(A) 2   (B) 3   (C) $\sqrt{13}$ (D) $\sqrt{15}$ (E) $3\sqrt{3}$

8. How far from the origin is the point $(3, 4)$?

(A) 3   (B) 4   (C) 5   (D) $5\sqrt{3}$ (E) $4\sqrt{5}$

9.   Find the distance between the point (– 4, 2) and (3, – 5).

(A)   3   (B) $3\sqrt{3}$ (C)   7   (D) $7\sqrt{2}$ (E) $7\sqrt{3}$

10.   The distance between points A and B is 10 units. If A has coordinates (4, – 6) and B has coordinates (– 2, y), determine the value of y.

(A)   – 6   (B)   – 2   (C)   0   (D)   1   (E)   2

11.   Find the midpoint between the points (– 2, 6) and (4, 8).

(A)   (3, 7)   (B)   (1, 7)   (C)   (3, 1)   (D)   (1, 1)   (E)   (– 3, 7)

12.   Find the coordinates of the midpoint between the points (– 5, 7) and (3, – 1).

(A)   (– 4, 4)   (B)   (3, – 1)   (C)   (1, – 3)   (D)   (– 1, 3)   (E)   (4, – 4).

13.   The y-coordinate of the midpoint of segment $\overline{AB}$ if A has coordinates (– 3, 7) and B has coordinates (– 3, – 2) is what value?

(A)   5/2   (B)   3   (C)   7/2   (D)   5   (E)   15/2

14.   One endpoint of a line segment is (5, – 3). The midpoint is (– 1, 6). What is the other endpoint?

(A)   (7, 3)   (B)   (2, 1.5)   (C)   (– 7, 15)

(D)   (– 2, 1.5)   (E)   (– 7, 12)

15.   The point (– 2, 6) is the midpoint for which of the following pair of points?

(A)   (1, 4) and (– 3, 8)   (B)   (– 1, – 3) and (5, 9)

(C)   (1, 4) and (5, 9)   (D)   (– 1, 4) and (3, – 8)

(E)   (1, 3) and (– 5, 9)

GEOMETRY DRILLS

ANSWER KEY

Drill 1–Lines and Angles

1.	(B)	5.	(D)	9.	(D)	13.	(B)
2.	(A)	6.	(C)	10.	(E)	14.	(E)
3.	(C)	7.	(B)	11.	(C)	15.	(A)
4.	(D)	8.	(A)	12.	(D)		

Drill 2–Regular Polygons

1.	(D)	4.	(A)	7.	(E)	10.	(B)
2.	(B)	5.	(D)	8.	(B)		
3.	(E)	6.	(C)	9.	(D)		

Drill 3–Triangles

1.	(D)	5.	(C)	9.	(A)	13.	(D)
2.	(B)	6.	(A)	10.	(C)	14.	(A)
3.	(C)	7.	(B)	11.	(C)	15.	(B)
4.	(E)	8.	(E)	12.	(B)		

Drill 4–Quadrilaterals

1.	(A)	6.	(A)	11.	(C)	16.	(A)
2.	(B)	7.	(D)	12.	(D)	17.	(B)
3.	(D)	8.	(C)	13.	(B)	18.	(C)
4.	(E)	9.	(B)	14.	(C)	19.	(D)
5.	(C)	10.	(C)	15.	(B)		

Drill 5–Circles

1.	(B)	6.	(D)	11.	(B)	16.	(C)
2.	(A)	7.	(C)	12.	(D)	17.	(B)
3.	(D)	8.	(B)	13.	(C)	18.	(D)
4.	(E)	9.	(E)	14.	(B)	19.	(A)
5.	(C)	10.	(D)	15.	(A)	20.	(C)

Drill 6–Solids

1. (D)   2. (B)   3. (C)

Drill 7–Coordinate Geometry

1.	(C)	5.	(A)	9.	(D)	13.	(A)
2.	(E)	6.	(B)	10.	(E)	14.	(C)
3.	(B)	7.	(C)	11.	(B)	15.	(E)
4.	(D)	8.	(C)	12.	(D)		

GLOSSARY: GEOMETRY

Acute Angle

An angle that is less than 90 degrees.

Acute Triangle

A triangle with all three angles under 90 degrees (i.e., all angles are acute).

Adjacent Angles

Angles with a vertex and side in common.

Altitude of a Parallelogram

A line segment between the opposite sides of a parallelogram, which is perpendicular to both sides.

Altitude of a Trapezoid

A line segment joining the two parallel sides of the trapezoid, which is perpendicular to each of these sides.

Altitude of a Triangle

The line segment from one vertex of the triangle to the opposite side such that it intersects the opposite side at a right angle.

Angle

What is formed by the intersection of two rays with a common endpoint. This intersection (endpoint) is the vertex of the angle. An angle is measured in terms of degrees.

Angle Bisector of a Triangle

A line segment from one vertex of the triangle to the opposite side, which bisects the interior angle of a triangle at the vertex.

Apothem of a Regular Polygon

The line segment joining the center of the polygon to the center of any side.

Arc of a Circle

A contiguous portion of a circle. An arc can be formed by the intersection of the lines forming a central angle and the circle. In this case, the measure of the arc equals the measure of the central angle.

Area

The space occupied by a figure.

Base of a Triangle

The unequal side of an isosceles triangle.

Bases of a Trapezoid

The two parallel sides of a trapezoid.

Bisect

Divide into two equal portions.

Center of a Circle

The point about which all points on the circle are equidistant.

Central Angle

An angle whose vertex is the center of a circle.

Chord of a Circle

A line segment joining two points on a circle. If it passes through the center of the circle, then the chord is a diameter.

Circle

The set of points in a plane at a fixed distance from a given point in that plane (the center of a circle).

Circumference

The length of a circle if it were to be "unwrapped." The circumference equals twice the length of the diameter of the circle.

Circumscribed Circle

A circle passing through each vertex of a polygon.

Collinear

Points that lie on a common line.

Complementary Angles

Angles whose measures sum to 90 degrees.

Concave Polygon

A polygon that does not contain all points on line segments joining all pairs of its vertices.

Concentric Circles

Circles with a common center.

Concurrent Lines

Lines with a point in common.

Congruent Angles

Angles of equal measure.

Congruent Circles

Circles with radii of the same length.

Consecutive Angles

Angles with vertices at adjacent sides of a polygon (i.e., the vertices have a common side).

Convex Polygon

A polygon containing all points on line segments connecting all pairs of its vertices.

Coordinate Axes

Two perpendicular lines (the *x*-axis and the *y*-axis) used for placing ordered pairs of reals relative to one another.

Coordinate Geometry

The study of geometry via algebraic principles.

Coplanar Lines

Lines in the same plane.

Cube

A six-faced solid in three dimensions in which each face is a square.

Decagon

A polygon with ten sides.

Degree

The unit of measurement for angles.

Diagonal of a Polygon

A line segment joining any two nonconsecutive vertices of a polygon.

Diameter of a Circle

The chord of a circle that passes through the center of the circle.

Equiangular Polygon

A polygon whose angles all have the same measure.

Equiangular Triangle

A triangle whose angles are all 60 degrees (an equilateral triangle).

Equidistant

The same distance from, or at a fixed distance from.

Equilateral Polygon

A polygon whose sides are all of equal length.

Equilateral Triangle

A triangle whose three sides all have the same length.

Exterior Angle of a Triangle

An angle supplementary to an interior angle of a triangle formed by extending one side of the triangle.

Hexagon

A polygon with six sides.

Horizontal Axis

The *x*-axis of the coordinate axes.

Hypotenuse

The longest side of a right triangle, it is the side facing the 90-degree angle.

Inscribed Angle

An angle whose vertex is on a circle and whose sides are chords of that circle.

Inscribed Circle

A circle within a (convex) polygon such that each side of the polygon is tangent to the circle.

Interior Angle of a Triangle

The smaller of the two angles formed by the intersection of two adjacent sides of a triangle (i.e., it never exceeds 180 degrees, while the larger angle always does).

Intersecting Lines

Lines that have a point in common.

Isosceles Right Triangle

A triangle with one 90-degree angle and two 45-degree angles.

Isosceles Trapezoid

A trapezoid whose nonparallel sides are of equal length.

Isosceles Triangle

A triangle with two angles of common measure.

Legs

The two shorter sides of a right triangle, these are adjacent to the right angle.

Line

A set of points of infinite length with the property that a line perpendicular to the given line at a certain point is parallel to any other line perpendicular to the given line at any other point. A line is said to be one-dimensional.

Line of Centers

A line joining the centers of circles.

Line Segment

The line portion that lies between two points.

Median of a Trapezoid

The line segment joining the midpoints of the nonparallel sides of a trapezoid.

Median of a Triangle

> The line segment from one vertex of the triangle to the midpoint of the opposite side.

Midline of a Triangle

> A line segment joining the midpoints of two adjacent sides of a triangle.

Midpoint

> The unique point on a line segment that is equidistant to each endpoint of the line segment.

Minute

> One sixtieth of a degree.

Nonagon

> A polygon with nine sides.

Obtuse Angle

> An angle whose measure exceeds 90 degrees.

Obtuse Triangle

> A triangle with an obtuse angle.

Octagon

> An eight-sided polygon.

Origin

> The intersection of the two coordinate axes. The origin corresponds to the ordered pair (0, 0).

Pair of Base Angles of a Trapezoid

> Two angles interior to the trapezoid, whose vertices have one of the parallel sides in common.

Parallel Lines

> Lines in the same plane that do not intersect.

Parallelogram

> A quadrilateral whose opposite sides are parallel.

Pentagon

> A five-sided polygon.

Perimeter

> The sum of the lengths of the sides of a polygon.

Perpendicular Bisector

> A bisector that is perpendicular to the segment it bisects.

Perpendicular Bisector of a Side of a Triangle

> A line segment that is perpendicular to and bisects one side of the triangle.

Perpendicular Lines

Lines that intersect, with the property that the angles whose vertex is the intersection are all right angles.

Plane

A set of points spanned by two intersecting lines and all the points between them. A plane is said to be two-dimensional.

Plane Figure

A figure in a plane (in two dimensions).

Plane Geometry

The study of plane figures.

Point

A specific location with no area. A point is said to be zero-dimensional.

Point of Tangency

The point at which a tangent intersects a circle.

Polygon

A closed figure with the same number of sides as angles.

Pythagorean Theorem

The rule that states that the square of the length of the hypotenuse of a right triangle equals the sum of the squares of the lengths of the two legs of that triangle.

Quadrilateral

A polygon with four sides.

Radii

Plural of radius.

Radius of a Circle

The line segment from the center of a circle to any point on the circle.

Radius of a Regular Polygon

The line segment joining the center of a polygon to any vertex.

Ray

The portion of a line that lies on one side of a fixed point.

Rectangle

A parallelogram with right interior angles.

Rectangular Solid

A solid with lateral faces and bases that are rectangles.

Reflex Angle

An angle whose measure exceeds 180 degrees but is less than 360 degrees.

Regular Polygon

A polygon that is both equiangular and equilateral.

Rhombus

A parallelogram with all four sides of equal length.

Right Angle

An angle measuring 90 degrees; it is formed by perpendicular lines.

Right Circular Cylinder

A three-dimensional solid whose horizontal cross sections are circles; these circles (for each horizontal location) have the same center and radius (i.e., can shaped).

Right Triangle

A triangle with one right angle.

Scalene Triangle

A triangle with no equal sides.

Secant of a Circle

A line segment joining two points on a circle.

Side of a Polynomial

Line segments whose endpoints are adjacent vertices of the polynomial.

Similar

Of the same shape, but not necessarily of the same size.

Solid Geometry

The study of figures in three dimensions.

Square

A rectangle with four equal sides. Alternatively, a rhombus with four right angles.

Straight Angle

An angle measuring 180 degrees, the two rays forming it form one line.

Supplementary Angles

Angles whose measures sum to 180 degrees.

Surface Area

The sum of the areas of all faces of a figure.

Tangent to a Circle

A line that intersects a circle at exactly one point.

Transitive Property

A relation, R, is transitive if, for all a, b, c the relations aRb and bRc imply aRc. For example, equality is transitive, since $a = b$ and $b = c$ together imply that $a = c$.

Transversal

A line that intersects two parallel lines.

Trapezoid

A quadrilateral with exactly two parallel sides.

Triangle

A three-sided polygon.

Vertex

A point at which adjacent sides of a polygon intersect.

Vertical Angles

Two angles formed by intersecting lines (not rays) and directly across from each other. They are also equal.

Vertical Axis

The y-axis of the coordinate axes.

Vertices

The points at which the adjacent sides of a polygon intersect.

Volume

Three-dimensional space occupied or displaced (i.e., if a three-dimensional solid were put into a full bathtub, its volume is the amount of water that would fall out).

CHAPTER 5

Student-Produced Response

➤ Arithmetic
➤ Algebra
➤ Geometry

STUDENT-PRODUCED
RESPONSE REVIEW

The student-produced response format of the SAT is designed to give the student a certain amount of flexibility in answering questions. In this section the student must calculate the answer to a given question and then enter the solution into a grid. The grid is constructed so that a solution can be given in either decimal or fraction form. Either form is acceptable unless otherwise stated.

The problems in the student-produced response section try to reflect situations arising in the real world. Here calculations will involve objects occurring in everyday life. There is also an emphasis on problems involving data interpretation. In keeping with this emphasis, students will be allowed the use of a calculator during the exam.

The Directions

Each student-produced response question will require you to solve the problem and enter your answer in a grid. There are specific rules you will need to know for entering your solution. If you enter your answer in an incorrect form, you will not receive credit, even if you originally solved the problem correctly. Therefore, you should carefully study the following rules now, so you don't have to waste valuable time during the actual test.

- Answers may be entered in either decimal or fraction form. For example, $\frac{3}{12}$ or .25 are equally acceptable.

- A mixed number, such as $4\frac{1}{2}$, must be entered either as 4.5 or $\frac{9}{2}$. If you entered 41/2, the machine would interpret your answer as $\frac{41}{2}$, not $4\frac{1}{2}$.

- There may be some instances where there is more than one correct answer to a problem. Should this be the case, grid only one answer.

- Be very careful when filling in ovals. Do not fill in more than one oval in any column, and make sure to completely darken the ovals.

- Make sure to fill in your answer in the boxes above each column. Although you will not be graded incorrectly if you do not write in your answer, it will help you fill in the corresponding ovals.

- The manner in which you enter decimals is very important. The rule is to grid the most accurate value possible. For example, if you need to grid a repeating decimal such as $0.66\overline{6}$, enter the answer as .666 or .667. Therefore, you should not enter a zero before the decimal point. In addition, if you gridded .66 or .67, your answer would be marked incorrect because you did not carry the decimal to the thousandths place, which would be the most accurate value.

SAMPLE QUESTION

How many pounds of apples can be bought with $5.00 if apples cost $.40 a pound?

SOLUTION

Converting dollars to cents we obtain the equation

$x = 500 \div 40$

$x = 12.5$

The solution to this problem would be gridded as

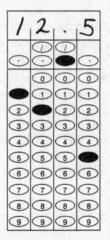

SECTION 1: ARITHMETIC

These arithmetic questions test your ability to perform standard manipulations and simplifications of arithmetic expressions. For some questions, there is more than one approach. There are six kinds of questions you may encounter in the student-produced response section. For each type of question, we will show how to solve the problem and grid your answer.

Question Type 1: Properties of a Whole Number *N*

This problem tests your ability to find a whole number with a given set of properties. You will be given a list of properties of a whole number and asked to find that number.

PROBLEM

The properties of a whole number *N* are

(A) *N* is a perfect square.

(B) *N* is divisible by 2.

(C) *N* is divisible by 3.

Grid in the second smallest whole number with the above properties.

SOLUTION

Try to first obtain the smallest number with the above properties. The smallest number with properties (B) and (C) is 6. Since property (A) says the number must be a perfect square, the smallest number with properties (A), (B), and (C) is 36.

$6^2 = 36$ is the smallest whole number with the above properties. The second smallest whole number (the solution) is

$$2^2 6^2 = 144.$$

The correct answer entered into the grid is

Question Type 2: Simplifying Fractions

This type of question requires you to simplify fractional expressions and grid the answer in the format specified. By canceling out terms common to both the numerator and denominator, we can simplify complex fractional expressions.

PROBLEM

Simplify $\dfrac{1}{2} \times \dfrac{3}{7} \times \dfrac{2}{8} \times \dfrac{14}{10} \times \dfrac{1}{3}$ as a decimal.

SOLUTION

Notice the point here is to cancel out terms common to both the numerator and denominator. Once the fraction is brought down to lowest terms the result is to be entered into the grid as a decimal.

After cancellation we are left with the fraction $\dfrac{1}{40}$. Equivalently,

$$\frac{1}{40} = \frac{1}{10} \times \frac{1}{4} = \frac{1}{10}(.25) = .025$$

Hence in our grid we enter

Note: If "decimal" were not specified, any correct version of the answer could be entered into the grid.

Question Type 3: Prime Numbers of a Particular Form

Here, you will be asked to find a prime number with certain characteristics. Remember—a prime number is a number that can only be divided by itself and 1.

PROBLEM

Find a prime number of the form $7k + 1 < 50$.

SOLUTION

This is simply a counting problem. The key is to list all the numbers of the form $7k + 1$ starting with $k = 0$. The first one that is prime is the solution to the problem.

The whole numbers of the form $7k + 1$ which are less than 50 are 1, 8, 15, 22, 29, 36, and 43. Of these, 29 and 43 are prime numbers. The possible solutions are 29 and 43.

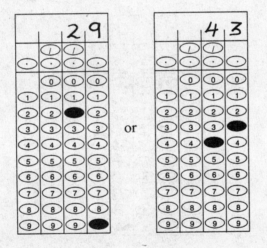

or

Question Type 4: Order of Operations

The following question type tests your knowledge of the arithmetic order of operations. Always work within the parentheses or with absolute values first, while keeping in mind that multiplication and division are carried out before addition and subtraction.

PROBLEM

Find a solution to the equation $x \div 3 \times 4 \div 2 = 6$.

SOLUTION

The key here is to recall the order of precedence for arithmetic operations. After simplifying the expression one can solve for x.

Since multiplication and division have the same level of precedence we simplify the equation from left to right to obtain

$$\frac{x}{3} \times 4 \div 2 = 6$$

$$\frac{4x}{3} \div 2 = 6$$

$$\frac{2x}{3} = 6$$

$$x = 9$$

As 9 solves the above problem our entry in the grid is

Question Type 5: Solving for Ratios

This type of question tests your ability to manipulate ratios given a set of constraints.

PROBLEM

Let A, B, C, and D be positive integers. Assume that the ratio of A to B is equal to the ratio of C to D. Find a possible value for A if the product of $BC = 24$ and D is odd.

SOLUTION

The quickest way to find a solution is to list the possible factorizations of 24:

$$1 \times 24$$
$$2 \times 12$$
$$3 \times 8$$
$$4 \times 6$$

As $AD = BC = 24$ and D is odd, the only possible solution is $A = 8$ (corresponding to $D = 3$).

In the grid below we enter

Question Type 6: Simplifying Arithmetic Expressions

Here you will be given an arithmetic problem that is easier to solve if you transform it into a basic algebra problem. This strategy saves valuable time by cutting down on the number and complexity of computations involved.

PROBLEM

Simplify $1 - \left(\dfrac{1}{2} + \dfrac{1}{4} + \dfrac{1}{8} + \dfrac{1}{16} + \dfrac{1}{32} + \dfrac{1}{64} \right)$

SOLUTION

This problem can be done one of two ways. The "brute force" approach would be to get a common denominator and simplify. An approach involving less computation is given below.

Set

$$S = 1 - \left(\frac{1}{2} + \frac{1}{4} + \frac{1}{8} + \frac{1}{16} + \frac{1}{32} + \frac{1}{64} \right)$$

Multiplying this equation by 2 we obtain

$$2S = 2 - \left(1 + \frac{1}{2} + \frac{1}{4} + \frac{1}{8} + \frac{1}{16} + \frac{1}{32} \right)$$

$$2S = 1 - \left(\frac{1}{2} + \frac{1}{4} + \frac{1}{8} + \frac{1}{16} + \frac{1}{32} \right)$$

$$2S = 1 - \left(\frac{1}{2} + \frac{1}{4} + \frac{1}{8} + \frac{1}{16} + \frac{1}{32} + \frac{1}{64} \right) + \frac{1}{64}$$

$$2S = S + \frac{1}{64}$$

$$S = \frac{1}{64}$$

We enter into the grid

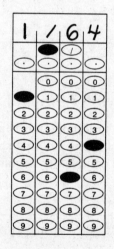

SECTION 2: ALGEBRA

Within the student-produced response section, you will also encounter numerous algebra questions which will test your ability to solve algebraic expressions in the setting of word problems. You may encounter the following six types of algebra questions during the SAT I. As in the previous section, we provide methods for approaching each type of problem.

Question Type 1: Solving a System of Linear Equations

This is a standard question which will ask you to find the solution to a system of two linear equations with two unknowns.

PROBLEM

Consider the system of simultaneous equations given by

$$y - 2 = x - 4$$

$$y + 3 = 6 - x$$

Solve for the quantity $6y + 3$.

SOLUTION

The problem can be solved in one of two ways. Naturally one can solve via the substitution method, i.e., plugging in the first equation into the second equation to solve for y. A more direct route is to solve for $6y + 3$ as in the solution below.

Adding both equations together we obtain

$$2y + 1 = 2.$$

Multiplying both sides by 3 we obtain

$$6y + 3 = 6.$$

In the grid we enter

Question Type 2: Word Problems Involving Age

When dealing with this type of question, you will be asked to solve for the age of a particular person. The question may require you to determine how much older one person is, how much younger one person is, or the specific age of the person.

PROBLEM

> Tim is 2 years older than Jane and Joe is 4 years younger than Jane. If the sum of the ages of Jane, Joe, and Tim is 28, how old is Joe?

SOLUTION

The most important aspect here (as with most math problems) is getting started. Define Jane's age to be the variable x and work from there.

Let

$$\text{Jane's age} = x$$

$$\text{Tim's age} = x + 2$$

$$\text{Joe's age} = x - 4.$$

Summing up the ages we get

$$x + x + 2 + x - 4 = 28$$

$$3x - 2 = 28$$

$$3x = 30$$

$$x = 10.$$

Joe's age $= 10 - 4 = 6$.

Hence, we enter into the grid below

Question Type 3: Word Problems Involving Money

Word problems involving money will test your ability to translate the information given into an algebraic statement. You will also be required to solve your algebraic statement.

PROBLEM

After receiving his weekly paycheck on Friday a man buys a television for $100, a suit for $200, and a radio for $50. If the total money he spent amounts to 40% of his paycheck, what is his weekly salary?

SOLUTION

Simply set up an equation involving the man's expenditures and the percentage of his paycheck that he used to buy them.

Let the amount of the man's paycheck equal x. We then have the equation

$$40\%x = 100 + 200 + 50$$

$$.4x = 350$$

$$x = \$875.$$

In the grid we enter

Question Type 4: Systems of Non-Linear Equations

This type of question will test your ability to perform the correct algebraic operations for a given set of equations in order to find the desired quantity.

PROBLEM

Consider the system of equations

$$x^2 + y^2 = 8$$

$$xy = 4$$

Solve for the quantity $3x + 3y$.

SOLUTION

Solve for the quantity $x + y$ and not for x or y individually.

First multiply the equation $xy = 4$ by 2 to get $2xy = 8$. Adding this to $x + y = 8$ we obtain

$$x^2 + 2xy + y^2 = 16$$

$$(x + y)^2 = 16$$

$$x + y = 4$$

or $$x + y = -4$$

Hence, $3x + 3y = 12$ or $3x + 3 = -12$. We enter 12 for a solution since -12 cannot be entered into the grid.

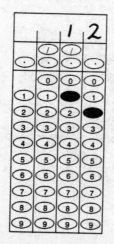

Question Type 5: Word Problems Involving Hourly Wage

When dealing with this type of question, you will be required to form an algebraic expression from the information based on a person's wages. You will then solve the expression to determine the person's wages (i.e., hourly, daily, annually, etc.).

PROBLEM

> Jim works 25 hours a week earning $10 an hour. Sally works 50 hours a week earning y dollars an hour. If their combined income every two weeks is $2,000, find the amount of money Sally makes in hour.

SOLUTION

Be careful. The combined income is given over a two-week period.

Simply set up an equation involving income. We obtain

$$2[(25)(10) + (50)(y)] = 2,000$$

$$[(25)(10) + (50)(y)] = 1,000$$

$$250 + 50y = 1,000$$

$$50y = 750$$

$$y = \$15 \text{ an hour.}$$

We enter in the grid

Question Type 6: Word Problems Involving Consecutive Integers

In this type of question, you will be asked to set up an equation involving consecutive integers based on the product of the integers, which is given.

PROBLEM

Consider two positive consecutive odd integers such that their product is 143. Find their sum.

SOLUTION

Be careful. Notice x and y are consecutive odd integers.

Set

1st odd integer = x

2nd odd integer = $x + 2$.

We get

$$x(x + 2) = 143$$
$$x^2 + 2x - 132 = 0$$
$$(x - 11)(x + 13) = 0$$

hence $x = 11$

and $x = -13$.

From the above we obtain the solution sets $\{11, 13\}$ and $\{-13, -11\}$ whose sums are 24 and -24, respectively. Since the problem specifies that the integers are positive we enter 24 below.

SECTION 3: GEOMETRY

In this section, we will explain how to solve questions which test your ability to find the area of various geometric figures. There are six types of questions you may encounter.

Question Type 1: Area of an Inscribed Triangle

This question asks you to find the area of a triangle which is inscribed in a square. By knowing certain properties of both triangles and squares, we can deduce the necessary information.

PROBLEM

Consider the triangle inscribed in the square below.

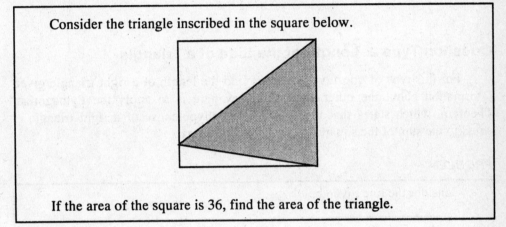

If the area of the square is 36, find the area of the triangle.

SOLUTION

Find the height of the triangle.

Let x be the length of the square. Since the four sides of a square are equal, and the area of a square is the length of a side squared, $x^2 = 36$. Therefore, $x = 6$.

The area of a triangle is given by

$$\frac{1}{2} \text{ (base) (height)}.$$

Here x is both the base and height of the triangle. The area of the triangle is

$$\frac{1}{2} (6) (6) = 18.$$

This is how the answer would be gridded.

Question Type 2: Length of the Side of a Triangle

For this type of question, one must find the length of a right triangle given information about the other sides. The key here is to apply the Pythagorean Theorem, which states that the square of the hypotenuse of a right triangle is equal to the sum of the squares of the other two sides.

PROBLEM

Consider the line given below

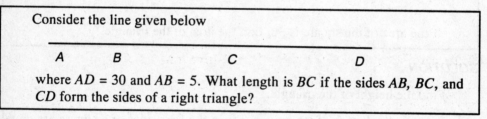

| A | B | C | D |

where $AD = 30$ and $AB = 5$. What length is BC if the sides AB, BC, and CD form the sides of a right triangle?

SOLUTION

Draw a diagram and fill in the known information.

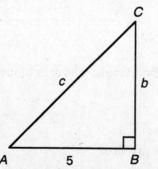

Next, apply the Pythagorean Theorem ($a^2 + b^2 = c^2$), filling in the known variables. Here, we are solving for BC (b in our equation). We know that $a = 5$, and since $AD = 30$ and $AB = 5$, $BD = 25$. Filling in these values, we obtain this equation:

$$5^2 + x^2 = (25 - x)^2$$

$$25 + x^2 = 625 - 50x + x^2$$

$$75x = 620$$

$$x = 12$$

This is one possible solution. If we had chosen $x = CD$ and $25 - x = BC$, one obtains $BC = 13$, which is another possible solution. The possible grid entries are given below.

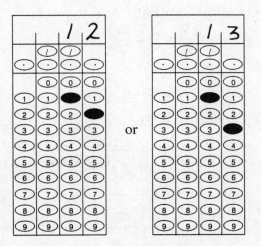

or

Question Type 3: Solving for the Degree of an Angle

Here you will be given a figure with certain information provided. You will need to deduce the measure of an angle based both on this information, as well as other geometric principles. The easiest way to do this is by setting up an algebraic expression.

PROBLEM

Find the angle y in the diagram below.

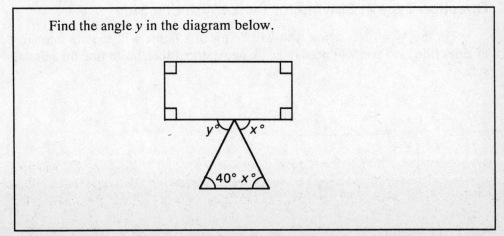

SOLUTION

Use the fact that the sum of the angles on the bottom side of the box is 180°.

Let z be the angle at the top of the triangle. Since we know the sum of the angles of a triangle is 180°,

$$z = 180 - (x + 40).$$

Summing all the angles at the bottom of the square we get

$$y + [180 - (x + 40)] + x = 180$$

$$y + 140 - x + x = 180$$

$$y + 140 = 180$$

$$y = 40$$

In the grid below we enter

Question Type 4: Solving for the Length of a Side

For this type of question, you will be given a figure with certain measures of sides filled in. You will need to apply geometric principles to find the missing side.

PROBLEM

Consider the figure below.

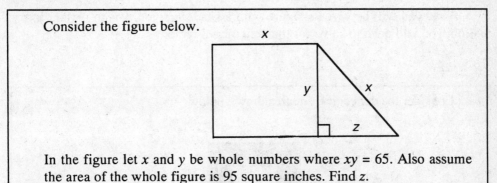

In the figure let x and y be whole numbers where $xy = 65$. Also assume the area of the whole figure is 95 square inches. Find z.

SOLUTION

The key point here is that x and y are whole numbers. Using the figure we only have a finite number of possibilities for z.

The equation for the area of the above figure is

$$xy + yz = 95.$$

Substituting $xy = 65$ into the above equation we get

$$yz = 60.$$

Using the fact that $xy = 65$ we know y can be either 1, 5, or 13. As $y = 13$ does not yield a factorization for $yz = 60$, y is either 1 or 5. If $y = 1$ this implies $x = 65$ and $z = 60$ which contradicts the Pythagorean Theorem (i.e., $1^2 + 60^2 = 13^2$). If $y = 5$ this implies $x = 13$ and $z = 12$ which satisfies $y^2 + z^2 = x^2$; hence, the solution is $y = 5$.

In our grid we enter

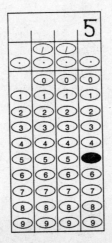

Question Type 5: Solving for the Area of a Region

Here, you will be given a figure with a shaded region. Given certain information, you will need to solve for the area of that region.

PROBLEM

Consider the concentric squares drawn below.

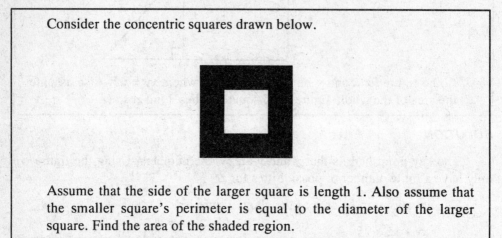

Assume that the side of the larger square is length 1. Also assume that the smaller square's perimeter is equal to the diameter of the larger square. Find the area of the shaded region.

SOLUTION

The key here is to find the length of the side for the smaller square.

By the Pythagorean Theorem the diameter of the square is

$$d^2 = 1^2 + 1^2$$

which yields $d = \sqrt{2}$. Similarly, the smaller square's perimeter is $\sqrt{2}$; hence, the smaller square's side = $\dfrac{\sqrt{2}}{4}$. Calculating the area for the shaded region we get

$$A = A_{\text{large}} - A_{\text{small}}$$

$$A = 1 - \left(\frac{\sqrt{2}}{4}\right)^2$$

$$A = 1 - \frac{2}{16}$$

$$A = \frac{7}{8}$$

In the grid we enter

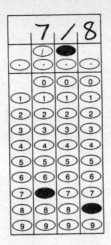

Question Type 6: Solve for a Sum the Lengths

The question here involves solving for a sum of lengths in the figure given knowledge pertaining to its area.

PROBLEM

Consider the figure below.

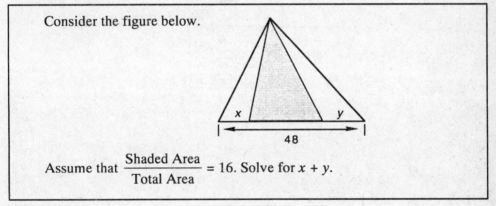

Assume that $\dfrac{\text{Shaded Area}}{\text{Total Area}} = 16$. Solve for $x + y$.

SOLUTION

Solve for $x + y$ and not for x or y individually. Denote by b the base of the smaller triangle. Then

$$48 - b = x + y.$$

From the information given

$$\frac{\frac{1}{2} 48h}{\frac{1}{2} bh} = 16$$

$$\frac{1}{2}48h = 16\left(\frac{1}{2}bh\right)$$

$$24 = 8b$$

$$3 = b$$

This yields

$$x + y = 48 - 3 = 45.$$

We enter in the grid below

STUDENT-PRODUCED RESPONSE DRILL

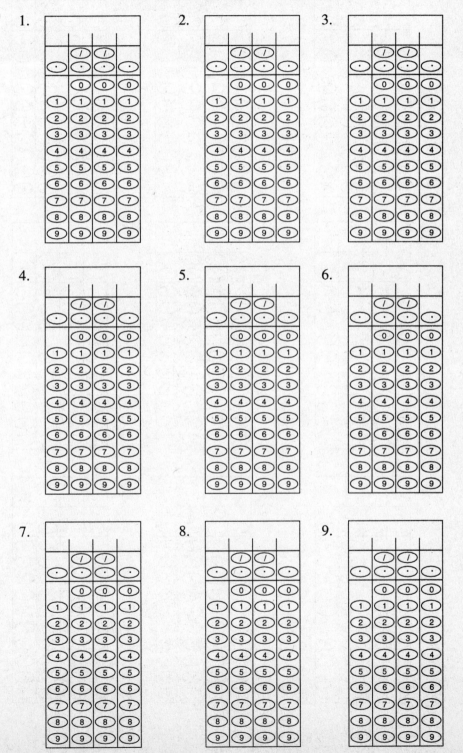

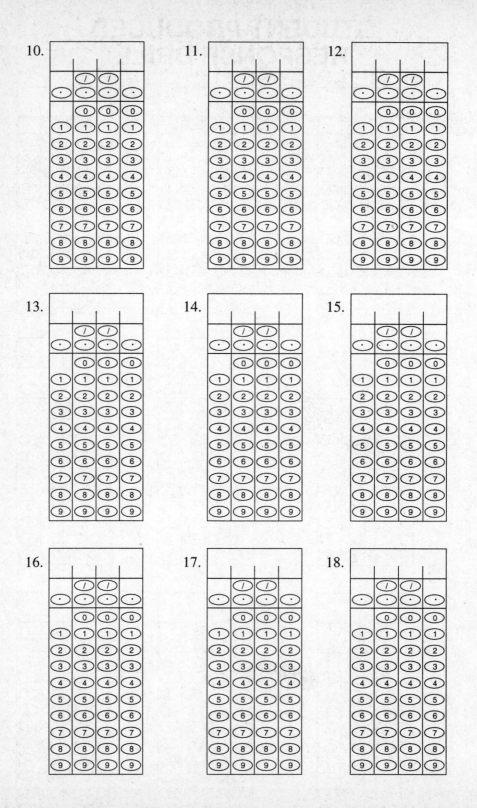

DRILL: STUDENT-PRODUCED RESPONSE QUESTIONS

DIRECTIONS: For each question, solve the problem and enter your answer in the grid.

1. At the end of the month, a woman pays $714 in rent. If the rent constitutes 21% of her monthly income, what is her hourly wage given the fact that she works 34 hours per week?

2. Find the largest integer which is less than 100 and divisible by 3 and 7.

3. The radius of the smaller of two concentric circles is 5 cm while the radius of the larger circle is 7 cm. Determine the area of the shaded region.

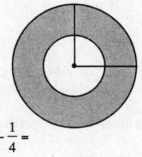

4. $\dfrac{1}{6} + \dfrac{2}{3} + \dfrac{1}{6} - \dfrac{1}{3} + 1 - \dfrac{3}{4} - \dfrac{1}{4} =$

5. The sum of the squares of two consecutive integers is 41. What is the sum of their cubes?

6. Find x.

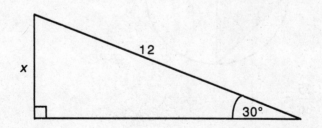

7. $|-8-4| \div 3 \times 6 + (-4) =$

8. A class of 24 students contains 16 males. What is the ratio of females to males?

9.   At an office supply store, customers are given a discount if they pay in cash. If a customer is given a discount of $9.66 on a total order of $276, what is the percent of discount?

10.   Let $RO = 16$, $HM = 30$. Find the perimeter of rhombus *HOMR*.

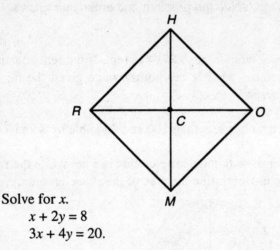

11.   Solve for x.
$$x + 2y = 8$$
$$3x + 4y = 20.$$

12.   Six years ago, Henry's mother was nine times as old as Henry. Now she is only three times as old as Henry. How old is Henry now?

13.   Find a prime number less than 40 which is of the form $5k + 1$.

14.   Find the area of the shaded triangles.

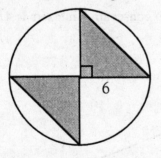

15. $\dfrac{7}{10} \times \dfrac{4}{21} \times \dfrac{25}{36} =$

16.   Find the solution for x in the pair of equations.
$$x + y = 7$$
$$x = y - 3$$

17.   Given the rhombus *RHOM,* find the length of the diagonal *RO.*

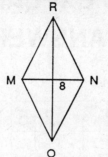

18.   Δ*MNO* is isosceles. If the vertex angle, ∠*N*, has a measure of 96°, find the measure of ∠*M*.

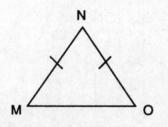

DETAILED EXPLANATIONS
OF ANSWERS

1.   The correctly gridded response is

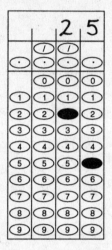

      To solve this problem, you must first calculate Wendy's monthly income. Since we know that $714 is 21% of her income,

$$\frac{21}{100} = \frac{714}{x}.$$

x therefore is $3,400. By dividing $3,400 by 4, we find that Wendy's weekly income is $850. Since she works 34 hours a week, her hourly wage is

$$\frac{850}{34} = \$25 \text{ an hour.}$$

2.   The correctly gridded answer is

To solve this problem, first multiply $3 \times 7 = 21$. Therefore, the answer must be divisible by 21. By finding multiples of 21, it quickly becomes apparent that the largest integer less than 100 and divisible by 3 and 7 is 84.

3.   The correct response is

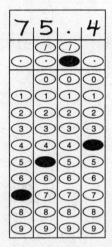

The area of the shaded region is equal to the area of the large circle minus the area of the small circle.

$A_{small} = \pi r^2$ $A_{large} = \pi r^2$

$A_{small} = \pi(5)^2$ $A_{large} = \pi(7)^2$

$A_{small} = 25\pi$ $A_{large} = 49\pi$

$49\pi - 25\pi = 24\pi$

Recall that $\pi = 3.14$. Therefore, the answer is

        $24(3.14) = 75.36$.

Round to 75.4.

4.   The correctly gridded response is

When adding and subtracting fractions, you must find a common denominator. In this case, the common denominator is 12. Converting all of the fractions would give us

$$\frac{2}{12}+\frac{8}{12}+\frac{2}{12}-\frac{4}{12}+\frac{12}{12}-\frac{9}{12}-\frac{3}{12}=$$

Remember that 1 can be expressed as a fraction with the same numerator and denominator. Adding all of the numerators together we get $\frac{8}{12}$. Simplify and get $\frac{2}{3}$.

5.   The correct answer is

The quickest way to solve this problem is by substitution, beginning with zero. You will find the two consecutive integers to be 4 and 5.

$$4^2 + 5^2 = 41$$

Once you have found these numbers, cube them to arrive at the answer:

$$x = 4^3 + 5^3$$
$$x = 64 + 125$$
$$x = 189$$

6.   The correct response is

Set up a proportion where

$$\frac{90°}{12} = \frac{30°}{x}.$$

Cross multiply to get

$$90x = 360$$

$$x = \frac{360}{90}$$

$$x = 4$$

7.   The correctly gridded response is

The first step is to do the portion in the absolute value symbol. When subtracting two negative numbers, they are added together giving a total of -12.

Take the absolute value of this number and move to the next sign. 12 divided by 3 yields an answer of 4. Moving on the next sign, we get 4×6 which equals 24. The next portion tells us to add a -4 to this total which gives us the final answer of 20.

8.   The correct answer is

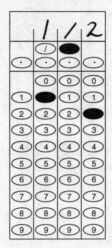

It is given that there are 24 students in all and 16 are male. By subtracting 16 from 24, we find that there are 8 females in the class. Setting up a ratio of females to males we get 8 to 16. Simplifying this we get 1 to 2, or written differently, $\frac{1}{2}$.

Note: Because this is a ratio, there is no other way to grid this response beside the one shown. Gridding .5 would not be acceptable in this case.

9.   The correct answer is

If you set this up as an equation, you get

$276x = 9.66.$

To solve for x (the percent), you must divide 9.66 by 276. When dividing into a number with a decimal point, you must be sure to set the positions correctly by moving the decimal point into your response and placing the right number of zeros (see below).

$$276 \overline{)9.66}^{.0}$$

Going through and doing the division gives us a response of .035. When converting to a percentile, you must move the decimal two places to account for the hundredths place in a percent. This will give you an answer of 3.5%.

Note: A percent sign cannot be marked in the grid and should therefore be left out when marking the response on an answer sheet.

10. The correctly gridded response is

In order to find the whole distance around the figure, we should find the length of just one side. We are given that *RO* is 16 and *HM* is 30 and if we take these lengths and divide them in half to form a triangle *CHO,* side *CH* would be 15 and side *CO* would be 8. Using the Pythagorean Theorem ($a^2 + b^2 = c^2$), we find side *HO* to be 17. There are 4 sides to a rhombus, so $4 \times 17 = 68$.

11.   The correct answer is

Solve the first equation for x in terms of y.

$$x = 8 - zy$$

Substitute $(8 - 2y)$ for all occurrences of x in the second equation.

$$3(8 - 2y) + 4y = 20 \rightarrow 24 - 6y + 4y = 20$$

Combine like terms and subtract $2y$ from both sides.

$$-2y = -4$$

Divide both sides by -2.

$$y = 2$$

Substitute 2 for y in the first equation

$$x + 2(2) = 8$$

$$x = 4$$

12.   The correctly gridded response is

Set a variable (y) to represent the current year. If six years ago ($y - 6$), Henry's mom was nine times as old as him, we could set up the equation

$$y - 6 = 9(x - 6).$$

We are also told that now she is only three times as old and can therefore set $y = 3x$. Substituting $3x$ for each occurrence of y in the equation, we get

$$3x - 6 = 9(x - 6).$$

Distribute the 9 and get

$$3x - 6 = 9x - 54$$

$$-6x = -48$$

$$x = 8$$

8 is Henry's current age.

13.   The correct answer is

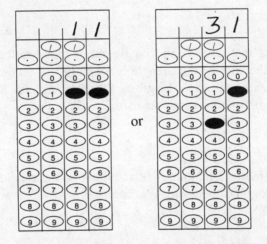

or

The best way to go about this problem is to simply plug all the numbers starting from zero until they add up to over 40. Any answer that is prime and under 40 is considered correct. If zero is plugged into the equation, the answer is 1. Remember, though, that 1 is not a prime number. By plugging in each consecutive number, we find that $k = 2$ gives an answer of 11. Eleven fits the criteria and is therefore one of the correct answers. (**Note:** remember that it is possible to have more than one correct answer.) If $k = 6$, we get an answer of 31, also a prime number under 40. We can stop plugging in numbers at 8 because $k = 8$ gives an answer of 41 and this number no longer fits the criteria.

14.   The correctly gridded response is

The area of a triangle can be found by using the formula

$$\frac{1}{2}b \times h$$

with b representing the base of the triangle and h representing the height of the triangle. Because the base of the triangle is the radius of a circle, we can assume that the height must be the same length as the base because it too is a radius of the circle. Putting our numbers into the formula, we get

$$\left(\frac{1}{2} \times 6\right) \times 6 = 18.$$

We can interpret from the diagram that the other triangle is identical to the first triangle and therefore has the same area. Multiplying by 2 to get the area for both triangles we get 36.

15.   The correctly gridded response is

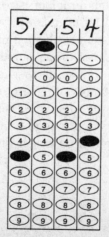

When multiplying fractions, you simply multiply all the numbers in the numerator together and multiply all the numbers in the denominator together and get one fraction, and then simplify. Multiplying through we get $\dfrac{700}{7,560}$. Simplifying the fraction by dividing through by 10 we get $\dfrac{70}{756}$. Dividing through by 7 we get $\dfrac{10}{108}$. Division by 2 leaves us with $\dfrac{5}{54}$ and this cannot be simplified any further.

16.   The correct response is

We are given that $x = y - 3$ in the second equation. By plugging this into the first equation, we get $(y - 3) + y = 7$. Combining like terms, we get $2y - 3 = 7$ which comes out to $2y = 10$ which gives 5 as the y value. Plugging this value into the second equation we get $x = 5 - 3$ or $x = 2$.

17.   The correctly gridded response is

We find that half of diagonal *RO* is a side to a triangle. We are given the lengths of the other sides of this triangle. Using the Pythagorean Theorem, we can determine the length of the third side. The Pythagorean Theorem states $a^2 + b^2 = c^2$. Plugging our given numbers into this equation we get

$$8^2 + b^2 = 17^2.$$

Multiplying out we get

$$64 + b^2 = 289.$$

Subtract the 64 from both sides and we have $b^2 = 225$. Take the square root of both sides and we get $b = 15$. We must remember to multiply by 2 in order to get the full length of the diagonal, which is what the question asks for. Therefore, our answer is

$$15 \times 2 = 30.$$

18.   The correct response is

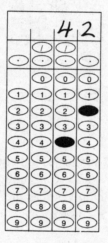

We are given the measure of one of the angles in the triangle. All of the interior angles of a triangle add up to 180°. We are told the vertex angle is 96°. Subtracting the vertex angle from our total of 180° leaves us with 84°. The two other angles must add up to 84°. We are also told that this is an isosceles triangle, meaning that the two indicated sides are the same length. If the length of the sides is the same, then their opposite, corresponding angles must be the same. If they are equal, we simply divide the remainder of our 180° by 2 which is 84 ÷ 2 which gives us 42.

CHAPTER 6

Word Problems

- ➤ Diagnostic Test
- ➤ Word Problems Review and Drills
- ➤ Glossary

WORD PROBLEMS DIAGNOSTIC TEST

1. Ⓐ Ⓑ Ⓒ Ⓓ Ⓔ		26. Ⓐ Ⓑ Ⓒ Ⓓ Ⓔ
2. Ⓐ Ⓑ Ⓒ Ⓓ Ⓔ		27. Ⓐ Ⓑ Ⓒ Ⓓ Ⓔ
3. Ⓐ Ⓑ Ⓒ Ⓓ Ⓔ		28. Ⓐ Ⓑ Ⓒ Ⓓ Ⓔ
4. Ⓐ Ⓑ Ⓒ Ⓓ Ⓔ		29. Ⓐ Ⓑ Ⓒ Ⓓ Ⓔ
5. Ⓐ Ⓑ Ⓒ Ⓓ Ⓔ		30. Ⓐ Ⓑ Ⓒ Ⓓ Ⓔ
6. Ⓐ Ⓑ Ⓒ Ⓓ Ⓔ		31. Ⓐ Ⓑ Ⓒ Ⓓ Ⓔ
7. Ⓐ Ⓑ Ⓒ Ⓓ Ⓔ		32. Ⓐ Ⓑ Ⓒ Ⓓ Ⓔ
8. Ⓐ Ⓑ Ⓒ Ⓓ Ⓔ		33. Ⓐ Ⓑ Ⓒ Ⓓ Ⓔ
9. Ⓐ Ⓑ Ⓒ Ⓓ Ⓔ		34. Ⓐ Ⓑ Ⓒ Ⓓ Ⓔ
10. Ⓐ Ⓑ Ⓒ Ⓓ Ⓔ		35. Ⓐ Ⓑ Ⓒ Ⓓ Ⓔ
11. Ⓐ Ⓑ Ⓒ Ⓓ Ⓔ		36. Ⓐ Ⓑ Ⓒ Ⓓ Ⓔ
12. Ⓐ Ⓑ Ⓒ Ⓓ Ⓔ		37. Ⓐ Ⓑ Ⓒ Ⓓ Ⓔ
13. Ⓐ Ⓑ Ⓒ Ⓓ Ⓔ		38. Ⓐ Ⓑ Ⓒ Ⓓ Ⓔ
14. Ⓐ Ⓑ Ⓒ Ⓓ Ⓔ		39. Ⓐ Ⓑ Ⓒ Ⓓ Ⓔ
15. Ⓐ Ⓑ Ⓒ Ⓓ Ⓔ		40. Ⓐ Ⓑ Ⓒ Ⓓ Ⓔ
16. Ⓐ Ⓑ Ⓒ Ⓓ Ⓔ		41. Ⓐ Ⓑ Ⓒ Ⓓ Ⓔ
17. Ⓐ Ⓑ Ⓒ Ⓓ Ⓔ		42. Ⓐ Ⓑ Ⓒ Ⓓ Ⓔ
18. Ⓐ Ⓑ Ⓒ Ⓓ Ⓔ		43. Ⓐ Ⓑ Ⓒ Ⓓ Ⓔ
19. Ⓐ Ⓑ Ⓒ Ⓓ Ⓔ		44. Ⓐ Ⓑ Ⓒ Ⓓ Ⓔ
20. Ⓐ Ⓑ Ⓒ Ⓓ Ⓔ		45. Ⓐ Ⓑ Ⓒ Ⓓ Ⓔ
21. Ⓐ Ⓑ Ⓒ Ⓓ Ⓔ		46. Ⓐ Ⓑ Ⓒ Ⓓ Ⓔ
22. Ⓐ Ⓑ Ⓒ Ⓓ Ⓔ		47. Ⓐ Ⓑ Ⓒ Ⓓ Ⓔ
23. Ⓐ Ⓑ Ⓒ Ⓓ Ⓔ		48. Ⓐ Ⓑ Ⓒ Ⓓ Ⓔ
24. Ⓐ Ⓑ Ⓒ Ⓓ Ⓔ		49. Ⓐ Ⓑ Ⓒ Ⓓ Ⓔ
25. Ⓐ Ⓑ Ⓒ Ⓓ Ⓔ		50. Ⓐ Ⓑ Ⓒ Ⓓ Ⓔ

WORD PROBLEMS
DIAGNOSTIC TEST

This diagnostic test is designed to help you determine your strengths and your weaknesses in word problems. Follow the directions for each part and check your answers.

Study this chapter for the following tests:
PSAT, SAT I, ACT, NTE, PPST, CBEST, ELM, GRE, GMAT, GED

---

50 Questions

DIRECTIONS: Choose the correct answer for each of the following problems. Fill in the answer on the answer sheet.

1. Two pounds of pears and one pound of peaches cost $1.40. Three pounds of pears and two pounds of peaches cost $2.40. How much is the combined cost of one pound of pears and one pound of peaches?

    (A) $2.00   (B) $1.50   (C) $1.60

    (D) $.80   (E) $1.00

2. Two dice are thrown, one red and one green. The probability that the number on the red exceeds the number showing on the green by exactly two is

    (A) $\dfrac{1}{18}$ (B) $\dfrac{1}{4}$ (C) $\dfrac{1}{9}$

    (D) $\dfrac{1}{36}$ (E) $\dfrac{1}{24}$

3. A man buys a book for $20 and wishes to sell it. What price should he mark on it if he wishes a 40% discount while making a 50% profit on the cost price?

    (A) $25   (B) $30   (C) $40

    (D) $50   (E) $55

4. A man who is 40 years old has three sons, ages 6, 3, and 1. In how many years will the combined age of this three sons equal 80% of his age?

(A) 5   (B) 10   (C) 15

(D) 20   (E) 25

5. Peter brought n compact disks for $\$m$. If in a second purchase he paid $\$q$, what was the increment per compact disk? ($q > m$)

(A) $(m - q)/n$ (B) $(m - q)n$ (C) $(q - m)/n$

(D) $(q - m)n$ (E) $(n - q)/m$

6. In a three-person, 100-meter race, Amy finishes 10 meters ahead of Brooke and 20 meters ahead of Carol. Assuming constant speeds for each runner, by how many meters did Brooke finish ahead of Carol?

(A) 9 meters   (B) 10 meters   (C) 11 meters

(D) $11^{1}/_{9}$ meters   (E) $11^{8}/_{9}$ meters

7. At a certain restaurant the cost of 3 sandwiches, 7 cups of coffee and 4 pieces of pie is $\$10.20$, while the cost of 4 sandwiches, 8 cups of coffee and 5 pieces of pie is $\$12.25$. What is the cost of a luncheon consisting of one sandwich, one cup of coffee and one piece of pie?

(A) $\$2.00$ (B) $\$2.05$ (C) $\$2.10$

(D) $\$2.15$ (E) $\$2.25$

8. Tilda's car gets 35 miles per gallon of gasoline and Naomi's car gets 8 miles per gallon. When traveling from Washington, D.C. to Philadelphia, they both used a whole number of gallons of gasoline. How far is it from Philadelphia to Washington, D.C.?

(A) 21 miles   (B) 32 miles   (C) 68 miles

(D) 136 miles   (E) 170 miles

9. In a chess match, a win counts 1 point, a draw counts $^{1}/_{2}$ point, and a loss counts 0 points. After 15 games, the winner was 4 points ahead of the loser. How many points did the loser have?

(A) $4^{1}/_{2}$ (B) $5^{1}/_{2}$ (C) 6

(D) 7   (E) 9

10. A sphere with diameter 1 meter has a mass of 120 kilograms. What is the mass, in kilograms, of a sphere of the same kind of material that has a diameter of 2 meters?

(A) 480   (B) 560   (C) 640

(D) 960   (E) 1080

Questions 11–15 refer to the following figure

Portion of Ph.D. Degrees in the Mathematical Sciences
Awarded to U.S. Citizens in 1986

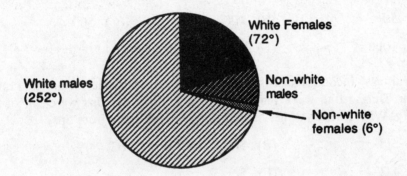

11. What percent of the Ph.D. degrees were awarded in 1986 to non-white males?

(A) 30   (B) $8^{1}/_{3}$ (C) $4^{1}/_{6}$

(D) 20   (E) None of the above

12. If 4000 Ph.D.s were awarded in Mathematical Sciences, how many were awarded to white female U.S. citizens?

(A) 800   (B) 2880   (C) 3200

(D) 1120   (E) None of the above

13. If the 600 white females represent 72° of the figure that depicts the total distribution of Ph.D.s awarded in the Mathematical Sciences in the U.S. in 1986, then how many were awarded to white males?

(A) 432   (B) 3000   (C) About 857

(D) 2100   (E) None of the above

14. Given the distribution of Ph.D.s awarded in Mathematical Sciences in the U.S. in 1986, what is the ratio of white male's degrees to non-white male's degrees?

(A) 1 to 5   (B) 3.5 to 1   (C) 8.4 to 1

(D) 42 to 1   (E) None of the above

15. If the non-white female category represents 6° of the distribution of a total of 6000 Ph.D.s awarded in the Mathematical Sciences, then how many Ph.D.s were awarded in this category?

(A) 50   (B) 100   (C) 500

(D) 1000   (E) None of the above

16. A waitress' income consists of her salary and tips. Her salary is $150 a week. During one week that included a holiday her tips were 5/4 of her salary. What fraction of her income for the week came from tips?

(A) 5/8   (B) 5/4   (C) 4/9

(D) 1/2   (E) 5/9

Question 17 refers to the following graph:

**Undergraduate Mathematics Enrollments in the U.S., 1965-85
(Thousands of enrollments, fall semester)**

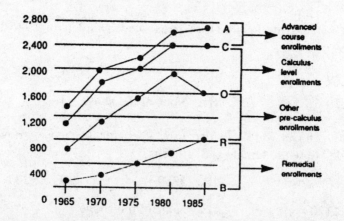

(Note: Area between line segments *B* and *R* represent remedial enrollments; between line segments *R* and *O* represent other precalculus enrollments; between line segments *O* and *C* represent calculus enrollments; and, between line segments *C* and *A* represent advanced course enrollments.)

17. What undergraduate enrollments category was fairly constant over the period of the graph?

    (A) Remedial   (B) Other precalculus

    (C) Calculus level   (D) Advanced course

    (E) None of the above

18. Jim is twice as old as Susan. If Jim were 4 years younger and Susan were 3 years older, their ages would differ by 12 years. What is the sum of their ages?

    (A) 19   (B) 42   (C) 56

    (D) 57   (E) None of the above

19. Joe and Jim together have 14 marbles. Jim and Tim together have 10 marbles. Joe and Tim together have 12 marbles. What is the maximum number of marbles that any one of these may have?

    (A) 7   (B) 8   (C) 9

    (D) 10   (E) 11

20. Emile receives a flat weekly salary of $240 plus 12% commission of the total volume of all sales he makes. What must his dollar volume be in a week if he is to make a total weekly salary of $540?

    (A) $2880   (B) $3600   (C) $6480

    (D) $2500   (E) $2000

21. A truck contains 150 small packages, some weighing 1 kg each and some weighing 2 kg each. How many packages weighing 2 kg each are in the truck if the total weight of all the packages is 264 kg?

    (A) 36   (B) 52   (C) 88

    (D) 124   (E) 114

22. I went to 'Las Vegas' Casino and in the first game I lost one third of my money, in the second game I lost half of the rest. If I still have $1000, how much money did I have when I arrived at the Casino?

    (A) $1000   (B) $2000   (C) $3000

    (D) $6000   (E) $12,000

23. A postal truck leaves its station and heads for Chicago, averaging 40 mph. An error in the mailing schedule is spotted and 24 minutes after the truck leaves, a car is sent to overtake the truck. If the car averages 50 mph, how long will it take to catch the postal truck?

    (A) 2.6 hours   (B) 3 hours   (C) 2 hours

    (D) 1.5 hours   (E) 1.6 hours

24. A gardener wishes to decorate a garden which is 576 square feet in area, and he must decide how to apportion each section of the garden with specific plants. He has decided to set aside 20% of the garden with roses and an additional 32.9 square feet for a tomato patch. How much of the garden is set aside for the roses and tomatoes?

    (A) 569.42 square feet   (B) 523.1 square feet   (C) 148.1 square feet

    (D) 52.9 square feet   (E) 53.9 square feet

25. A man sold two-thirds of his pencils for 20 cents each. If he has 7 pencils left, how much money did he collect for the pencils he sold?

    (A) $2.10   (B) $2.80   (C) $1.40

    (D) $2.00   (E) $2.20

26. The cost of digging a basement for a house 30 feet long and 27 feet wide was $975. If the excavating cost was $3.75 per cubic yard, how deep was the basement?

    (A) $11\frac{2}{3}$ ft   (B) $8\frac{2}{3}$ ft   (C) 11 ft

    (D) 9 ft   (E) 8 ft

27. Stanley and Mitchell made a bet about Stanley's math test. Mitchell told Stanley that he would give him $8 for each problem he got correct on the test if Stanley would pay him $5 for each problem that he got wrong. There were going to be 26 problems on the test. The next day, after getting his test back, Stanley told Mitchell that neither owed the other any money. How many problems did Stanley get right?

    (A) 8   (B) 13   (C) 11

    (D) 10   (E) 16

28. The owners of a business divided up the profits as follows: The share of the second was 3 times that of the third and the share of the first was 4 times that of the second. The first received $1,210 more than the third. How much did the first receive?

(A) $1,320   (B) $1,400   (C) $1,550

(D) $2,300   (E) $2,400

29. A company was forced out of business by its competitor. It was able to pay 25 cents on the dollar, but had the company been able to collect a certain debt of $800, it could have paid 30 cents on the dollar. How much did the company owe at the time of its closing?

(A) $1,600   (B) $160,000   (C) $16,000

(D) $1,455   (E) $14,550

30. An investor earns $930 from two accounts in a year. If she has three times as much invested at 8% as she does at 7%, how much does she have invested at 8%?

(A) $9,000   (B) $3,207   (C) $9,621

(D) $3,000   (E) $11,500

31. Cyndi invests part of $2,000 in a certificate of deposit that pays simple annual interest of 9% and the remainder in a passbook savings account that pays 5% simple annual interest. If she receives $148 interest in one year how much did she invest in the certificate of deposit?

(A) $800   (B) $1,000   (C) $1,200

(D) $1,500   (E) $1,800

32. The average of 12 test scores is 55. When the 2 highest and 2 lowest scores are dropped, the average of the remaining scores is 50. The average of the scores dropped is

(A) 65   (B) 60   (C) 55

(D) 52.5   (E) 50

33. A computer is marked up 50 percent and then later marked down 30 percent. If the final price is $3,360, the original price was

(A) $2,240   (B) $3,200   (C) $4,200

(D) $4,800   (E) $5,600

34. At $6.75 per hour, the minimum number of hours that Joel needs to work to earn at least $150 is

(A) 20   (B) 22   (C) 23

(D) 24   (E) 25

35. Eva can wallpaper a room in 4 hours and Kathy can wallpaper the same room in 6 hours. Kathy works on her own for one hour, and is then joined by Eva. Assuming these rates, how many hours did Kathy and Eva together take to finish the job?

    (A) $2^2/_5$ (B) 2   (C) $1^4/_5$

    (D) $1^1/_5$ (E) 1

36. SPLINT, a "we try harder" telephone company advertises that it charges 51 cents for the first minute and 34 cents for each additional minute for a long-distance call from New Jersey to New York. If the number of additional minutes after the first minute is x and the cost, in cents, is y, then the equation representing the total cost of the call is $y = 34x + 51$. AC&C, its competitor, has a cost equation for the same call of the form $y = 31x + 60$. After how many additional minutes will the two companies charge an equal amount?

    (A) 9   (B) 3

    (C) 2   (D) 4

    (E) The two companies will never charge an equal amount because SPLINT is always cheaper than AC&C.

37. At Martin's Market each piece of bubble gum ordinarily sells for 9¢. Mary paid $1.55 for some of these pieces of bubble gum when they were on sale. How many did she buy?

    (A) 21   (B) 28   (C) 31

    (D) 35   (E) 37

38. In a four-child family, the four children could all be of one sex (4–0), or there could be three of one sex and one of the other sex (3–1), or there could be two of each sex (2–2). Concerning a four-child family, which of the following is a true sentence?

    (A) A family of all of one sex is most likely (4–0).

    (B) A family of three of one sex and one of the other sex is most likely (3–1).

    (C) A family of two of each sex is most likely (2–2).

    (D) The three types of families (4–0), (3-1), and (2-2), are equally likely to occur.

    (E) All of the above are false.

39. Mary has $29^1/_2$ yards of material available to make uniforms. Each uniform requires $^3/_4$ yard of material. How many uniforms can she make and how much material will she have left?

    (A) 39 uniforms with $^1/_3$ yard left over

    (B) 39 uniforms with $^1/_4$ yard left over

    (C) 39 uniforms with $^1/_2$ yard left over

    (D) 27 uniforms with $^1/_3$ yard left over

    (E) 27 uniforms with $^1/_2$ yard left over

40. In a certain city, a taxi ride cost 85¢ for the first $^1/_{10}$ of a mile and 10¢ for every $^1/_{10}$ of a mile after the first. If x is the number of additional $^1/_{10}$-miles after the first $^1/_{10}$ of a mile, write an equation for the cost $f(x)$, in cents of a taxi ride and use it to find the cost of a 2-mile ride.

    (A) 175¢   (B) 185¢   (C) 285¢

    (D) 200¢   (E) 275¢

41. A pitcher holds 6 times as much water as a paper drinking cup. Three pitchers hold 39 ounces more than 5 drinking cups. How many ounces does a cup hold?

    (A) 6   (B) 5   (C) 4

    (D) 3   (E) 2

42. At a garage sale, Sarah sold two kitchen gadgets at $2.40 each. Based on the cost her profit on one was 20% and her loss on the other was 20%. On the sale she:

    (A) gained 8¢   (B) lost 8¢   (C) broke even

    (D) gained 20¢   (E) lost 20¢

43. A miller took $^1/_{10}$ of the wheat he ground as his fee. How much did he grind if a customer had exactly one bushel left after the fee had been subtracted?

    (A) $1^1/_9$ (B) $1^1/_{10}$ (C) $1^1/_3$

    (D) $1^1/_2$ (E) $1^1/_5$

44. Of the freshmen at a college, 24% failed remedial mathematics. If 360 students failed remedial mathematics, how many freshmen are enrolled at the college?

    (A) 500   (B) 1200   (C) 1500

    (D) 18   (E) 81

45. Julie holds 100 shares each of Companies *A*, *B* and *C*. On January 1 the prices per share, respectively, were $10, $12, and $18. Shares of Company *B* split 2 for 1 and those of Company *C* split 3 for 2. On December 31, the price per share of Companies *A*, *B* and *C* respectively was $12, $6 and $16. There were no dividends. What was the annual return on Julie's portfolio of stocks?

    (A) 16.7%   (B) 20%   (C) 25%

    (D) 30%   (E) 33.3%

46. Ten years ago a house was insured for $10,500 which represented three-fourths of its value. If property values have increased by 150% since then, for how much should the house be insured to represent seven-eighths of its present value?

    (A) $17,226.56   (B) $18,375   (C) $30,625

    (D) $22,968.75   (E) $35,000

47. The average speed of today's plane is twice that of a plane of 5 years ago and takes $1^1/_4$ hours less time to fly the same distance of 1500 miles. Find the average speed of a plane of 5 years ago.

    (A) 450   (B) 1200   (C) 600

    (D) 500   (E) 375

48. Tickets for a particular concert cost $5 each if purchased in advance and $7 each if bought at the box office on the day of the concert. For this particular concert, 1,200 tickets were sold and the receipts were $6,700. How many tickets were bought at the box office on the day of the concert?

    (A) 500   (B) 700   (C) 600

    (D) 350   (E) 200

49. A paint mixture contains 2 parts of green paint and 6 parts of white paint. How many gallons of green paint must be added to 16 gallons of this mixture to obtain a new mixture which has 40% green paint?

    (A) 2   (B) 3   (C) 4

    (D) 5   (E) 6

50. How many ounces of a metal other than gold must be added to 56 ounces of pure gold to make a composition 70% gold?

    (A) 39.2   (B) 16.8   (C) 9.8

    (D) 56   (E) 24

WORD PROBLEMS
DIAGNOSTIC TEST

ANSWER KEY

1. (E)	11. (B)	21. (E)	31. (C)	41. (D)
2. (C)	12. (A)	22. (C)	32. (A)	42. (E)
3. (D)	13. (D)	23. (E)	33. (B)	43. (A)
4. (B)	14. (C)	24. (C)	34. (C)	44. (C)
5. (C)	15. (B)	25. (B)	35. (B)	45. (B)
6. (D)	16. (E)	26. (B)	36. (B)	46. (C)
7. (B)	17. (D)	27. (D)	37. (C)	47. (C)
8. (D)	18. (D)	28. (A)	38. (B)	48. (D)
9. (B)	19. (B)	29. (C)	39. (B)	49. (C)
10. (D)	20. (D)	30. (A)	40. (E)	50. (E)

DETAILED EXPLANATIONS
OF ANSWERS

1. **(E)**
    X : cost of one pound of pears.
    Y : cost of one pound of peaches.

    $$2X + Y = 1.4 \tag{1}$$

    $$3X + 2Y = 2.4 \tag{2}$$

    (1) times (2)

    $$4X + 2Y = 2.8 \tag{3}$$

    $$3X + 2Y = 2.4 \tag{2}$$

    (3) – (2)

    $$X = .4$$

    Substitute $X = .4$ in (1)

2. **(C)** The total number of possible combinations on a pair of dice is $(6)^2$ = 36 combinations.

    We are looking for combinations where the number showing on the red die exceeds the number on the green die by 2. This occurs only for the following combinations.

Red	Green
3	1
4	2
5	3
6	4

Thus there are four combinations that satisfy the constraints, out of 36 possible combinations.

   The probability is equal to $^4/_{36} = {}^1/_9$.

3. **(D)** The man originally buys the book for \$20. He wishes to make a 50% profit on the book. To do this he must sell the book for:

    $$20 + (50\%)(20) = \$30.$$

He would like the $30 price to appear as if it is a markdown from an even higher price. We must find this phony price. Let this price be p. Then:

$$p - (40\%)(p) = 30$$

$$(.60)p = 30$$

$$p = \$50.$$

4.   **(B)** n years later, the ages will be

father	$40 + n$
son #1	$6 + n$
son #2	$3 + n$
son #3	$1 + n$

Therefore

$$6 + n + 3 + n + 1 + n = (80/100) * (40 + n)$$

$$10 + 3n = .8(40 + n)$$

$$10 + 3 = 32 + .8n$$

$$2.2n = 22$$

$$n = 10.$$

5.   **(C)**   The first time Peter paid $^m/_q$ dollars/disk and the second time he paid $^q/_n$ dollars/disk. The increment was

$$\frac{q}{n} = \frac{m}{n} = \frac{q-m}{n} = (q - m)/n.$$

6.   **(D)**   Let a, b and c be the rates of Amy, Brooke and Carol, respectively. Using the formula

$$\text{time} = \frac{\text{distance}}{\text{rate}},$$

and the fact that Amy's time for 100 yards was the same as Brooke's time for 90 yards and Carol's time for 80 yards

$$\frac{100}{a} = \frac{90}{b} = \frac{80}{c}.$$

Then $^b/_c = ^9/_8$. Let $x =$ the distance Brooke finishes ahead of Carol. Then

$$\frac{100}{b} = \frac{100 - x}{c} \text{ and } \frac{b}{c} = \frac{100}{100 - x}.$$

Then

$$\frac{100}{100 - x} = \frac{9}{8} \; x = \frac{100}{9}$$

$$x = 11\frac{1}{9}$$

7.   **(B)**   Let *a, b* and *c* be the cost of one sandwich, one cup of coffee and one piece of pie respectively. Then

$$3a + 7b + 4c = 10.20$$

$$4a + 8b + 5c = 12.25$$

$$a + b + c = 2.05$$

8.   **(D)**   Tilda's car gets 34 miles per gallon of gasoline, and Naomi's car gets 8 miles per gallon. Since each of them used a whole number of gallons of gasoline in traveling from Washington, D.C. to Philadelphia, it follows that the distance between the two cities must be a multiple of the two numbers 34 and 8. In fact, it has to be the least common multiple of 34 and 8.

The least common multiple of two (or more) whole numbers is the smallest non-zero whole number that is a multiple of both (all) of the numbers.

The least common multiple of 34 and 8 can be found by factoring each of 34 and 8 into their prime factors expressed in exponential form as follows:

$$8 = 2 \cdot 2 \cdot 2 = 2^3$$

$$34 = 2 \cdot 17.$$

Then the least common multiple of 34 and 8 is equal to $2^3 \cdot 17 = 136$.

Another procedure for finding the least common multiple of two whole numbers is called the intersection-of-sets method. First, find the set of all positive multiples of both numbers, then find the set of all common multiples of both numbers, and, finally, pick the least element in the set.

In this problem, multiples of 8 are:

8, 16, 24, 32, 40, 48, 56, 64, 72, 80, 88, 96, 104,

112, 120, 128, 136, 144, 152, 160, 168, ...

Multiples of 34 are:

34, 68, 102, 136, 170, ...

The intersection of the multiples of 8 and 34 is the set

{136, 272, 408, ...}

Because 136 is the smallest common multiple of 8 and 34, it follows that the least common multiple of 34 and 8 is 136. Thus, the distance from Washington D.C. to Philadelphia is 136 miles.

Yet another way to attack this problem is to check if any of the answer choices is a common multiple of both 34 and 8. Checking the answer choices given yields,

(A)   21 is not a multiple of 34 or 8.

(B)   32 is a multiple of 8, but not of 34.

(C)   68 is a multiple of 34, but not of 8.

(D)   136 is a multiple of both 34 and 8.

(E)   170 is a multiple of 34, but not of 8.

9.   **(B)**   A total of 1 point is accumulated for each game. Thus in 15 games, 15 points are accumulated. Let x be the number of points for the loser. Then $x + 4$ is the number of points for the winner, and

$$x + (x + 4) = 15$$

$$2x = 11$$

$$x = 5\frac{1}{2}.$$

10.   **(D)**   The ratio of their volumes is the cube of the ratio of their diameters.

Since the mass of a sphere is directly proportional to the volume, the ratio of their masses is equal to the ratio of their volumes.

$$\therefore \quad \frac{\text{Mass of the bigger sphere}}{\text{Mass of the smaller sphere}} = \left(\frac{2}{1}\right)^3$$

$$\text{Mass of the bigger} = (120)(2)^3$$

$$= 120 \times 8$$

$$= 960.$$

11.   **(B)**   Since the non-white males category is the only portion (in degrees) not shown in the graph, simply add the given degrees in the circle and subtract the sum from 360 degrees to obtain 30 degrees. Then form the ratio of 30 to 360 and find the percent which is simply $8\frac{1}{3}\%$.

Answer choice (A) indicates the number of degrees in the circle that represents the non-white males category. Answer choice (D) indicates the number of degrees in the circle that represents the white females category. Answer choice

(C) represents only one-half of the correct percent for the non-white males category.

12.　**(A)**　Observe that 20% of the total number of Ph.D.s awarded went to white female U.S. citizens, that is, 72/360 = 20%. Then, multiply 20% (that is 0.20) by 4000 to obtain 800, which is the correct answer.

Answer choice (B) is obtained by incorrectly multiplying 0.72 by 4000 to get 2880. Notice that the portion of the circle representing the white females category is 72 degrees of the whole. One may wrongly consider this as 72/100 or 0.72. Answer choice (C) is obtained by incorrectly subtracting 800 from 4000 and answer choice (D) is obtained by incorrectly subtracting 2880 from 4000.

13.　**(D)**　Let x denote the number of Ph.D.s awarded to white males. Then, form ratios 72/600 and 252/x. Then form a proportion $^{72}/_{600} = 252/x$ and solve for x to obtain the number of Ph.D.s awarded to white males. The results is as follows:

$$\frac{72}{600} = \frac{252}{x} \text{ or } 72\,x = 600\,(252) \text{ or } 72x = 151200 \text{ or } x = 2100.$$

Answer choice (A) represents a value that is too small. The same is true about answer choice (C) since the white male category represents more than 3 times the area of the white female category. Answer choice (B) is obtained by dividing 600 by 20%, which is incorrect.

14.　**(C)**　The ratio of degrees awarded to white males to those awarded to non-white males is given by using 252 to 30, the corresponding portions of the circle representing these categories. So, the ratio is 252/30 or 8.4/1 (that is, 8.4 to 1). Hence, the answer choice is (C).

Answer choice (B) is obtained by finding the ratio of 252 to 72; choice (D) is obtained by finding the ratio of 252 to 6; and choice (A) is illogical.

15.　**(B)**　Observe that 6 degrees represent 6/360 of the whole circle. Since the entire circle represents a distribution of 6000 one can find the number of the total that 6 degrees represents as follows:

$$\frac{6}{360} \times 6000 = 100.$$

16.　**(E)**　Note that tips for the week were (5/4) (150). Thus the total income was as follows:

$$(1)(150 + (5/4)) = (4/4)\,(150) + (5/4)\,(150)$$

$$= (9/4)\,(150).$$

Therefore, tips made up

$$\frac{(5/4)(150)}{(9/4)(150)} = \frac{5/4}{9/4} = \frac{5}{9}$$

of her income.

Notice that one could figure out the total income in order to arrive at the solution, however, this would be a waste of time.

17.   **(D)**   The only category of enrollments in the graph that shows the least amount of variance from year to year is the advanced course enrollments. Notice that the line that represents this category is about the same distance from the calculus level enrollments for each year in the graph.

18.   **(D)**   The easiest way to determine the result for this problem is to represent the unknown ages, set up an equation, and solve it. Begin by letting x = the age of Susan now. Then, $2x$ = the age of Jim now. The next step is to represent Jim's age 4 years ago and Susan's age 3 years from now. Thus, $2x - 4$ = Jim's age 4 years ago. Then, $x + 3$ = Susan's age 3 years from now. Finally an equation can be set up by noting that the age represented by $2x - 4$ differs from the age represented by $x + 3$ by 12 years. So, the equation is given by the following:

$$(2x - 4) - (x + 3) = 12.$$

Solving for x one gets

$$2x - 4 - x - 3 = 12$$

$$x - 7 = 12$$

$$x - 7 + 7 = 12 + 7$$

$$x = 19, \text{ Susan's age now.}$$

$$2x = 38, \text{ Jim's age now.}$$

The sum of their ages (19 + 38) is 57.

19.   **(B)**   Let x = Joe's marbles, y = Jim's marbles and z = Tim's marbles. It is given that:

$$x + y = 14 \tag{1}$$

$$y + z = 10 \tag{2}$$

$$x + z = 12 \tag{3}$$

Solve equation (2) for y and equation (3) for x. Then substitute their values in equation (1) and solve for z.

$$y + z = 10 \Rightarrow y + z - z = 10 - z \Rightarrow y = 10 - z$$

and

$$x + z = 12 \Rightarrow x + z - z = 12 - z \Rightarrow x = 12 - z$$

Thus,

$$x + y = 14 \Rightarrow (12 - z) + (10 - z) = 14$$

$$-2z + 22 = 14$$

$$-2z + 22 + (-22) = 14 + (-22)$$

$$-2z = -8$$

$$z = 4, \text{Tim's marbles.}$$

Now substitute the value of z in equations (2) and (3), respectively, and solve. The results are:

$$y + z = 10 \Rightarrow y + 4 - 4 = 10 - 4$$

$$y = 6, \text{Jim's marbles.}$$

and

$$y + z = 12 \Rightarrow x + 4 - 4 = 12 - 4$$

$$x = 8, \text{Joe's marbles.}$$

Joe's marbles, 8, is the maximum number of marbles anyone can have.

20.   **(D)**   Since we do not know Emile's dollar volume during the week in question, we can assign this amount the value of x.

Now, Emile's total salary of $540 can be divided into two parts; one part is his flat salary of $240, and the other part is his salary from commissions, which amounts to $540 − $240 = $300. This part of his salary is equal to 12% of his dollar volume, x. Thus, 12% of x = $300. This means

$$(0.12)x = 300$$

$$x = 300/0.12 = \$2500.$$

Another way to attack this problem is to test each answer choice as follows:

(A)   (0.12) ($2800)   = $345.60 ≠ $300   (wrong)

(B)   (0.12) ($3600)   = $432 ≠ $300   (wrong)

(C)   (0.12) ($6400)   = $768 ≠ $300   (wrong)

(D)   (0.12) ($2500)   = $300   (correct)

(E)   (0.12) ($2000)   = $240 ≠ $300   (wrong)

21.   **(E)**   One way to attack this problem is to solve it algebraically.

Let x represent the number of packages weighing 2 kg each. Then $(150 - x)$ represents the number of packages weighing 1 kg each.

Therefore,

$$2x + 1(150 - x) = 264$$

$$2x + 150 - x = 264$$

$$x = 264 - 150$$

$$x = 114.$$

Thus, there are 114 packages weighing 2 kg each on the truck.

Another way to solve this problem is to test each of the answer choices (A), (B), (C), (D) and (E). Note that if, for example, the number of packages weighing 2 kg each is 36 (answer choice (A)), then the number of packages weighing 1 kg each will be $(150 - 36) = 114$. Testing the answer choices yields:

(A) $(36)(2) + (150 - 36)(1)$ $=$ $72 + 114 = 186$ (wrong)

(B) $(52)(2) + (150 - 52)(1)$ $=$ $104 + 98 = 202$ (wrong)

(C) $(88)(2) + (150 - 88)(1)$ $=$ $176 + 62 = 238$ (wrong)

(D) $(124)(2) + (150 - 124)(1)$ $=$ $248 + 26 = 274$ (wrong)

(E) $(114)(2) + (150 - 114)(1)$ $=$ $228 + 36 = 264$ (correct)

22.   **(C)**   Let x = amount of money that I have when I arrive at Casino Las Vegas. After the first game

$$x - \frac{1}{3}x = \frac{2}{3}x$$

After the second game

$$\frac{2}{3}x - \frac{1}{2}\left(\frac{2}{3}x\right) = \frac{1}{3}x$$

and at this moment I have $1000. Therefore

$$1000 = \frac{1}{3}x \quad x = 3000.$$

23.   **(E)**   This question asks about the time of travel. This requires the use of the formula

Distance = Rate × Time

One way to solve this problem is to create an algebraic equation. To do so, let t be the time, in hours, it takes the car to catch up with the postal truck, then the time of travel of the truck should be $(t + {}^{24}/_{60})$ hours. Note that 24 minutes = ${}^{24}/_{60}$ hours = 0.4 hours.

When the car catches up with the truck, the distance traveled by the truck in $(t + {}^{24}/_{60})$ hours at a rate of 40 mph will be the same as the distance traveled by the car at a rate of 50 mph for a period of t hours. Let d denotes that distance. Then for the

(i) Truck: d = Rate × Time

$$= 40\,(t + 0.4)$$

$$= 40t + 16$$

(ii) Car: d = Rate × Time

$$= (50) \times (t)$$

$$= 50t$$

Hence, $50t = 40t + 16$

$50t - 40t = 16$

$10t = 16$

$t = 1.6$

Thus, it takes the car 1.6 hours to catch up with the postal truck.

Another way to solve this problem is to test each of the answer choices given. Remember that if the time of travel of the car is t hours, then the time of travel of the truck is $(t + .4)$ hours, and the distance traveled by the car is the same distance traveled by the truck. Thus, testing the answer choices yields

Answer choice	Time of Travel (hours)		Rate of Travel (mph)		Distance Traveled (miles)		
	Car	Truck	Car	Truck	Car		Truck
(A)	2.6	3	50	40	130	≠	120
(B)	3.0	3.4	50	40	150	≠	136
(C)	2.0	2.4	50	40	100	≠	96
(D)	1.5	1.9	50	40	75	≠	95
(E)	1.6	2.0	50	40	80	=	80

24.   **(C)**

576 square feet × .20 garden for roses = 115.2 square feet

32.9 square feet for tomato patch + 115.2 square feet for roses
= 148.1 square feet

Answer choice (A) is incorrect because it shows

32.9 square feet × .20 = 6.58 square feet

and   576 – 6.58 = 569.42 square feet

Answer choice (B) is incorrect because it shows

576 square feet – 20 square feet – 32.9 square feet = 523.10 square feet

Answer choice (D) is incorrect because it shows

20 square feet + 32.9 square feet = 52.9 square feet

25.   **(B)**   Let x = the number of pencils the man had.

Then $x - \frac{2}{3}x = 7$

$$\frac{1}{3}x = 7$$

$$x = 21$$

Since $\frac{2}{3} \cdot 21 = 14$, he sold 14 pencils. Since $14 \cdot 20 = 280$, he collected $2.80.

26.   **(B)**   To see how many cubic feet there are in the basement, divide $975 by $3.75 and then multiply by 27 because there are 27 cubic feet in one cubic yard.

$$\frac{975}{3.75} = 260 \times 27 = 7020 \text{ cu. ft.}$$

Let x = depth of basement and using

$$LWH = 30(27)x = 7020$$

gives $810x = 7020$ so that $x = 8\frac{2}{3}$ ft.

27.   **(D)**   Let x = number of problems Stanley got right. Then $26 - x$ is the number he got wrong. Since neither owed the other money, the "break even" equation is

$$8x = 5(26) - x, \ 8x = 130 - 5x, \ 13x = 130$$

$$\therefore x = 10.$$

To check, $10(8) = 80$ and $16(5) = 80$.

28.　　**(A)**　Let x = share of the third; y = share of the second = 3 x; and z = share of the first =

$$4y = 4(3x) = 12x.$$

Then the first received \$1,210 more than the third gives the equation

$$12x = x + 1210 \text{ or } 11x = 1210.$$

Therefore $x = 110$ the share of the third so that the share of the first is $110 + 1210 = 1320$.

29.　　**(C)**　Let x = the number of dollars the company owed. Then

$$.25x + 800 = .30x, 800 = .05x, x = {}^{800}/_{.05} = 16,000.$$

Choices (A) and (B) come from the correct setup but a decimal point mistake in the division of 800 by .05. Choices (D) and (E) come from dividing 800 by .55, the sum of .25 and .30. Choice (D) does the division incorrectly.

30.　　**(A)**

Let x = amount at 8%

y = amount at 7% then

$x = 3y$

The interest equation is $.08x + .07y = 930$. Multiplying each term by 100 gives

$$8x + 7y = 93,000$$

and substituting $x = 3y$ in for x gives

$$24y + 7y = 93,000 \text{ or } 31y = 93,000,$$

then $y = 3000$ so $x = 9000$. Choices (B) and (C) come from the mistake of letting $y = 3x$ then the equation becomes $29x = 93000$ or $x = 3207$ (rounded to nearest dollar) and $y = 9621$ (also rounded). Choice (D) is the amount at 7%, which was not asked for.

31.　　**(C)**　If Cyndi invests \$$X$ in the certificate of deposit at 9% interest and \$$(2000 - X)$ in the passbook savings account at 5% interest, then

$$.09X + .05(2000 - X) = 148.$$

This is equivalent to

$$.04X + 100 = 148, \text{ or } .04X = 48,$$

which gives $X = 1200$.

32. **(A)**   The total of 12 test scores is 12(55) = 660. When the two highest and the two lowest test scores are dropped, the total of the remaining 8 test scores is 8(50) = 400. Hence the total of the 4 dropped scores is 660 − 400 = 260, and the average of scores dropped is 260/4 = 65.

33. **(B)**   If X is the original price, then the 50 percent markup price is (1.5)X. Since this price is marked down by 30%, the final price is

$$(.7)(1.5)X = 1.05X.$$

Therefore

$$1.05X = 3360, \text{ or, } X = 3360/1.05 = \$3200.$$

34. **(C)**   If Joel works X hours at $6.75 per hour, he earns \$(6.75)X. Therefore we want to find the smallest integer X such that

$$6.75X \geq 150, \text{ or,}$$

$$X \geq 150/6.75 = 150(4/27) = 200/9.$$

Thus X must be 23.

35. **(B)**   In one hour, Eva can wallpaper $\frac{1}{4}$ of the room and Kathy $\frac{1}{6}$ of the room. Therefore, working together they can wallpaper $\frac{1}{4} + \frac{1}{6} = \frac{5}{12}$ of the room in one hour. Since Kathy works on her own for one hour, she finishes $\frac{1}{6}$ of the room. The remaining $\frac{5}{6}$ of the room is wallpapered by Kathy and Eva in $(\frac{5}{6})/(\frac{5}{12}) = 2$ hours.

36. **(B)**   The solution involves finding the x-coordinate of the point of intersection of the lines

$$y = 34x + 51$$

and

$$y = 31x + 60.$$

Setting the equations equal to each other gives

$$34x + 51 = 31x + 60, 3x = 9, x = 3.$$

37. **(C)**   Since 155 = 5 • 31, each piece of bubble gum must cost 5¢, and Mary must have bought 31 pieces of bubble gum.

38. **(B)**   If b represents the birth of a boy and if g represents the birth of a girl, then the possible family birth sequences are

bbbb, bbbg, bbgb, bgbb, gbbb, bbgg, bgbg, bggb, gbbg, gbgb, ggbb,

bggg, gbgg, ggbg, gggb and *gggg.*

A family of three of one sex and one of the other sex is most likely.

39.   **(B)**

$$29^1/_2 \div {}^3/_4 = {}^{59}/_2 \cdot {}^4/_3$$
$$= 39^1/_3.$$

Thus, Mary had enough material to make 39 uniforms and enough material left over to "make" $^1/_3$ of a uniform. But $^1/_3 \cdot {}^3/_4 = {}^1/_4$, so she would have $^1/_4$ of a yard left over.

40.   **(E)**   The function is

$$f(x) = 10x + 85$$

and 2 miles $20 \cdot {}^1/_{10}$ or twenty $^1/_{10}$-miles so, there are 19 additional $^1/_{10}$-miles,

$$f(19) = 10(19) + 85 = 275.$$

The most common mistake is to evaluate

$$f(20) = 10(20) + 85 = 285$$

which is choice (C). Choice (D) comes from forgetting the 85¢.

41.   **(D)**   Let x = drink cup and y = pitcher, then

$$y = 6x \text{ and } 3y = 5x + 39,$$

substituting $y = 6x$ into this equation gives

$$18x = 5x + 39 \text{ or } 13x = 39, \text{ so that } x = 3.$$

42.   **(E)**   Let x = cost of gadget whose profit was 20% and let y = cost of other gadget. Then

$$x + .20x = 2.40 \text{ or } 1.20x = 2.40 \text{ and } x = 2.00$$

or her profit is 40¢. The other gadget:

$$y - .20y = 2.40 \text{ or } .8y = 2.40 \text{ and } y = 3.00$$

or her loss is 60¢. Therefore, her total loss is $60 - 40 = 20$¢. Choice (A) comes from $2.40(.2) = .48$ or 8¢.

43.   **(A)**   Let x = amount of wheat originally. Then $x - {}^1/_{10} x = 1$ bushel. Multiply each term by 10: $10x - x = 10$ or $9x = 10$ and $x = 1^1/_9$ bushels.

44.   **(C)**   If X is the number of freshmen at the college, then $(.24)X = 360$. Therefore,

$$X = 360/(.24) = 1500.$$

45. **(B)** Julie's portfolio of stocks on January 1 has a total market value of
$[100(10) + 100(12) + 100(18)] = \$4000$.

On December 31, she has 100 shares of *A*, 200 shares of *B*, and 150 shares of *C* with a market value of

$[100(12) + 200(6) + 150(16)] = \$4800$.

Therefore her return for the year was

$$\left(\frac{4800}{4000} - 1\right) \times 100 = 20\%.$$

46. **(C)** Let x = previous value.
$^3/_4 x = 10{,}500$, $x = 14{,}000$.

The value of the house after property increased by 150% is
$14{,}000 + (1.5)14{,}000 = 35{,}000$.

Taking $^7/_8$ of 35,000 is 30,625.
   Choice (A) comes from taking $^3/_4$ of 10,500, which is 7,875, then proceeding as above. Choice (B) comes from taking 14,000 times 1.5 and not adding another 14,000 to it. Choice (D) comes from not taking $^4/_3$ of 10,500 but just taking $10{,}500(1.5) + 10{,}500 = 26{,}250$ times $^7/_8 = 22{,}968.75$. Choice (E) comes from not taking $^7/_8$ of 35,000, in correct solution.

47. **(C)** Let x = speed of plane 5 years ago and y = speed of plane now. We know that $y = 2x$. Since the planes are flying the same distance, we use

$D = RT$

which gives the equation
   $xt = y(t - 1^1/_4)$ and $xt = 1500$, $t = {}^{1500}/_x$

so substituting the value of t in the equation, we have

$$x \cdot \frac{1500}{x} = 2x\left(\frac{1500}{x} - \frac{5}{4}\right) \text{ or } 1500 = 3000 - \frac{5}{2}x,$$

$3000 = 6000 - 5x$, $x = 600$ mph.

48. **(D)** This problem can be solved by creating an algebraic formula in one unknown variable, then solve it for the variable. To do so, let x be the number of tickets that were bought at the box office. Then the number of tickets that were purchased at the advance sale is $(1200 - x)$. Hence, we can set up the formula as follows:

$$5(1,200 - x) + 7x = 6,700$$

$$6,000 - 5x + 7x = 6,700$$

$$2x = 6,700 - 6,000$$

$$2x = 700$$

$$x = 350$$

Hence, the number of tickets that were bought at the box office is 350.

One can also solve this problem by testing each of the answer choices given. If, for example, the number of tickets that were bought at the box office at $7 each is 500, then the number of tickets that were bought at the advance sale at the rate of $5 each is $(1200 - 500) = 700$. In this case, the total amount of receipts should be $500(\$5) + 700(\$7)$. If the total amount of receipts is $6,700, then the answer choice with the answer 500 is correct. Thus,

(A) $(500)(\$7) + (1,200 - 500)(\$5) = 500(\$7) + (700)(\$5)$

$$= \$3,500 + \$3,500$$

$$= \$7,000$$

$$\neq \$6,700$$

(B) $(700)(\$7) + (1,200 - 700)(\$5) = 700(\$7) + (500)(\$5)$

$$= \$4,900 + \$3,500$$

$$= \$8400$$

$$\neq \$6,700$$

(C) $(600)(\$7) + (1,200 - 600)(\$5) = 600(\$7) + (600)(\$5)$

$$= \$4,200 + \$3,000$$

$$= \$7,200$$

$$\neq \$6,700$$

(D) $(350)(\$7) + (1,200 - 350) = 350(\$7) + (850)(\$5)$

$$= \$2,450 + \$4,250$$

$$= \$6,700$$

(E) $(200)(\$7) + (1,200 - 200)(\$5) = 200(\$7) + (1,000)(\$5)$

$$= \$1,400 + \$5,000$$

$$= \$6,400$$

$$\neq \$6,700$$

49. **(C)** In the 16 gallons of paint mixture, there are

$$(2/(6 + 2))16 = 4$$

gallons of green paint and $16 - 4 = 12$ gallons of white paint. Let X = number of gallons of green paint to be added to produce 40% green paint. Then,

$$(X + 4)/(16 + X) = .4, \text{ or } (X + 4) = .4(16 + X).$$

Therefore, $.6X = 2.4$, or $X = 4$.

50. **(E)** Let x = # oz. other metal. The percentage of gold in x is 0 so we get an equation:

$$56 + (0)x = .70(56 + x) \text{ or } 56 = .7(56 + x).$$

Therefore, $56 - 39.2 = .7x$ and $.7x = 16.8$ so that $x = 16.8/.7 = 24$ oz.

Choice (A) comes from $56(.70) = 39.2$.

Choice (B) comes from $56(.30) = 16.8$.

Choice (C) comes from $56 + x = .7(x = 56)$ or $56 + x = .7x + 39.2$ and $1.7x = 16.8$, $x = 9.8$.

Choice (D) comes from $1.7x = 95.2$ or $x = 56$.

WORD PROBLEMS REVIEW

One of the main problems students have in mathematics involves solving word problems. The secret to solving these problems is being able to convert words into numbers and variables in the form of an algebraic equation.

The easiest way to approach a word problem is to read the question and ask yourself what you are trying to find. This unknown quantity can be represented by a variable.

Next, determine how the variable relates to the other quantities in the problem. More than likely, these quantities can be explained in terms of the original variable. If not, a separate variable may have to be used to represent a quantity.

Using these variables and the relationships determined among them, an equation can be written. Solve for a particular variable and then plug this number in for each relationship that involves this variable in order to find any unknown quantities.

Lastly, reread the problem to be sure that you have answered the questions correctly and fully.

1. Algebraic

The following illustrates how to formulate an equation and solve the problem.

EXAMPLE

Find two consecutive odd integers whose sum is 36.

Let x = the first odd integer

Let $x + 2$ = the second odd integer

The sum of the two numbers is 36. Therefore,

$$x + (x + 2) = 36$$

Simplifying,

$$2x + 2 = 36$$

$$2x = 34$$

$$x = 17$$

Substituting 17 for x, we find the second odd integer = $(x + 2) = (17 + 2) = 19$. Therefore, we find that the two consecutive odd integers whose sum is 36 are 17 and 19 respectively.

Drill 1: Algebraic

1. The sum of two numbers is 41. One number is one less than twice the other. Find the larger of the two numbers.

(A) 13   (B) 14   (C) 21   (D) 27   (E) 41

2. The sum of two consecutive integers is 111. Three times the larger integer less two times the smaller integer is 58. Find the value of the smaller integer.

(A) 55   (B) 56   (C) 58   (D) 111   (E) 112

3. The difference between two integers is 12. The sum of the two integers is 2. Find both integers.

(A) 7 and 5   (B) 7 and − 5   (C) − 7 and 5

(D) 2 and 12   (E) − 2 and 12

2. Rate

One of the formulas you will use for rate problems will be:

Rate × Time = Distance

PROBLEM

> If a plane travels five hours from New York to California at a speed of 600 miles per hour, how many miles does the plane travel?

SOLUTION

Using the formula rate × time = distance, multiply 600 mph × 5 hours = 3000 miles.

The average rate at which an object travels can be solved by dividing the total distance traveled by the total amount of time.

PROBLEM

> On a 40-mile bicycle trip, Cathy rode half the distance at 20 mph and the other half at 10 mph. What was Cathy's average speed on the bike trip?

SOLUTION

First you need to break down the problem. On half of the trip, which would be 20 miles, Cathy rode 20 mph. Using the rate formula, $distance/_{rate}$ = time, you would compute,

$$\frac{20 \text{ miles}}{20 \text{ miles per hour}} = 1 \text{ hour}$$

to travel the first 20 miles. During the second 20 miles, Cathy traveled at 10 miles per hour, which would be

$$\frac{20 \text{ miles}}{10 \text{ miles per hour}} = 2 \text{ hours}$$

Thus, the average speed Cathy traveled would be $^{40}/_3 = 13.33$ miles per hour.

In solving for some rate problems you can use cross multiplication involving ratios to solve for x.

PROBLEM

> If 2 pairs of shoes cost $52, then what is the cost of 10 pairs of shoes at this rate?

SOLUTION

$$\frac{2}{52} = \frac{10}{x}, \, 2x = 52 \times 10, \, x = \frac{520}{2}, \, x = \$260.$$

Drill 2: Rate

1. Two towns are 420 miles apart. A car leaves the first town traveling toward the second town at 55 mph. At the same time, a second car leaves the other town and heads toward the first town at 65 mph. How long will it take for the two cars to meet?

    (A) 2 hr   (B) 3 hr   (C) 3.5 hr   (D) 4 hr   (E) 4.25 hr

2. A camper leaves the campsite walking due east at a rate of 3.5 mph. Another camper leaves the campsite at the same time but travels due west. In two hours the two campers will be 15 miles apart. What is the walking rate of the second camper?

    (A) 2.5 mph   (B) 3 mph   (C) 3.25 mph

    (D) 3.5 mph   (E) 4 mph

3. A bicycle racer covers a 75-mile training route to prepare for an upcoming race. If the racer could increase his speed by 5 mph, he could complete the same course in 3/4 of the time. Find his average rate of speed.

    (A) 15 mph   (B) 15.5 mph   (C) 16 mph

    (D) 18 mph   (E) 20 mph

3. Work

In work problems, one of the basic formulas is

$$\frac{1}{x} + \frac{1}{y} = \frac{1}{z}$$

where x and y represent the number of hours it takes two objects or people to complete the work and z is the total number of hours when both are working together.

PROBLEM

> Otis can seal and stamp 400 envelopes in 2 hours while Elizabeth seals and stamps 400 envelopes in 1 hour. In how many hours can Otis and Elizabeth, working together, complete a 400-piece mailing at these rates?

SOLUTION

$$\frac{1}{2} + \frac{1}{1} = \frac{1}{z}, \frac{1}{2} + \frac{2}{2} = \frac{3}{2}, \frac{3}{2} = \frac{1}{z}, \quad 3z = 2$$

$z = {}^2/_3$ of an hour or 40 minutes. Working together, Otis and Elizabeth can seal and stamp 400 envelopes in 40 minutes.

Drill 3: Work

1.   It takes Marty 3 hours to type the address labels for his club's newsletter. It only takes Pat $2^1/_4$ hours to type the same amount of labels. How long would it take them working together to complete the address labels?

(A) $^7/_9$ hr   (B) $1\,^2/_7$ hr   (C) $1\,^4/_5$ hour

(D) $2\,^5/_8$ hr   (E) $5\,^1/_4$ hr

2.   It takes Troy 3 hours to mow his family's large lawn. With his little brother's help, he can finish the job in only 2 hours. How long would it take the little brother to mow the entire lawn alone?

(A) 4 hr   (B) 5 hr   (C) 5.5 hr   (D) 6 hr   (E) 6.75 hr

3.   A tank can be filled by one inlet pipe in 15 minutes. It takes an outlet pipe 75 minutes to drain the tank. If the outlet pipe is left open by accident, how long would it take to fill the tank?

(A) 15.5 min   (B) 15.9 min   (C) 16.8 min

(D) 18.75 min   (E) 19.3 min

4. Mixture

Mixture problems present the combination of different products and ask you to solve for different parts of the mixture.

PROBLEM

> A chemist has an 18% solution and a 45% solution of a disinfectant. How many ounces of each should be used to make 12 ounces of a 36% solution?

Solution

Let x = Number of ounces from the 18% solution, and

y = Number of ounces from the 45% solution.

$$x + y = 12 \tag{1}$$

$$.18x + .45y = .36(12) \tag{2}$$

Note that .18 of the first solution is pure disinfectant and that .45 of the second solution is pure disinfectant. When the proper quantities are drawn from each mixture the result is 12 ounces of mixture which is .36 pure disinfectant.

The second equation cannot be solved with two unknowns. Therefore, write one variable in terms of the other and plug it into the second equation.

$$x = 12 - y \tag{1}$$

$$.18(12 - y) + .45y = .36(12) \tag{2}$$

Simplifying,

$$2.16 - .18y + .45y = 4.32$$

$$.27y = 4.32 - 2.16$$

$$.27y = 2.16$$

$$y = 8$$

Substituting for y in the first equation,

$$x + 8 = 12$$

$$x = 4$$

Therefore, 4 ounces of the first and 8 ounces of the second solution should be used.

PROBLEM

Clark pays $2.00 per pound for 3 pounds of peanut butter chocolates and then decides to buy 2 pounds of chocolate covered raisins at $2.50 per pound. If Clark mixes both together, what is the cost per pound of the mixture?

SOLUTION

The total mixture is 5 pounds and the total value of the chocolates is

$$3(\$2.00) + 2(\$2.50) = \$11.00$$

The price per pound of the chocolates is $\$11.00/_{5 \text{ pounds}}$ = $2.20.

Drill 4: Mixture

1. How many liters of a 20% alcohol solution must be added to 80 liters of a 50% alcohol solution to form a 45% solution?

(A) 4   (B) 8   (C) 16   (D) 20   (E) 32

2. How many kilograms of water must be evaporated from 50 kg of a 10% salt solution to obtain a 15% salt solution?

(A) 15   (B) 15.75   (C) 16   (D) 16.$\overline{66}$ (E) 16.75

3. How many pounds of coffee *A* at $3.00 a pound should be mixed with 2.5 pounds of coffee *B* at $4.20 a pound to form a mixture selling for $3.75 a pound?

(A) 1   (B) 1.5   (C) 1.75   (D) 2   (E) 2.25

5. Interest

If the problem calls for computing simple interest, the interest is computed on the principal alone. If the problem involves compounded interest, then the interest on the principal is taken into account in addition to the interest earned before.

PROBLEM

How much interest will Jerry pay on his loan of $400 for 61 days at 6% per year?

SOLUTION

Use the formula:

Interest = Principal × Rate × Time ($I = P \times R \times T$).

$400 × 6%/year × 61 days = $400 × .06 × $\frac{1}{6}$

= $400 × $\frac{1}{100}$ = $4.00.

Jerry will pay $4.00.

PROBLEM

Mr. Smith wishes to find out how much interest he will receive on $300 if the rate is 3% compounded annually for three years.

SOLUTION

Compound interest is interest computed on both the principal and the interest it has previously earned. The interest is added to the principal at the end of every year. The interest on the first year is found by multiplying the rate by the principal. Hence, the interest for the first year is

3% × $300 = .03 × $300 = $9.00.

The principal for the second year is now $309, the old principal ($300) plus the interest ($9). The interest for the second year is found by multiplying the rate by the new principal. Hence, the interest for the second year is

3% × $309 = .03 × $309 = $9.27.

The principal now becomes $309 + $9.27 = $318.27.

The interest for the third year is found using this new principal. It is

3% × $318.27 = .03 × $318.27 = $9.55.

At the end of the third year his principal is $318.27 + 9.55 = $327.82. To find how much interest was earned, we subtract his starting principal ($300) from his ending principal ($327.82), to obtain

$327.82 – $300.00 = $27.82.

Drill 5: Interest

1. A man invests $3,000, part in a 12-month certificate of deposit paying 8% and the rest in municipal bonds that pay 7% a year. If the yearly return from both investments is $220, how much was invested in bonds?

(A) $80   (B) $140   (C) $220   (D) $1000   (E) $2000

2. A sum of money was invested at 11% a year. Four times that amount was invested at 7.5%. How much was invested at 11% if the total annual return was $1,025?

(A) $112.75   (B) $1025   (C) $2500

(D) $3400   (E) $10,000

3. One bank pays 6.5% a year simple interest on a savings account while a credit union pays 7.2% a year. If you had $1500 to invest for three years, how much more would you earn by putting the money in the credit union?

(A) $10.50   (B) $31.50   (C) $97.50   (D) $108   (E) $1500

6. Discount

If the discount problem asks to find the final price after the discount, first multiply the original price by the percent of discount. Then subtract this result from the original price.

If the problem asks to find the original price when only the percent of discount and the discounted price are given, simply subtract the percent of discount from 100% and divide this percent into the sale price. This will give you the original price.

PROBLEM

A popular bookstore gives 10% discount to students. What does a student actually pay for a book costing $24.00?

SOLUTION

10% of $24 is $2.40 and hence the student pays $24 – $2.40 = $21.60.

PROBLEM

Eugene paid $100 for a business suit. The suit's price included a 25% discount. What was the original price of the suit?

SOLUTION

Let x represent the original price of the suit and take the complement of .25 (discount price) which is .75.

$.75x = \$100$ or $x = 133.33$

So, the original price of the suit is $133.33

Drill 6: Discount

1. A man bought a coat marked 20% off for $156. How much had the coat cost originally?

(A) $136   (B) $156   (C) $175   (D) $195   (E) $205

2. A woman saved $225 on the new sofa, which was on sale for 30% off. What was the original price of the sofa?

(A) $25   (B) $200   (C) $225   (D) $525   (E) $750

3. At an office supply store, customers are given a discount if they pay in cash. If a customer is given a discount of $9.66 on a total order of $276, what is the percent of discount?

(A) 2%   (B) 3.5%   (C) 4.5%   (D) 9.66%   (E) 276%

---

7. Profit

The formula used for the profit problems is

Profit = Revenue – Cost   or

Profit = Selling Price – Expenses.

PROBLEM

Four high school and college friends started a business of remodeling and selling old automobiles during the summer. For this purpose they paid $600 to rent an empty barn for the summer. They obtained the cars from a dealer for $250 each, and it takes an average of $410 in materials to remodel each car. How many automobiles must the students sell at $1,440 each to obtain a gross profit of $7,000?

SOLUTION

Total Revenues – Total Cost = Gross Profit

Revenue – [Variable Cost + Fixed Cost] = Gross Profit

Let a = number of cars

Revenue = $1,440$a$

Variable Cost = ($250 + 410)$a$

Fixed Cost = $600

The desired gross profit is $7,000.

Using the equation for the gross profit,

$$1,440a - [660a + 600] = 7,000$$

$$1,440a - 660a - 600 = 7,000$$

$$780a = 7,600$$

$$a = 9.74$$

or to the nearest car, $a = 10$.

PROBLEM

A glass vase sells for $25.00. The net profit is 7%, and the operating expenses are 39%. Find the gross profit on the vase.

SOLUTION

The gross profit is equal to the net profit plus the operating expenses. The net profit is 7% of the selling cost; thus it is equal to 7% × $25.00 = .07 × $25 = $1.75. The operating expenses are 39% of the selling price, thus equal to 39% × $25 = .39 × $25 = $9.75.

$$
\begin{array}{ll}
\$1.75 & \text{net profit} \\
+ \ \$9.75 & \text{operating expenses} \\
\hline
\$11.50 & \text{gross profit}
\end{array}
$$

Drill 7: Profit

1. An item cost a store owner $50. She marked it up 40% and advertised it at that price. How much profit did she make if she later sold it at 15% off the advertised price?

(A) $7.50   (B) $9.50   (C) $10.50   (D) $39.50   (E) $50

2. An antique dealer made a profit of 115% on the sale of an oak desk. If the desk cost her $200, how much profit did she make on the sale?

(A) $230   (B) $315   (C) $430   (D) $445   (E) $475

3. As a graduation gift, a young man was given 100 shares of stock worth $27.50 apiece. Within a year the price of the stock had risen by 8%. How much more were the stocks worth at the end of the first year than when they were given to the young man?

(A) $110   (B) $220   (C) $1220   (D) $2750   (E) $2970

8. Sets

A **set** is any collection of well defined objects called elements.

A set which contains only a finite number of elements is called a **finite set**; a set which contains an infinite number of elements is called an **infinite set**. Often the sets are designated by listing their elements. For example: $\{a, b, c, d\}$ is the set which contains elements a, b, c, and d. The set of positive integers is $\{1, 2, 3, 4, \ldots\}$.

Venn diagrams can represent sets. These diagrams are circles which help to visualize the relationship between members or objects of a set.

PROBLEM

In a certain Broadway show audition, it was asked of 30 performers if they knew how to either sing or dance, or both. If 20 auditioners said they could dance and 14 said they could sing, how many could sing and dance?

SOLUTION

Divide the 30 people into 3 sets: those who dance, those who sing and those who dance and sing. S is the number of people who both sing and dance. So $20 - S$ represents the number of people who dance and $14 - S$ represents the number of people who sing.

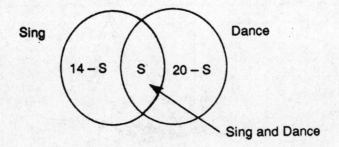

The equation for this problem is as follows:

$$(20 - S) + S + (14 - S) = 30.$$

$$20 + 14 - 30 = S$$

$$34 - 30 = S$$

$$4 = S$$

So, 4 people in the audition both sing and dance.

Drill 8: Sets

1. In a small school there are 147 sophomores. Of this number, 96 take both Biology and Technology I. Eighty-three take both Chemistry and Technology I. How many students are taking Technology I?

(A) 32   (B) 51   (C) 64   (D) 83   (E) 96

2. In a survey of 100 people, 73 owned only stocks. Six of the people invested in both stocks and bonds. How many people owned bonds only?

(A) 6   (B) 21   (C) 73   (D) 94   (E) 100

3. On a field trip, the teachers counted the orders for a snack and sent the information in with a few people. The orders were for 77 colas only and 39 fries only. If there were 133 orders, how many were for colas and fries?

(A) 17   (B) 56   (C) 77   (D) 95   (E) 150

9. Geometry

PROBLEM

A boy knows that his height is 6 ft. and his shadow is 4 ft. long. At the same time of day, a tree's shadow is 24 ft. long. How high is the tree? (See following figure.)

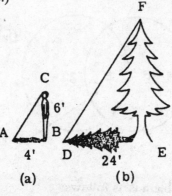

(a)   (b)

SOLUTION

Show that $\triangle ABC \approx \triangle DEF$, and then set up a proportion between the known sides AB and DE, and the sides BC and EF.

First, assume that both the boy and the tree are $\perp$ to the earth. Then, $\overline{BC} \perp \overline{BA}$ and $\overline{EF} \perp \overline{ED}$. Hence,

$\angle ABC \cong \angle DEF$.

Since it is the same time of day, the rays of light from the sun are incident on both the tree and the boy at the same angle, relative to the earth's surface. Therefore,

$\angle BAC \cong \angle EDF$.

We have shown, so far, that 2 pairs of corresponding angles are congruent. Since the sum of the angles of any triangle is 180°, the third pair of corresponding angles is congruent (i.e. $\angle ACB \cong \angle DFE$). By the Angle Angle Angle (A.A.A.) Theorem

$\angle ABC \approx \angle DEF$.

By definition of similarity,

$$\frac{FE}{CB} = \frac{ED}{BA}.$$

$CB = 6'$, $ED = 24'$, and $BA = 4'$. Therefore,

$$FE = (6')(24'/4') = 36'.$$

Drill 9: Geometry

1. $\triangle PQR$ is a scalene triangle. The measure of $\angle P$ is 8 more than twice the measure of $\angle R$. The measure of $\angle Q$ is two less than three times the measure of $\angle R$. Determine the measure of $\angle Q$.

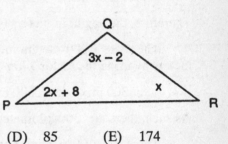

(A) 29   (B) 53   (C) 60   (D) 85   (E) 174

2. Angle A and angle B are supplementary. The measure of angle B is 5 more than four times the measure of angle A. Find the measure of angle B.

(A) 35   (B) 125   (C) 140   (D) 145   (E) 155

3. Triangle RUS is isosceles with base $\overline{SU}$. Each leg is 3 less than 5 times the length of the base. If the perimeter of the triangle is 60 cm, find the length of a leg.

(A) 6   (B) 12   (C) 27   (D) 30   (E) 33

10. Measurement

When measurement problems are presented in either metric or English units which involve conversion of units, the appropriate data will be given in the problem.

PROBLEM

> The Eiffel Tower is 984 feet high. Express this height in meters, in kilometers, in centimeters, and in millimeters.

SOLUTION

A meter is equivalent to 39.370 inches. In this problem, the height of the tower in feet must be converted to inches and then the inches can be converted to meters. There are 12 inches in 1 foot. Therefore, feet can be converted to inches by using the factor 12 inches/1 foot.

$$984 \text{ feet} \times 12 \text{ inches}/1 \text{ foot} = 11808$$

Once the height is found in inches, this can be converted to meters by the factor 1 meter/39.370 inches.

$$11808 \text{ inches} \times 1 \text{ meter}/39.370 \text{ inches} = 300 \text{ m.}$$

Therefore, the height in meters is 300 m.

There are 1,000 meters in one kilometer. Meters can be converted to kilometers by using the factor 1 km/1000 m.

$$300 \text{ m} \times 1 \text{ km}/1000 \text{ m} = .300 \text{ km.}$$

As such, there are .300 kilometers in 300 m.

There are 100 centimeters in 1 meter, thus meters can be converted to centimeters by multiplying by the factor 100 cm/1 m.

$$300 \text{ m} \times 100 \text{ cm}/1 \text{ m} = 300 \times 10^2 \text{ cm.}$$

There are 30,000 centimeters in 300 m.

There are 1,000 millimeters in 1 meter; therefore, meters can be converted to millimeters by the factor 1000 mm/1 m.

$$300 \text{ m} \times 1,000 \text{ mm}/1 \text{ m} = 300 \times 10^3 \text{ mm.}$$

There are 300,000 millimeters in 300 meters.

PROBLEM

> The unaided eye can perceive objects which have a diameter of 0.1 mm. What is the diameter in inches?

SOLUTION

From a standard table of conversion factors, one can find that 1 inch = 2.54 cm. Thus, cm can be converted to inches by multiplying by 1 inch/2.54 cm. Here, one is given the diameter in mm, which is .1 cm. Millimeters are converted to cm by multiplying the number of mm by .1 cm/1 mm. Solving for cm, you obtain:

0.1 mm × .1 cm/1 mm = .01 cm.

Solving for inches:

0.01 cm × $^{1\ \text{inch}}/_{2.54\ \text{cm}}$ = 3.94 × 10^{-3} inches.

Drill 10: Measurement

1.   A brick walkway measuring 3 feet by 11 feet is to be built. The bricks measure 4 inches by 6 inches. How many bricks will it take to complete the walkway?

(A)   132   (B)   198   (C)   330   (D)   1927   (E)   4752

2.   A wall to be papered is three times as long as it is wide. The total area to be covered is 192 ft². Wallpaper comes in rolls that are 2 feet wide by 8 feet long. How many rolls will it take to cover the wall?

(A)   8   (B)   12   (C)   16   (D)   24   (E)   32

3.   A bottle of medicine containing 2 kg is to be poured into smaller containers that hold 8 grams each. How many of these smaller containers can be filled from the 2 kg bottle?

(A)   0.5   (B)   1   (C)   5   (D)   50   (E)   250

11. Data Interpretation

Some of the problems test ability to apply information given in graphs and tables.

PROBLEM

In which year was the least number of bushels of wheat produced?(See Figure on following page.)

SOLUTION

By inspection of the graph, we find that the shortest bar representing wheat production is the one representing the wheat production for 1976. Thus, the least number of bushels of wheat was produced in 1976.

Number of bushels (to the nearest 5 bushels) of wheat and corn produced by farm RQS from 1975 – 1985

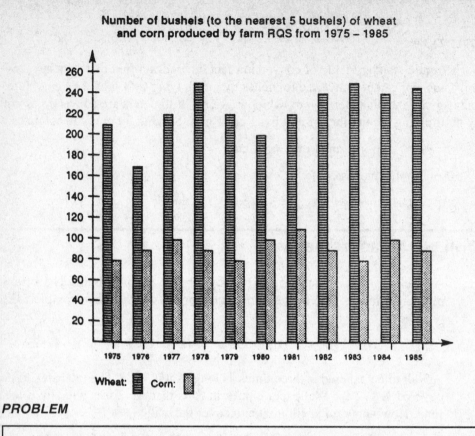

Wheat: ▓ Corn: ▓

PROBLEM

What was the ratio of wheat production in 1985 to that of 1975?

SOLUTION

From the graph representing wheat production, the number of bushels of wheat produced in 1975 is equal to 210 bushels. This number can be found by locating the bar on the graph representing wheat production in 1975 and then drawing a horizontal line from the top of that bar to the vertical axis. The point where this horizontal line meets the vertical axis represents the number of bushels of wheat produced in 1975. This number on the vertical axis is 210. Similarly, the graph indicates that the number of bushels of wheat produced in 1985 is equal to 245 bushels.

Thus, the ratio of wheat production in 1985 to that of 1975 is 245 to 210, which can be written as $245/210$. Simplifying this ratio to its simplest form yields

$$\frac{245}{210} = \frac{5 \cdot 7 \cdot 7}{2 \cdot 3 \cdot 5 \cdot 7} = \frac{7}{2 \cdot 3} = \frac{7}{6} \text{ or } 7:6$$

Drill 11: Data Interpretation

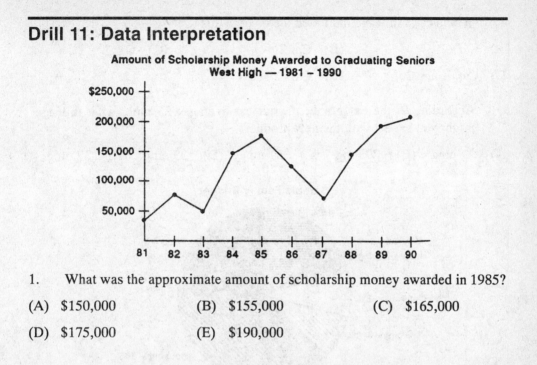

Amount of Scholarship Money Awarded to Graduating Seniors
West High — 1981 – 1990

1. What was the approximate amount of scholarship money awarded in 1985?

(A) $150,000   (B) $155,000   (C) $165,000

(D) $175,000   (E) $190,000

Changes In Average Mileage

2. By how much did the scholarship money increase between 1987 and 1988?

(A) $25,000   (B) $30,000   (C) $50,000

(D) $55,000   (E) $75,000

3. By how much did the mileage increase for Car 2 when the new product was used?

(A) 5 mpg   (B) 6 mpg   (C) 7 mpg   (D) 10 mpg   (E) 12 mpg

4.   Which car's mileage increased the most in this test?

(A)   Car 1   (B)   Car 2   (C)   Car 3

(D)   Cars 1 and 2   (E)   Cars 2 and 3

5.   According to the bar graph, if your car averages 25 mph, what mileage might you expect with the new product?

(A)   21 mpg   (B)   29 mpg   (C)   31 mpg   (D)   35 mpg   (E)   37 mpg

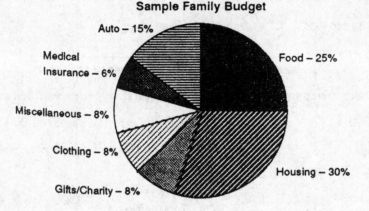

Sample Family Budget

Auto – 15%
Medical Insurance – 6%
Miscellaneous – 8%
Clothing – 8%
Gifts/Charity – 8%
Food – 25%
Housing – 30%

6.   Using the budget shown, a family with an income of $1500 a month would plan to spend what amount on housing?

(A) $300   (B) $375   (C) $450   (D) $490   (E) $520

7.   In this sample family budget, how does the amount spent on an automobile compare to the amount spent on housing?

(A) $1/3$ (B) $1/2$ (C) $2/3$ (D) $1 1/2$ (E)   2

8.   A family with a monthly income of $1240 spends $125 a month on clothing. By what amount do they exceed the sample budget?

(A) $1.00   (B) $5.20   (C) $10.00   (D) $25.80   (E) $31.75

CALORIE CHART — BREADS

Bread	Amount	Calories
French Bread	2 oz	140
Bran Bread	1 oz	95
Whole Wheat	1 oz	115
Oatmeal Bread	0.5 oz	55
Raisin Bread	1 oz	125

9.   One dieter eats two ounces of french bread. A second dieter eats two
      ounces of bran bread. The second dieter has consumed how many more
      calories than the first dieter?

(A)   40   (B)   45   (C)   50   (D)   55   (E)   65

10.   One ounce of whole wheat bread has how many more calories than an
      ounce of oatmeal bread?

(A)   5   (B)   15   (C)   60   (D)   75   (E)   125

WORD PROBLEM DRILLS

ANSWER KEY

Drill 1—Algebraic
1.	(D)	2.	(A)	3.	(B)

Drill 2—Rate
1.	(C)	2.	(E)	3.	(A)

Drill 3—Work
1.	(B)	2.	(D)	3.	(D)

Drill 4—Mixture
1.	(C)	2.	(D)	3.	(B)

Drill 5—Interest
1.	(E)	2.	(C)	3.	(B)

Drill 6—Discount
1.	(D)	2.	(E)	3.	(B)

Drill 7—Profit
1.	(B)	2.	(A)	3.	(B)

Drill 8—Sets
1.	(A)	2.	(B)	3.	(A)

Drill 9—Geometry
1.	(D)	2.	(D)	3.	(C)

Drill 10—Measurement
1.	(B)	2.	(B)	3.	(E)

Drill 11—Data Interpretation
1.	(D)	4.	(E)	7.	(B)	10.	(A)
2.	(E)	5.	(B)	8.	(D)		
3.	(B)	6.	(C)	9.	(C)		

DETAILED EXPLANATIONS
OF ANSWERS

Drill 1 – Algebraic

1. **(D)**   Let x and y represent the two numbers. Since their sum is 41, one equation is $x + y = 41$.

Then if one of the two numbers, say x, is one less than twice the other, the second equation can be written $x = 2y - 1$.

So the two equations are

$$x + y = 41$$

and $x = 2y - 1$.

Solve the first equation for x:

$$x = 41 - y.$$

Substitute $(41 - y)$ for x in the second equation:

$$41 - y = 2y - 1.$$

Solve for y:

$$41 - y = 2y - 1$$
$$42 - y = 2y$$
$$42 = 3y$$
$$14 = y$$

Then if $y = 14$ and $x + y = 41$, $x = 27$.

Check: $27 + 14 = 41$ $27 = 2(14) - 1$

$41 = 41$ $27 = 28 - 1$

$27 = 27$

2. **(A)**   If a represents the smaller integer, then its consecutive integer is represented by $a + 1$. So the first equation becomes

$$a + (a + 1) = 111.$$

Three times the larger integer is $3(a + 1)$ while two times the smaller integer is $2a$. "Less" indicates subtraction, so the second equation becomes

$$3(a + 1) - 2a = 58.$$

Solve this equation for a:

$$3(a + 1) - 2a = 58$$
$$3a + 3 - 2a = 58$$
$$a + 3 = 58$$
$$a = 55$$

Since a represented the smaller integer, we have answered the question.

Check: $55 + (55 + 1) = 111$ $3(55 + 1) - 2(55) = 58$
                      $55 + 56 = 111$ $168 - 110 = 58$
                          $111 = 111$ $58 = 58$

3.   **(B)**   Let X and Y represent two integers.

"Difference" indicates subtraction, so the first equation can be written as $X - Y = 12$.

"Sum" indicates addition, so the second equation is $X + Y = 2$.

Solve these two equations simultaneously by adding them together. (The Y's are eliminated.)

$$X - Y = 12$$
$$\underline{X + Y = 2}$$
$$2X \quad = 14$$
$$X \quad = 7$$

Then substitute X into either one of the two original equations to find Y.

$$7 - Y = 12$$
$$-Y = 5$$
$$Y = -5$$

Check: $7 - (-5) = 12$ $7 + (-5) = 2$
                    $7 + 5 = 12$ $2 = 2$
                      $12 = 12$

Drill 2 – Rate

1.   **(C)**   For a problem such as this, a diagram, a chart, and the formula $D = RT$ are necessary.

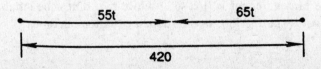

As the diagram indicates, this is an addition problem. The distance covered by the first car must be added to the distance covered by the second car to obtain the distance between the two cities.

The chart uses the three parts of the equation $D = RT$. Since the time is the unknown in this problem, it is represented by t.

Car	Rate	Time	Distance
1	55	t	$55t$
2	65	t	$65t$

Now add together the two distances from the chart and set them equal to the total distance.

$$55t + 65t = 420$$

Solve for t
$$120t = 420$$
$$t = 3.5\,\text{hr}$$

Check:
$$55(3.5) + 65(3.5) = 420$$
$$192.5 + 227.5 = 420$$
$$420 = 420$$

2. **(E)** A diagram, a chart, and the formula $D = RT$ are used to solve this problem.

Let x represent the walking rate of the second camper.

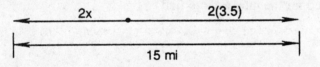

The diagram indicates that we need to add the two individual distances to equal the entire distance of 15 miles.

In the chart, we fill in the rate and the time for each camper. The formula $D = RT$ is used to find the value in the last column.

	Rate	Time	Distance
1st	3.5	2	7
2nd	x	2	$2x$

Now add the two individual distances together and set them equal to the total distance:

$$7 + 2x = 15$$

Solve for x:

$$7 + 2x = 15$$
$$2x = 8$$
$$x = 4\,\text{mph}$$

Check: 7 + 2(4) = 15

7 + 8 = 15

15 = 15

3.   **(A)**   Let r = the initial average rate and let t = the initial time. Then since $D = RT$, 75 = rt.

If the rate is increased by 5 mph, it would be written $r + 5$. If the time is re-duced by $^3/_4$, it becomes $^3/_4 t$. Using the same formula, $D = RT$, 75 = $(r + 5) (^3/_4 t)$.

Use the Distributive Property in the second equation.

75 = $(r + 5) (^3/_4 t)$

75 = $^3/_4 rt + ^{15}/_4 t$

Multiply both sides of the equation by 4.

300 = $3rt + 15rt$

Since the first equation is $rt = 75$, substitute 75 for the expression rt.

300 = $3(75) + 15t$

Solve for t.

300 = $225 + 15t$

75 = $15t$

5 = t

Since the problem asked for the rate, use t to find r.

$rt = 75$

$r(5) = 75$

$r = 15$ mph

Check: 15(5) = 75 $(15 + 5) * ^3/_4 (5) = 75$

75 = 75   20 * 3.75 = 75

75 = 75

Drill 3 – Work

1.   **(B)**   To solve this problem, decide on a convenient unit of time — here the hour is the easiest choice. Next, write the amount of work that each person can do in that amount of time (this is the *rate* of work):

In one hour, Louise can do $^1/_3$ of the job.

In one hour, Pat can do

$$\frac{1}{2\frac{1}{4}} \text{ or } \frac{1}{\frac{9}{4}} \text{ or } \frac{4}{9} \text{ of the job.}$$

The unknown in this problem is the amount of time it will take the two working together — call this unknown x. Then multiply each person's rate of work by the amount of time spent working together to obtain the portion of the total job each person did. Louise did $x/3$ and Pat did $4x/9$ of the work.

Next add each person's part of the work together and set it equal to 1; this represents one completed task. Now the equation looks like this:

$$\frac{x}{3} + \frac{4x}{9} = 1.$$

Find the Least Common Denominator (LCD) and multiply both sides of the equation by the LCD.

$$9\left(\frac{x}{3} + \frac{4x}{9}\right) = (1)(9)$$

$$3x + 4x = 9$$

$$7x = 9$$

$$x = \frac{9}{7} \text{ hr or } 1\frac{2}{7} \text{ hr}$$

2.   **(D)**   Let x represent the time it would take for the brother to mow the lawn alone.

Since Troy does the lawn in 3 hours, he does $1/3$ of the lawn in one hour. Since the brother takes x hours to mow the lawn, in one hour he does $1/x$ of the job. Both rates are multiplied by 2 since they complete the job in 2 hours.

	In One Hour	Time	Part of Job
Troy	$1/3$	2	$2/3$
Brother	$1/x$	2	$2/x$

Now add the part that each person does and set the sum equal to 1. The 1 represents one complete job.

$$2/3 + 2/x = 1$$

Multiply by the LCD of $3x$.

$$(2/3)(3x) + (2/x)(3x) = 1(3x)$$

$$2x + 6 = 3x$$

Solve for x.

$$6 = x$$

It would take the little brother 6 hours to mow the lawn by himself.

Check: $2/3 + 2/6 = 1$

$$2/3 + 1/3 = 1$$

$$1 = 1$$

3. **(D)** Let x represent the time to fill the tank.

Since it takes 15 minutes for the inlet pipe to fill the tank, in one minute it can fill $^1/_{15}$ of the tank. Since the outlet pipe drains the tank in 75 minutes, in one minute it can drain $^1/_{75}$ of the tank. The amount done in one minute is multiplied by the time to get the part of the job done in x minutes.

	In One Minute	Time	Part of Job
Inlet	$^1/_{15}$	x	$^x/_{15}$
Outlet	$^1/_{75}$	x	$^x/_{75}$

In setting up the equation, the part of the job done by the outlet pipe must be *subtracted* from that part done by the inlet pipe. The difference is set equal to one to represent one completed job.

The equation is

$$\frac{x}{15} - \frac{x}{75} = 1$$

Multiply by the LCD, 75.

$$(75)\frac{x}{15} - (75)\frac{x}{75} = (75)1$$
$$5x - x = 75$$
$$4x = 75$$
$$x = 18\frac{3}{4} \text{ minutes}$$

Check: $\dfrac{18.75}{15} - \dfrac{18.75}{75} = 1$

$$1.25 - 0.25 = 1$$
$$1 = 1$$

Drill 4 – Mixture

1. **(C)** For each solution, fill in the chart with the amount of the solution, the percent of alcohol it contains, and the amount of alcohol it contains.

Solution	Amount of Solution	% of Alcohol	Amount of Alcohol
1st	x	.20	$.20x$
2nd	80	.50	$.50(80)$
mix	$(x + 80)$	.45	$.45(x + 80)$

Since we don't know how much of the first solution there is, the amount of the first solution is represented by x.

Add the first two amounts of alcohol together and set the sum equal to the amount of alcohol in the mixture. Solve the equation for x.

$$.20x + .50(80) = .45(x + 80)$$
$$.20x + 40 = .45x + 36$$
$$4 = .25x$$
$$x = 16$$

So 16 liters of the 20% alcohol solution must be added to the 50% solution.

Check: $\quad .20(16) + .50(80) = .45(16 + 80)$
$$3.2 + 40 = .45\,(96)$$
$$43.2 = 43.2$$

2.   **(D)**   Fill in the chart with the amount of each solution, the percent of salt each solution is, and the amount of salt contained in each solution. Let x represent the amount of water to be evaporated.

Solution	Amount	%	Amount of Salt
Original	50	0.10	0.10(50)
Water	x	0	0
New Sol.	$(50 - x)$	0.15	$0.15(50 - x)$

The amount of salt in the original solution less the amount of salt in the water evaporated (which is 0) equals the amount of salt in the new solution.

$$0.10(50) - 0 = 0.15(50 - x)$$

Solve for x.

$$5 - 0 = 7.5 - 0.15x$$
$$-2.5 = -0.15x$$
$$16^2/_3 = x$$
$$16.\overline{66} = x$$

Sixteen and two-thirds kilograms of water must be evaporated from the original solution.

Check: $\quad 5 = 7.5 - 0.15(16^2/_3)$
$$5 = 7.5 - {}^{15}/_{100} * {}^{50}/_3$$
$$5 = 7.5 - 2.5$$
$$5 = 5$$

3.　**(B)**　Fill the chart in with the amount of each coffee, the price per pound of each coffee, and the total price.

Since the amount of coffee A is the unknown, call it x.

Coffee	Amount	Price/lb	Total Price
A	x	3.00	$3x$
B	2.5	4.20	2.5(4.2)
Mix	$(x + 2.5)$	3.75	$3.75(x + 2.5)$

Add the total prices of the two coffees together and set the sum equal to the total price of the mixture. Solve for x.

$$3x + 2.5(4.2) = (2.5 + x)(3.75)$$
$$3x + 10.50 = 9.375 + 3.75x$$
$$1.125 = 0.75x$$
$$1.5 \text{ lb} = x$$

The amount of coffee A to be added to the mixture is 1.5 lb.

Check:　$3(1.5) + 2.5(4.2) = (2.5 + 1.5)(3.75)$

$$4.5 + 10.5 = 4(3.75)$$
$$15 = 15$$

Drill 5 – Interest

1.　**(E)**　Let x = the amount invested at 8%. Then, since the total amount is $3,000, the remaining part is $(3000 - x)$.

Multiply the amount invested by the % of interest and add these two amounts together to equal the total interest.

$$0.08x + 0.07(3000 - x) = 220$$
$$0.08x + 210 - 0.07x = 220$$
$$0.01x = 10$$
$$x = 1000$$
$$3000 - x = 2000$$

The amount invested in Bonds is $2000.

Check:　$0.08(1000) + 0.07(2000) = 220$

$$80 + 140 = 220$$
$$220 = 220$$

2.   **(C)**   Let x = the amount invested at 11%, then $4x$ = the amount invested at 7.5%.

Multiply the amount invested by the interest rate to determine the individual interest. Add these two individual interests together and set the sum equal to the total interest.

$$0.11x + 0.075(4x) = \$1025$$
$$0.11x + 0.3x = 1025$$
$$0.41x = 1025$$
$$x = \$2500$$

$2500 was invested at 11%.

Check: $0.11(2500) + 0.075(4 * 2500) = 1025$
$$275 + 750 = 1025$$
$$1025 = 1025$$

3.   **(B)**   Use the simple interest formula, $I = PRT$, to find the interest earned on each account.

Bank: $I = \$1500 * 0.065 * 3 = \$292.50$

Credit Union: $I = \$1500 * 0.072 * 3 = \$324$

Subtract the amounts of interest to see how much more you would earn by keeping the money in the credit union.

$$\$324 - \$292.50 = \$31.50$$

Drill 6 – Discount

1.   **(D)**   Let x be the original price of the coat.

The original price minus 20% of the original price equals $156.

Or, $x - 0.20(x) = 156$

Or, $0.80(x) = 156$

so $x = 156/0.80 = 195$

The coat originally cost $195.

Check: $195 - 0.20(195) = 156$
$$195 - 39 = 156$$
$$156 = 156$$

2.   **(E)**   If x = the original price of the sofa, then $0.30x$ = the amount saved, which was $225.

So, $0.30x = 225$.

Then $x = 225/0.30 = \$750$

The original price of the sofa was $750.

Check: $0.30(750) = 225$

$225 = 225$

3.   **(B)**   A good technique to use in this problem is the formula

$$\frac{\text{Percentage}}{\text{Base}} = \frac{\text{Rate}}{100}$$

In this problem you are asked for the percent of discount, which is the same as the rate — call it r.

The percentage is $9.66 and the base, or total amount, is $276.

The equation becomes

$$\frac{9.66}{276} = \frac{r}{100}.$$

Use cross products to solve.

$9.66(100) = 276r$ so $r = 966/276 = 3.5$.

The percent of discount is 3.5%.

Drill 7 – Profit

1.   **(B)**   The profit is the sale price less the initial cost. The initial cost was $50. The sale price is 15% off the advertised price.

The advertised price is marked up 40% over the initial price — or $50 + 0.40 ($50). This advertised price is $70.

Then the sale price is the advertised price less 15% of the advertised price, or $70 – 0.15(70)$, or $59.50.

Finally, the profit is $59.50 – 50 = \$9.50$.

2.   **(A)**   The profit is 115% of the initial cost of the desk.

$P = 1.15(\$200) = \$230$.

3.   **(B)**   The profit on the stocks is the new value less the original value.

Original value = $\$27.50 * 100 = \$2750$

New value = 2750 + 0.08(2750) = $2970

Profit = $2970 − $2750 = $220.

Drill 8 − Sets

1.   **(A)**   Draw two overlapping circles to represent the numbers of people in each group. If 96 take Biology and Tech. I and 83 take Chemistry and Tech. I, this gives a total of 179. But there are only 147 students in all, so subtract to find the number in Tech. I.

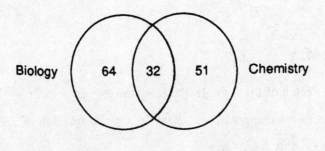

179 − 147 = 32

2.   **(B)**   Draw two overlapping circles and let one represent stocks and the other represent bonds.

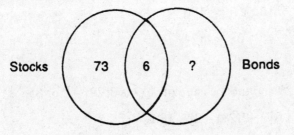

If 73 only own stocks and 6 own stocks and bonds, that leaves the remainder of the 100 people to own bonds only.

100 − (73 + 6) = 21.

Twenty-one people own bonds only.

3.   **(A)**   Draw two overlapping circles to represent the orders − one for fries and the other for colas. The part of the cola circle outside the overlapping part represents 77 people. The part of the fries circle outside the overlapping part represents the 39 people ordering the fries only.

Add the two parts together and subtract the sum from 133 to get the number in the overlapping part.

$$133 - (77 + 39) = 17.$$

There were 17 orders for both fries and cola.

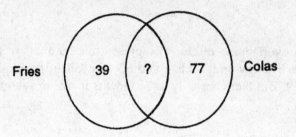

Drill 9: Geometry

1. **(D)** Draw a sketch of the triangle and label the angles.

    Two of the angles are compared to $\angle R$, so let x = the measure of $\angle R$. Then
    $$\angle P = 2x + 8 \text{ and } \angle Q = 3x - 2.$$

The sum of the measures of the angles of a triangle is 180, so add the measures of all three angles and this will equal 180.

$$x + (2x + 8) + (3x - 2) = 180$$
$$6x + 6 = 180$$
$$6x = 174$$
$$x = 29$$

The measure of $\angle R$ is 29 and the measure of $\angle Q$ is $3(29) - 2$ or 85.

Check: $29 + [2(29) + 8] + [3(29) - 2] = 180$
$$29 + 66 + 85 = 180$$
$$180 = 180$$

2. **(D)** Let A = the measure of angle A and let B = the measure of angle B. Since the two angles are supplementary, one equation is
    $$A + B = 180.$$

Since B is 5 more than four times the measure of angle A, either subtract 5 from the measure of angle B or add 5 to four times the measure of angle A. The equation becomes

$$B = 4A + 5.$$

Now substitute the value of B into the first equation to get

$$A + (4A + 5) = 180.$$

Solve the equation for A:

$$5A + 5 = 180$$
$$5A = 175$$
$$A = 35$$

Then $B = 4(35) + 5 = 145$.

Check: $35 + 145 = 180$ $145 = 4(35) + 5$
         $180 = 180$ $145 = 145$

3.   **(C)**   Draw an isosceles triangle and label each side. Let the length of the base be x. Then each leg is five times the base less 3, or $5x - 3$.

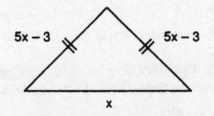

The perimeter is the sum of the sides, so the equation becomes

$$x + (5x - 3) + (5x - 3) = 60.$$

Solve for x:

$$11x - 6 = 60$$
$$11x = 66$$
$$x = 6$$

and $5(6) - 3 = 27$

The length of each leg is 27.

Check: $6 + 27 + 27 = 60$
         $60 = 60$

Drill 10 – Measurement

1.   **(B)**   Convert the measurements of the walkway to inches:

$$3 * 12 = 36 \text{ inches and } 11 * 12 = 132 \text{ inches.}$$

The area to be covered is 36 in $*132$ in $= 4752$ in^2.

Each brick has an area of 4 in $*$ 6 in $= 24$ in^2.

Divide the area of the brick into the area to be covered to determine how many bricks are needed:

$$4752 \text{ in}^2 \div 24 \text{ in}^2 = 198.$$

There are 198 bricks needed to cover the walkway.

2. **(B)** Let x = the width of the wall.

The length of the wall is then $3x$.

The area of the wall is the length multiplied by the width, or

$$x * 3x = 192.$$

So, $3x^2 = 192$.

Then $x^2 = 64$, so $x = 8$ ft.

The width of the wall is $3 * 8 = 24$ ft.

If a roll of paper is 2 feet wide, it will take 12 rolls to cover the wall.

3. **(E)** First change 2 kg into grams by multiplying by 1000 (1 kg = 1000 g). Then divide by 8 to determine the number of smaller containers that can be filled.

$$(2 * 1000) \div 8 = 250.$$

Two hundred and fifty smaller bottles can be filled.

GLOSSARY: WORD PROBLEMS

Annual

Once a year.

Balance

The amount of money in an account (this may change over time if interest is paid).

Biannual

Twice a year.

Compound Interest

Interest that applies to both principal and previously earned interest.

Consecutive

In a row, or next (e.g., 4, 5, and 6 are consecutive integers).

Difference

The result of subtracting one number from another

Discount Problems

Problems in which there are an original price, a discount rate, and a sales price. Two of these quantities are given, and the third must be solved for.

Dividend

The amount of interest paid.

Finite

Not infinite, or equal to a real number.

Finite Set

A set with a finite number of elements. A finite set cannot be put into a one-to-one correspondence with any of its proper subsets.

Infinite

Exceeding every real number.

Infinite Set

A set with an infinite number of elements. An infinite set can be put into a one-to-one correspondence with one of its proper subsets. For example, the integers can be put into a one-to-one correspondence with the even integers by matching the integer a to the even integer $2a$. Thus the set of integers is infinite.

Interest Problems

Problems in which principal is invested for a period of time at a certain interest rate (either simple or compound). Typically, one is asked to find the interest rate, the duration of the investment, the initial principal, or the final balance.

Intersection

The set consisting of all elements in all the sets under consideration.

Mixture Problems

Problems in which two or more mixtures are combined in various proportions, with each mixture containing different amounts of a key ingredient. Typically, one is asked to find either how much of one mixture is added, or what proportion a mixture contains of the key ingredient.

One-to-One Correspondence

A mapping from one set to another in which each element of one set is matched with exactly one from the other set.

Principal

The amount of money initially invested.

Product

The result of multiplying two or more numbers together.

Profit

Revenue in excess of cost expense, or selling price in excess of expense.

Proper Subset

A subset of a set, which does not equal that set.

Quarterly

Four times a year.

Quotient

The result of division.

Semiannual

Twice a year.

Set

A collection of members or elements.

Simple Interest

Interest that applies to principal but not to previously earned interest.

Subset

A collection of elements drawn from a specified set (i.e., each element in the subset is also in the original set).

Sum

The result of adding two or more numbers together.

Union

> The set consisting of all the elements belonging to at least one of the sets under consideration.

Venn Diagram

> A visual aid that helps to illustrate various sets, as well as their unions and intersections.

Work Problems

> Problems in which two or more people work on a common task at varying rates. Typically, one is asked to find how long it will take to complete the task.

CHAPTER 7

Quantitative Ability

➤ Quantitative Ability Review
➤ Practice Test

QUANTITATIVE ABILITY PRACTICE TEST

1. Ⓐ Ⓑ Ⓒ Ⓓ Ⓔ
2. Ⓐ Ⓑ Ⓒ Ⓓ Ⓔ
3. Ⓐ Ⓑ Ⓒ Ⓓ Ⓔ
4. Ⓐ Ⓑ Ⓒ Ⓓ Ⓔ
5. Ⓐ Ⓑ Ⓒ Ⓓ Ⓔ
6. Ⓐ Ⓑ Ⓒ Ⓓ Ⓔ
7. Ⓐ Ⓑ Ⓒ Ⓓ Ⓔ
8. Ⓐ Ⓑ Ⓒ Ⓓ Ⓔ
9. Ⓐ Ⓑ Ⓒ Ⓓ Ⓔ
10. Ⓐ Ⓑ Ⓒ Ⓓ Ⓔ
11. Ⓐ Ⓑ Ⓒ Ⓓ Ⓔ
12. Ⓐ Ⓑ Ⓒ Ⓓ Ⓔ
13. Ⓐ Ⓑ Ⓒ Ⓓ Ⓔ
14. Ⓐ Ⓑ Ⓒ Ⓓ Ⓔ
15. Ⓐ Ⓑ Ⓒ Ⓓ Ⓔ
16. Ⓐ Ⓑ Ⓒ Ⓓ Ⓔ
17. Ⓐ Ⓑ Ⓒ Ⓓ Ⓔ
18. Ⓐ Ⓑ Ⓒ Ⓓ Ⓔ
19. Ⓐ Ⓑ Ⓒ Ⓓ Ⓔ
20. Ⓐ Ⓑ Ⓒ Ⓓ Ⓔ
21. Ⓐ Ⓑ Ⓒ Ⓓ Ⓔ
22. Ⓐ Ⓑ Ⓒ Ⓓ Ⓔ
23. Ⓐ Ⓑ Ⓒ Ⓓ Ⓔ
24. Ⓐ Ⓑ Ⓒ Ⓓ Ⓔ
25. Ⓐ Ⓑ Ⓒ Ⓓ Ⓔ

QUANTITATIVE ABILITY

DIRECTIONS: Read the following tips, techniques, and examples, and take the diagnostic test.

Study this chapter for the following tests:
PSAT, SAT I, GRE

Quantitative Ability questions include quantitative comparison, discrete quantitative, and data interpretation skills. Quantitative Ability measures basic mathematical ability, quantitative reasoning, problem solving, and understanding of mathematical concepts. These questions require a review of basic arithmetic, algebra, geometry, and familiarity with word problems.

The following material introduces the types of questions you may be asked in the section.

QUANTITATIVE COMPARISON

The quantitative comparison questions challenge ability to determine accurately and quickly the relative sizes of two quantities. It also measures the ability to see whether enough information is given in order to pick a correct choice.

The directions in this section read as follows:

Numbers: All numbers are real numbers.

Figures: Position of points, angles, regions, etc. are assumed to be in the order shown and angle measures are assumed to be positive.

Lines: Assume that lines shown as straight are indeed straight.

Directions: Each of the following given set of quantities is placed into either column A or B. Compare the two quantities to decide whether:

A.   the quantity in Column A is greater

B.   the quantity in Column B is greater

C.   the two quantities are equal

D.   the relationship cannot be determined from the information given

---

Note: Do not choose (E) since there are only four choices.

Common Information: Information which relates to one or both given quantities is centered above the two columns. A symbol which appears in both columns will indicate the same item in Column A and Column B.

EXAMPLES

Column A	Column B

The length of a ruler is *"L"*. This value is increased by 10%, and then decreased by 10%.

1. L final length

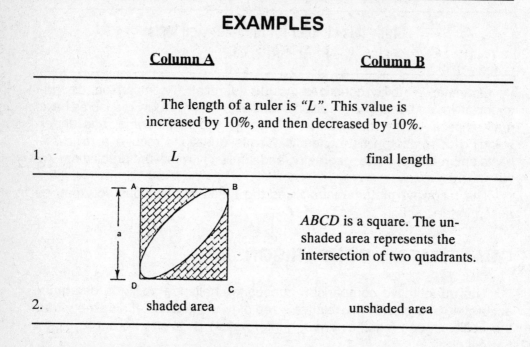

ABCD is a square. The unshaded area represents the intersection of two quadrants.

2. shaded area   unshaded area

Suggested Strategies:

• Memorize and understand the directions since they present abundant information. You will be able to save more time to work on the problems instead of spending time reading the directions.

• It is better to simplify both given quantities as little as possible to come to a conclusion rather than extensively work out the problem. This will save time and still will allow you to arrive at the correct answer.

• The answer can be reduced to three choices [(A), (B), or (C)] if both quantities being compared present no variables. If this is the case, the answer can never be (D), which states the relationship **cannot be determined from the information given.**

• If it is established that (A) is greater when considering certain numbers but (B) is greater when considering other certain numbers, then choose (D) immediately.

- If it is established that (A) is greater when considering certain numbers, then you can rule out choices (B) and (C) immediately.

- If it is established that (B) is greater when considering certain numbers, then you can rule out choices (A) and (C) immediately.

EXPLANATIONS

1.   **(A)**   The original length = "L". When the ruler increases by 10%, the length will be

$$L + 10\% \text{ of } L = L + (10/100)L = 1.1\,L$$

Then the ruler is decreased by 10%:

$$1.1L - 10\% \text{ of } 1.1L = 1.1L - (10/100)1.1L = .99L$$

Note: In the second part, the 10% refers to $1.1L$. Therefore, the final length is $.99L$ and the answer is (A) because $L > .99L$.

2.   **(B)**   First, evaluate the shaded area with the following procedure:

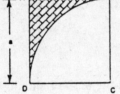

The half-shaded area can be expressed by

half-shaded area = (Sq. area – Quadrant area)

half-shaded area = $a^2 - \pi\,a^2/4 = a^2(1 - \pi/4)$

because the quadrant represents one-fourth of the area of a circle with the radius a. Therefore, the shaded area in the problem will be

shaded area = $2a^2\,(1 - \pi/4) \approx .43a^2$

The unshaded area can be expressed by

unshaded area = (Sq. area – Shaded area)

unshaded area = $a^2 - 2a^2(1 - \pi/4)$

unshaded area = $a^2(\pi/2 - 1) \approx .57a^2$

Therefore, the unshaded area > the shaded area. The answer is (B).

DISCRETE QUANTITATIVE

Discrete Quantity questions test the ability to apply given information in an abstract situation in order to solve a problem.

> **Directions:** For the following questions, select the best answer choice to the given question.

EXAMPLES

1. Which of the following has the smallest value?

   (A) $\frac{1}{0.2}$ (B) $\frac{0.1}{2}$ (C) $\frac{0.2}{1}$

   (D) $\frac{0.2}{0.1}$ (E) $\frac{2}{0.1}$

2. A square is inscribed in a circle of area 18π. What is the length of a side of the square?

   (A) 6   (B) 3   (C) $3\sqrt{2}$

   (D) $6\sqrt{2}$ (E) Cannot be determined

Suggested Strategies:

* Determine first what form the answer should be put in looking at the forms in the multiple choices.

* If the question requires an approximation, get an idea of the degree of approximation by scanning the multiple choices.

EXPLANATIONS

1. **(B)** Note that

   $\dfrac{.1}{2} = \dfrac{.1 \times 10}{2 \times 10} = \dfrac{1}{20}$ for Response (B). For choice (A),

   $\dfrac{1}{.2} = \dfrac{1 \times 10}{.2 \times 10} = \dfrac{10}{2} = 5$ which is larger than $\dfrac{1}{20}$. For choice (C),

   $\dfrac{.2}{1} = \dfrac{.2 \times 10}{1 \times 10} = \dfrac{2}{10} = \dfrac{1}{5}$ which is larger than $\dfrac{1}{20}$. For choice (D),

$\dfrac{.2}{.1} = \dfrac{.2 \times 10}{.1 \times 10} = \dfrac{2}{1} = 2$ which is larger than $\dfrac{1}{20}$. For choice (E),

$\dfrac{2}{.1} = \dfrac{2 \times 10}{.1 \times 10} = \dfrac{20}{1} = 20$ which is larger than $\dfrac{1}{20}$.

2. **(A)** The formula for the area of a circle is $A = \pi r^2$. Since the area of the square is 18π, then it is true that

$$\pi r^2 = 18\pi \quad \text{or} \quad r^2 = 18 \quad \text{or} \quad r = \sqrt{18} = 3\sqrt{2}.$$

Then, the diameter of the circle is

$$2r = 2(3\sqrt{2}) = 6\sqrt{2}.$$

Using the Pythagorean Theorem:

$$x^2 + x^2 = (6\sqrt{2})^2$$

$$2x^2 = 36(2); \ x^2 = 36$$

$x = 6$ is the length of the side of the square.

DATA INTERPRETATION

Data interpretation questions test the ability to read graphs and tables and apply information given in order to come to a decision. The questions are based upon graphs or tables. Most of the graphs presented are grid graphs, pie charts, tables, and bar graphs.

> **Directions:** The following questions refer to the chart and information below. Select the best answer choice to the given question.

EXAMPLES

Table of Weight Distribution of a 70,000–Gram Man
(Weights of some organs given)

Organ	Weight in Grams	Organ	Weight in Grams
Skeleton	10,000	Muscles	30,000
Blood	5,000	Intestinal tract	2,000
Liver	1,700	Lungs	1,000
Brain	1,500		

1. If 40 percent of the weight of the blood is made up of cells, what percent (to the nearest tenth) of the total body weight is made up of blood cells?

    (A) 7.1   (B) 3.6   (C) 1.4

    (D) 2.8   (E) 9.9

2. What expression represents the total body weight if the weight of the skeleton is represented by S grams?

    (A) $7S$ (B) $70000S$ (C) $60S$

    (D) $S + 6$ (E) Cannot be determined

Suggested Strategies

*   Try not to spend too much time understanding the data. Become more familiar with the data as you read and answer the questions.

*   It is more efficient to estimate rather than to compute the average.

*   When a question seems too involved, it is helpful to break it down into parts.

*   Avoid figuring large computations by estimating products and quotients.

*   Become familiar with the different types of charts discussed above.

EXPLANATIONS

1. **(D)** Since 40% of the weight of blood is made up of cells, then the weight of the cells is 0.4 times 5000 grams or 2000 grams. So, to find the percent of the total body weight that is made up of blood cells, form the following ratio and change the result to percent.

$$\frac{2,000}{70,000} = \frac{1}{35} = .028 = 2.8\%$$

2. **(A)** To find the solution one needs to set up a proportion. Thus, let x denote the total body weight in grams and S denote the weight of the skeleton. Then, the following proportion can be formed.

$$\frac{\text{weight of skeleton}}{\text{total body weight}} = \frac{10,000 \text{ grams}}{70,000 \text{ grams}} = \frac{S}{x}$$

QUANTITATIVE ABILITY
PRACTICE TEST

NUMBERS: All numbers are real numbers.

FIGURES: Position of points, angles, regions, etc. are assumed to be in the order shown and angle measures are assumed to be positive.

LINES: Assume that lines shown as straight are indeed straight.

DIRECTIONS: Each of the following given set of quantities is placed into either column A or B. Compare the two quantities to decide whether:

(A) the quantity in Column A is greater

(B) the quantity in Column B is greater

(C) the two quantities are equal

(D) the relationship cannot be determined from the information given.

NOTE: Do not choose (E) since there are only four choices.

COMMON INFORMATION: Information which relates to one or both given quantities is centered in the two columns. A symbol which appears in both columns will indicate the same item in Column A and Column B.

Column A	**Column B**
1. $\frac{1}{5}$ of 0.2% of $1000	$(\frac{1}{5})$% of 0.2 of $1000

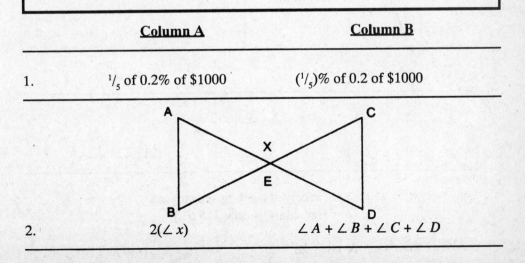

2. $2(\angle x)$	$\angle A + \angle B + \angle C + \angle D$

Column A	**Column B**

$w : x = y : x$ and z are not zero

3.	$w + x$	$y + z$

$$w : x = y : z$$
$$x \neq 0, \quad z \neq 0$$

4.	$wz - xy$	0

		Area of triangle plus area of square = 125 and perimeter of square is 40
5.	Twice the length of line segment *BD*	The shortest distance from point *A* to line segment *DE*

6.	angle 5	$k \parallel m$ angle 2 = 60 degrees 60 degrees

$W = 4, X = 3,$ and $Y = -2$

7.	$(2WY)^2$	$(2Y)^2 (4X)$

Gail received a 7% raise last year.
Her salary is now $15,515.

8.	Gail's salary last year	$14,000

Column A	Column B

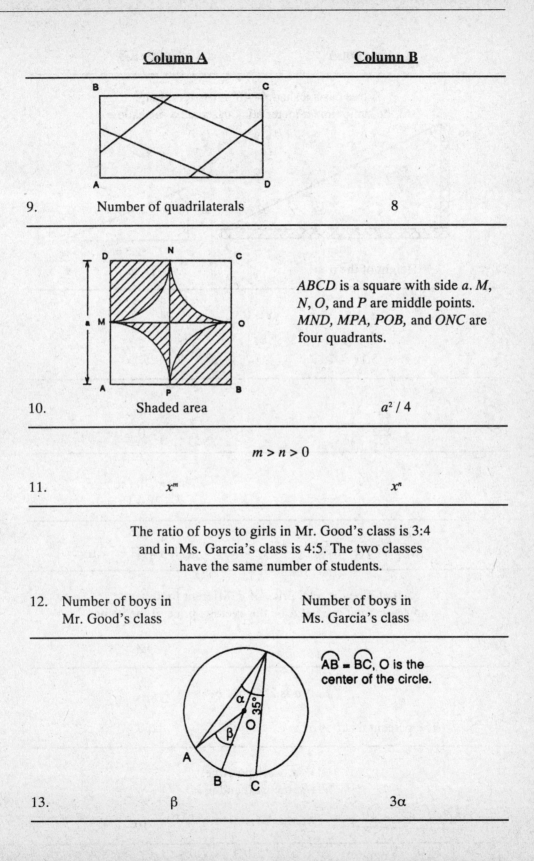

9. Number of quadrilaterals — 8

ABCD is a square with side *a*. *M*, *N*, *O*, and *P* are middle points. *MND*, *MPA*, *POB*, and *ONC* are four quadrants.

10. Shaded area — $a^2 / 4$

$$m > n > 0$$

11. x^m — x^n

The ratio of boys to girls in Mr. Good's class is 3:4 and in Ms. Garcia's class is 4:5. The two classes have the same number of students.

12. Number of boys in Mr. Good's class — Number of boys in Ms. Garcia's class

---

$\overset{\frown}{AB} = \overset{\frown}{BC}$, O is the center of the circle.

13. β — 3α

Column A	Column B

A tree casts a shadow 40 m (meters) long.
At the same time a meter stick casts a 2.5 m shadow.

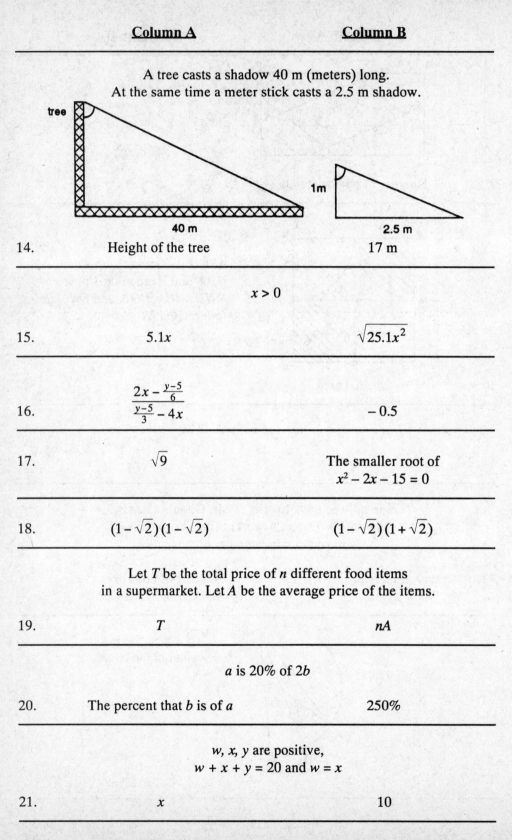

14. Height of the tree | 17 m

$x > 0$

15. $5.1x$ | $\sqrt{25.1x^2}$

16. $\dfrac{2x - \frac{y-5}{6}}{\frac{y-5}{3} - 4x}$ | -0.5

17. $\sqrt{9}$ | The smaller root of $x^2 - 2x - 15 = 0$

18. $(1 - \sqrt{2})(1 - \sqrt{2})$ | $(1 - \sqrt{2})(1 + \sqrt{2})$

Let T be the total price of n different food items
in a supermarket. Let A be the average price of the items.

19. T | nA

a is 20% of $2b$

20. The percent that b is of a | 250%

w, x, y are positive,
$w + x + y = 20$ and $w = x$

21. x | 10

	Column A	**Column B**

The sum of three consecutive numbers is $3x$.

22.	The smallest of the three	x

The three-digit number 4 ■ 4 is divisible by 8.

23.	■	8

$$f(x,y) = \frac{2x+y}{y^2}$$

24.	$f(1, 1)$	$f(1, 2)$

$$\underbrace{3+3+3+\ldots}_{m \text{ times}} > \underbrace{4+4+4+4+4\ldots}_{p \text{ times}}$$

25.	$\dfrac{m}{p}$	2

QUANTITATIVE ABILITY
PRACTICE TEST

ANSWER KEY

1. (C)	6. (C)	11. (D)	16. (C)	21. (D)
2. (C)	7. (C)	12. (B)	17. (A)	22. (B)
3. (D)	8. (A)	13. (B)	18. (A)	23. (B)
4. (C)	9. (A)	14. (B)	19. (C)	24. (A)
5. (A)	10. (A)	15. (A)	20. (C)	25. (D)

DETAILED EXPLANATIONS
OF ANSWERS

1.   **(C)**   First notice that in Column A, $^1/_5$ of 0.2% of 1000 means that we multiply the values together after 0.2% is changed to the decimal 0.002. Thus, we get $^1/_5 \times 0.002 \times 1000 = 0.4$. In Column B, the expression $(^1/_5)\%$ of 0.2 of 1000 means $(^1/_5)\% \times 0.2 \times 1000 = 0.002 \times 0.2 \times 1000 = 0.4$. Choice of response (B) would probably indicate that $(^1/_5)\%$ in the expression $(^1/_5)\%$ of 0.2 of 1000 was interpreted as 20% instead of 0.2%. Similarly, if choice (A) was selected, then perhaps the decimal equivalent for 0.2% was incorrectly determined in the expression.

2.   **(C)**   To explain this answer one needs to first know that the exterior angle of a triangle equals the sum of the measure of both remote interior angles of the triangle. The exterior angle of triangle *CDE is* angle x and the remote interior angles are C and D. So, the sum of angles C and D equals to angle x. Similarly, the exterior angle of triangle *ABE* is angle x and the remote interior angles are A and B. So, the sum of angles A and B equals to angle x. Hence, by substitution, one gets that the quantities in the two Columns are equal as follows:

$$\angle x + \angle x = (\angle A + \angle B) + (\angle C + \angle D) \text{ or}$$

$$2(\angle x) = \angle A + \angle B + \angle C + \angle D.$$

3.   **(D)**   Note that $w: x = w/x$ and $y: z = y/z$. Thus, $w/x = y/z$ is a proportion. Simplify the proportion by recalling that the product of the extremes equal the product of the means. The result is $wz = xy$. Since the values of w, x, y and z are both positive and negative real numbers, there is not enough information that will allow comparison of the quantities $w + x$ and $y = z$.

4.   **(C)**   Note that $w: x = w/x$ and $y: z = y/z$. Thus, $w/x = y/z$. Adding the opposite of y/z to both sides of the equation we get

$$w/x + (-y/z) = y/z + (-y/z)$$

$$w/x - y/z = 0.$$

Multiplying through by xz, the LCD, we have

$$(xz)(w/x) - (xz)(y/z) = (xz)(0)$$

$$wz - xy = 0.$$

Hence, the quantities in both columns are equal.

5.   **(A)**   Observe that each side of the square must be 10 since its perimeter is 40. So the information in Column A yields the value 2(10) = 20 units, twice the length of line segment *BD*.

In Column B the length of the shortest distance from point A to line segment *DE* is given by the length of a side of the square plus the height of the triangle. The distance from *DE* to the base of the triangle is 10 units.

The length of the base of the triangle is also 10 units. In order to find the height of the triangle the area must be known first. The area of the combined figures is given to be 125 square units. But, the

area of the square = e^2 = $(10)^2$ = 100 square units.

Thus, the area of the triangle is 25 square units since the total area of the figures is 125 square units.

The formula for the area of the triangle is $A = (1/2)bh$. Thus, the height of the triangle is given by

h = 2A/b = 2(25)/10 = 50/10 = 5 units.

So, the value of the quantity in Column B is 10 + 5 = 15 units. Hence, the quantity in Column A is larger.

6.   **(C)**   By definition angles 4 and 5 are vertical angles and by a theorem vertical angles are equal. Since line segments *k* and *m* are parallel, by a theorem the corresponding angles are equal. What are the corresponding angles? They are angles 1, 3 and 5 on the left side of the diagonal *d* and angles 2, 4 and 6 on the right side of the diagonal. It is given that angle 2 = 60 degrees. Since angle 4 = angle 2, then angle 4 equals 60 degrees. Finally, since angles 4 and 5 are equal vertical angles then angle 5 equals 60 degress. So the quantities in both columns are equal.

7.   **(C)**   To determine the value of each quantity one needs only to simplify the expressions and substitute as follows:

$(2WY)^2 = 2^2W^2Y^2 = 4(4)^2 (-2)^2 = 4(16) (4) = 256$

and $(2Y)^2 (4W) = 2^2Y^2(4W) = 4(-2)^2(4) (4) = 4(4)(4)(4) = 256$.

Hence, the quantities in both columns are equal.

8.   **(A)**   One strategy to solve this problem is to calculate Gail's salary this year as compared with her salary last year as follows:

Let $x represent Gail's salary last year. Since she received a 7% increase over last year's salary, it follows that her salary this year is equal to $x + 7% of $x. Thus,

$$x + 0.07x = 15,515$$
$$1.07x = 15,515$$
$$x = 15,515/1.07$$
$$= 14,500$$

So the quantity in Column A is greater.

Another strategy that can be used to solve this problem is to take 7% of the quantity in Column B, $14,000, and add it to $14,000. If the final result is $15,515, then the two quantities are equal. If the final result is less than $15,515, then the quantity in Column B is greater.

$$\text{Thus, 7\% of } 14{,}000 + 14{,}000 = (0.07)(14{,}000) + 14{,}000$$

$$= 980 + 14{,}000$$

$$= 14{,}980.$$

which is less than 15,515. Hence, Gail's salary last year was more than $14,000.

9. **(A)** Re-label the figure. Using the letters,

$E, F, G, H, I, J, K, L, M, N, O$ and P, we have:

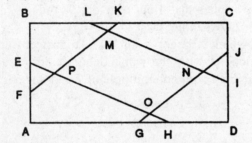

The quadrilaterals are:

ABCD	FPHA	GOEA	HOJD	INGD
JNLC	KMIC	LMFB	EPKB	MNOP

The total number is 10.

10. **(A)** The shaded area can be arranged as presented in the following figure:

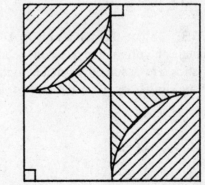

Since the shaded area = half the square area, the shaded area

$= \dfrac{a^2}{2}$.

11. **(D)**

If $x = 0, x^m = x^n$

If $x > 0, x^m > x^n$

If $x < 0$ the result can be $x^m = x^n$

$$x^m > x^n$$

$$x^m < x^n$$

Thus, the relationship cannot be determined.

12.   **(B)**   Since Mr. Good's class and Ms. Garcia's class have the same number of students and we do not know this number, we can start by letting x be the number of students in each of the two classes.

From the center information, the ratio of boys to girls in Mr. Good's class is 3:4. This means 3 out of every 7 students in Mr. Good's class are boys. Hence, the ratio of the number of boys in Mr. Good's class is 3:7 or $^3/_7$, that is, the number of boys in his class is $^3/_7 x = ^{3x}/_7$.

Similarly, the center information tells us that the ratio of boys to girls in Ms. Garcia's class is 4:5. This implies that 4 out of every 9 students in her class are boys. That is, the number of boys in her class is $^4/_9 x = ^{4x}/_9$.

The question now is, which is larger $^3/_7$ or $^{4x}/_9$? To answer this question, we need to express both fractions with the same denominator, usually the least common denominator. The least common multiple of 7 and 9 is 63. Hence,

$$\frac{3x}{7} = \frac{9(3x)}{63} = \frac{27x}{63}$$
$$\frac{4x}{9} = \frac{7(4x)}{63} = \frac{28x}{63}$$

Thus, the quantity in Column A is equal to $^{27x}/_{63}$ and the quantity in Column B is equal to $^{28x}/_{63}$.

So the quantity in Column B is greater.

13.   **(B)**   Given $\overset{\frown}{AB} = \overset{\frown}{BC}$ then $\alpha = 35°$ and $\beta = 70°$. Therefore

$$3\alpha = 105° > 70° = \beta.$$

14.   **(B)**   Since the sun's rays make the same angles with the horizontal for the triangles involving the tree and the meter stick, and since both the tree and the meter stick are assumed to make right angles with the horizontal, $\triangle ABC$ and $\triangle DEF$ are similar, as indicated in the following figure.

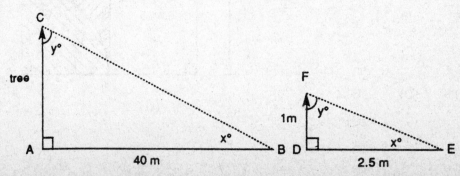

Recall that two triangles are similar if and only if corresponding angles are congruent (have the same angle measure) and corresponding sides are proportional.

Thus, angle C is congruent to angle *F*, angle *A* is congruent to angle *D*, and angle *B* is congruent to angle *E* . Also, if *AB* represents the length of side *AB*, then

$$\frac{AB}{DE} = \frac{AC}{DF} = \frac{BC}{EF}$$

Hence, using the proportion $\frac{AC}{DF} = \frac{AB}{DE}$, yields

$$\frac{AC}{1} = \frac{40}{2.5}$$

Cross-multiplication yields,

$$2.5(AC) = 40$$

$$AC = \frac{40}{2.5} = 16$$

Thus, the tree is 16 meters high.

So the quantity in Column B is greater.

15. **(A)**   Notice that $(5.1x)^2 = 26.01x^2$. Thus, one can write

$$\sqrt{(5.1x)^2} = \sqrt{26.01x^2} = 5.1x.$$

But, $25.1x^2 < 26.01x^2$. Hence,

$$\sqrt{25.1x^2} < \sqrt{26.01x^2} = 5.1x,$$

which means that the quantity in Column A is larger than the quantity in Column B.

16. **(C)**   Simplify the expression in Column A. The LCD for the rational expressions in the numerator and denominator is 6. So,

$$\frac{6(2x) - 6\left(\frac{y-5}{6}\right)}{6\left(\frac{y-5}{3}\right) - 6(4x)} = \frac{12x - y + 5}{2y - 10 - 24x}$$

$$= \frac{12x - y + 5}{-2(12x - y + 5)} = \frac{1}{-2} = -.05$$

Hence, the quantity in Column A is equal to the quantity in Column B.

17. **(A)**   Factoring the polynomial in the second column, we get

$$x^2 - 2x - 15 = (x - 5)(x + 3) = 0,$$

and the roots are therefore $x = 5$ and $x = -3$. Therefore, the smaller root is $x = -3$ and since $\sqrt{9} = 3$, and $3 > -3$, the first column represents the bigger number.

18.　**(A)**　In Column A expand the indicated product by using the foil method or some other method. Thus, the product of

$$
\begin{aligned}
(1 - \sqrt{2})(1 - \sqrt{2}) &= 1 - \sqrt{2} - \sqrt{2} + (\sqrt{2})(\sqrt{2}) \\
&= 1 - 2\sqrt{2} + \sqrt{4} \\
&= 1 - 2\sqrt{2} + 2 \\
&= 3 - 2\sqrt{2},
\end{aligned}
$$

which is positive.

Similarly, in Column B one expands the indicated product to get

$$
\begin{aligned}
(1 - \sqrt{2})(1 + \sqrt{2}) &= 1 - \sqrt{2} + \sqrt{2} - (\sqrt{2})(\sqrt{2}) \\
&= 1 - \sqrt{4} \\
&= 1 - 2 \\
&= -1.
\end{aligned}
$$

Thus, the quantity in Column A is larger.

19.　**(C)**　The average price is the total price divided by the number of items. In this case, $A = T / n$. Consequently, $T = nA$ and the two columns are equal.

20.　**(C)**　From the information given,

$$a = 0.2 \times 2b = 0.4b.$$

Solving for b, we see that

$$b = a/0.4 = 2.5a.$$

Therefore, $b/a = 250\%$ and the numbers in the two columns are equal.

21.　**(D)**　We know that w and x are equal. Set x (the value you are looking for) at the highest possible amount: 10. Since

$$w = x$$

x and w can be 10 and $y = 0$.

Therefore, it cannot be determined that $x < 10$ because x can be equal to 10.

22.　**(B)**　Let $x - 1$, x, $x + 1$ be three consecutive numbers, then

$$(x + 1) + x + (x - 1) = 3x,$$

and the smallest of the three is $x - 1$ which is less than x.

23.   **(B)**   Since 400 is divisible by 8, it is sufficient to examine those two-digit numbers ending in 4 that are divisible by 8. They are 24 and 64 only. Thus, ■ = 2 or 6, and in either case, that is less than 8. So, **Column B is bigger.**

24.   **(A)**   Replacing x and y with 1, we have

$$f(1, 1) = [(2 \times 1) + 1]/1^2 = 3.$$

In the second case, $x = 1$, $y = 2$,

$$f(1, 2)] [(2 \times 1) + 2]/2^2 = 4/4 = 1.$$

Thus, $f(1, 1) > f(1, 2)$.

25.   **(D)**   We can rewrite the statement as

$$3m > 4p,$$

therefore

$$^m/_p > ^4/_3,$$

but not necessarily bigger than 2.

CHAPTER 8

Data Sufficiency

➤ Data Sufficiency Review
➤ Practice Test

DATA SUFFICIENCY DIAGNOSTIC TEST

1. Ⓐ Ⓑ Ⓒ Ⓓ Ⓔ
2. Ⓐ Ⓑ Ⓒ Ⓓ Ⓔ
3. Ⓐ Ⓑ Ⓒ Ⓓ Ⓔ
4. Ⓐ Ⓑ Ⓒ Ⓓ Ⓔ
5. Ⓐ Ⓑ Ⓒ Ⓓ Ⓔ
6. Ⓐ Ⓑ Ⓒ Ⓓ Ⓔ
7. Ⓐ Ⓑ Ⓒ Ⓓ Ⓔ
8. Ⓐ Ⓑ Ⓒ Ⓓ Ⓔ
9. Ⓐ Ⓑ Ⓒ Ⓓ Ⓔ
10. Ⓐ Ⓑ Ⓒ Ⓓ Ⓔ
11. Ⓐ Ⓑ Ⓒ Ⓓ Ⓔ
12. Ⓐ Ⓑ Ⓒ Ⓓ Ⓔ
13. Ⓐ Ⓑ Ⓒ Ⓓ Ⓔ
14. Ⓐ Ⓑ Ⓒ Ⓓ Ⓔ
15. Ⓐ Ⓑ Ⓒ Ⓓ Ⓔ
16. Ⓐ Ⓑ Ⓒ Ⓓ Ⓔ
17. Ⓐ Ⓑ Ⓒ Ⓓ Ⓔ
18. Ⓐ Ⓑ Ⓒ Ⓓ Ⓔ
19. Ⓐ Ⓑ Ⓒ Ⓓ Ⓔ
20. Ⓐ Ⓑ Ⓒ Ⓓ Ⓔ
21. Ⓐ Ⓑ Ⓒ Ⓓ Ⓔ
22. Ⓐ Ⓑ Ⓒ Ⓓ Ⓔ
23. Ⓐ Ⓑ Ⓒ Ⓓ Ⓔ
24. Ⓐ Ⓑ Ⓒ Ⓓ Ⓔ
25. Ⓐ Ⓑ Ⓒ Ⓓ Ⓔ

DATA SUFFICIENCY

DIRECTIONS: Read the following tips, techniques, and examples, and take the diagnostic test.

Study this chapter for the following test:
GMAT

Data Sufficiency measures the ability to analyze a problem quantitatively, to choose which information is relevant to the situation, and to determine where and when there is sufficient information to solve the problem. Each problem consists of a question followed by pertinent information and two numbered statements. You must decide whether the information provided is sufficient to answer the question given by either (1) or (2) individually or combined. Data Sufficiency usually includes basic arithmetic, algebra, geometry and word problems.

Learn and understand the DIRECTIONS so you don't waste valuable time reading them on the day of the exam.

The directions and given information for this section read as follows:

Directions: Each of the data sufficiency problems below contains a question and two statements, labeled (1) and (2), in which certain data are given. Decide whether the data given in the statements are sufficient for answering the question. Using the data given in the statements plus your knowledge of mathematics and everyday facts choose:

A.   if Statement (1) ALONE is sufficient, but Statement (2) alone is not sufficient to answer the question asked;

B.   if Statement (2) ALONE is sufficient, but Statement (1) alone is not sufficient to answer the question asked;

C.   if BOTH Statements (1) and (2) TOGETHER are sufficient to answer the question asked, but NEITHER statement ALONE is sufficient;

D.   if EACH statement ALONE is sufficient to answer the question asked;

E.   if Statements (1) and (2) TOGETHER are NOT sufficient to answer the question asked, and additional data specific to the problem are needed.

Numbers: All numbers are real numbers.

Figures: A figure in this section will conform to the information given, but will not necessarily conform to the additional information given in the numbered statements (1) and (2).

Lines are straight if shown as straight and angle measures are greater than zero.

The position of points, angles, regions, etc., exist in the order shown.

All figures lie in a plane unless otherwise stated.

In case you did not understand the directions as given, here is a simplified version:

A. Only Statement 1. answers the question.

B. Only Statement 2. answers the question.

C. Both statements are needed to answer the question.

D. Each statement individually answers the questions.

E. Neither statement, alone nor combined, can answer the question.

EXAMPLES

1. Consider the path of a ball on a billiard table (no pockets) starting from the lower-left corner and making 45 degree angles with the sides. The ball stops when it strikes any corner. When does the ball stop in the upper-right corner?

    (1) The table's dimensions are the same.

    (2) The reduced ratio of the table's dimensions is an odd number compared to an odd number.

2. An observer at point *A* sees an object at point *B*. Assume the circle is the earth with a radius of 4000 miles. How high is point *B* above the earth?

    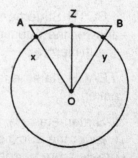

    (1) Measure of *AX* is 100 feet.

    (2) Measure of *AB* is 100 miles.

3.   A bicyclist riding due north and into the wind wants to return along the same route and be back at his starting point in 1 hour. The wind is constant during the ride. How far north may the cyclist ride?

(1)   The average speed going north is 14 mph and without the wind the cyclist knows his speed would be 17 mph.

(2)   The speed going south is 20 mph.

4.   A family is touring in two cars. At 9 A.M., the first car stops for 15 minutes while the second car continues on at a constant rate of speed. At what time will the first car "catch" the second car if the difference in their speeds is 16 mph?

(1)   Speed of the second car is 48 mph.

(2)   The distance the second car travels is 48 miles.

5.   If x and y are real numbers, is $|x - y| = y - x$?

(1) $y > x$

(2) $|y| > |x|$.

Suggested Techniques for Answering Data Sufficiency Questions:

- In most problems, it is not necessary to solve the problem. Figure the estimations to determine if the information given is sufficient.

- Go to Statement (2) if you get stuck on Statement (1).

- Choices can logically be eliminated. If it is determined that Statement (1) is sufficient, the answer may be A or D. If Statement (2) alone is sufficient but you are not sure about Statement (1), the answer can be either B or D. If neither statement alone is sufficient, the answer can be either C or E.

- Don't assume anything. If a problem tells you that everyone at a movie had either popcorn or soda, and that of 40 people at the movie, 20% had popcorn, don't assume that there were only 40 people at the movie.

- When reading the two statements, cover up the one you just read before reading the next. This will help you concentrate on the one you are reading.

- Look for clues that tell you how to solve the problem, then see whether the two statements provide you with enough information to answer the question.

- The math content of both the Data Sufficiency section and the Problem Solving section is exactly the same. Much of your knowledge of math can be applied to this section.

- On "yes and no" questions, a statement must always give us the same answer in order to be "sufficient." It must always answer "yes" or always answer "no." The statement is "insufficient" if the answer is "yes" one time and "no" the next.

- The numbers used on the Data Sufficiency section will only be real numbers. No imaginary numbers will appear or be implied on this test.

- All diagrams on the Data Sufficiency section are drawn to scale with the information provided in the question. However, the diagram may no longer be drawn to scale with the addition of the new data provided in Statements 1 and 2.

- If either statement answers the question in the affirmative or in the negative, the statement is "sufficient."

- As with the Problem Solving section, know all the important concepts in the Mathematics Review.

- Avoid lengthy computations. If a problem is taking a long time to figure out, go on to another question or come back to it if time remains.

EXPLANATIONS

1.   **(D)**   A ball moving at a 45 degree angle with respect to the sides of the table will approach all sides at a 45 degree angle and bounce away at a 45 degree angle. Therefore the legs of the right triangle formed by the path of the ball and the sides of the table are equal. When the table's dimensions are the same (Statement (1)), the ball's first contact with the sides would be the upper-right corner. A simple case of an odd to odd ratio is a one by three table. The ball will bounce twice — right side, left side — and then stop at the upper-right corner, having moved up one unit at each touch of the table's sides. By inductive reasoning, Statement (2) is also sufficient.

2.   **(C)**   Statement (1) gives sufficient information to find the measure of *AZ* (Pythagorean theorem). The angles at point *O* are not necessarily equal. There-

fore, the measure of *BY* is not necessarily the same height as *AX*. By including Statement (2), the measure of *BZ* can be found by subtracting the measure of *AZ* from 100 miles and again applying the Pythagorean theorem to find the measure of *BY*.

3.   **(A)**   Statement (2) is dependent on Statement (1), but it does not give the speed in either direction, and hence it alone is insufficient to solve the problem. From Statement (1) we know that the biker's speed travelling north is 14 mph, and south is is 20 mph. Let *D* denote the distance travelled north. Then at 14 mph the biker can cover this distance in *D*/14 hours. At 20 mph the biker can cover this distance in *D*/20 hours. Thus we require *D* to satisfy $D/14 + D/20 = 1$. This is equivalent to $10D + 7D = 140$, or $D = 140/17$ miles. To check this solution it would take the biker *D*/14 hours = 10/17 hours to travel north and $D/20 = 7/17$ hours to travel south. Thus the total time elapsed would be one hour.

4.   **(D)**   The basic relationship is $D = RT$. From Statement (1) we know the second car's speed and can deduce the first car's speed. The time the cars travel after the pit-stop until the first car catches the second car is the same. The distance the second car travels during this time is 36 miles

$$({}^{x}/_{48} = (x + 12)/64).$$

The first car travels 36 + 12 miles, where 12 miles is the distance the second car goes while the first car has stopped $(12 = 48 \ ¥ \ .25)$. 10:00 A.M. is the answer to the question. Statement (2) is sufficient because we know the distance each car travels and their relative speeds. Once again the time is the same for both cars after the pit-stop

$$(48 - x)/(s - 16) = 48/s \text{ (where } x = .25(s - 16).$$

5.   **(A)**   The absolute value of a number is positive since

$$y > x, y - x > 0 .$$

Statement (2) is insufficient. By counterexample: let $y = -3$ and $x = -2$. Clearly

$$|-3| > |-2|, \text{ but } |3 - (-2)| \neq -3 - (-2).$$

DATA SUFFICIENCY
PRACTICE TEST

TIME: 30 Minutes

25 Questions

DIRECTIONS: Each of the data sufficiency problems below contains a question and two statements, labeled (1) and (2), in which certain data are given. Decide whether the data given in the statements are sufficient for answering the question. Using the data given in the statements plus your knowledge of mathematics and everyday facts choose:

(A)   if statement (1) ALONE is sufficient, but statement (2) alone is not sufficient to answer the question asked;

(B)   if statement (2) ALONE is sufficient, but statement (1) alone is not sufficient to answer the question asked;

(C)   if BOTH statements (1) and (2) TOGETHER are sufficient to answer the question asked, but NEITHER statement ALONE is sufficient;

(D)   if EACH statement ALONE is sufficient to answer the question asked;

(E)   if statements (1) and (2) TOGETHER are NOT sufficient to answer the questions asked, and additional data specific to the problem is needed.

NUMBERS: All numbers are real numbers.

FIGURES: A figure in this section will conform to the information given, but will not necessarily conform to the additional information given in the numbered statements (1) and (2).

NOTES: Lines are straight if shown as straight, and angle measures are greater than zero.

The position of points, angles, regions, etc., exist in the order shown.

All figures line in a plane unless otherwise stated.

1. Paul ordered a certain number of books, by mail, from Academic Press publishers. If he had to enclose payment, which includes sales tax and a payment for postage and handling, in the amount of $91.40, what was the price of each book?

   (1) The sales tax for each book was 8%.

   (2) Payment for postage and handling was $1.25 per book.

2. If $\dfrac{x+1}{y-2} = -1$, what is the value of $\dfrac{x}{y-2}$?

   (1) $y = 4$

   (2) $\dfrac{3}{2-y} = \dfrac{1}{5}$

3. A train runs from City A to City B, back and forth, at a constant speed. What is its speed?

   (1) Round trip tickets cost $81.25.

   (2) The train fare is $.50 per mile.

4. In the figure, it took Michael one hour to get from A to C, via B. If he was driving from A to B at a constant speed of 25 miles per hour and walked at a constant speed of 5 miles per hour from B to C, how long did it take him to get from A to B?

   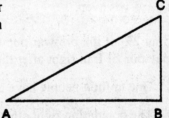

   (1) $AC = 100$ miles

   (2) $BC = .3$ miles.

5. In the 1988–89 academic year, 40% of the students in public schools are boys while 60% are girls. What percentage of the 10th graders are girls?

   (1) $\frac{1}{3}$ of the girls in public school are 10th graders.

   (2) $\frac{3}{5}$ of the boys in public school are 10th graders.

6. In the figure, if A is the center of the circle, what is the perimeter of $\triangle ABC$?

   (1) $|AB| = 4$ and $|BC| = |AC|$.

   (2) $|AB| = 4$ and $\angle BAC = 60°$.

   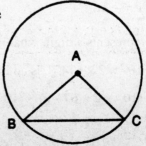

7. Is x less than y?

    (1) $y + |x| > 0$.

    (2) $y - |x| > 0$.

8. For a certain group of 10 people, what is their average income in 1988?

    (1) Their average income was $80,000 in 1987.

    (2) Five of the people had twice as much income in 1988 as in 1987; while the remaining five had the same income in 1988 as in 1987.

9. In the figure shown what is the area of the rectangle *ABEF*?

    (1) $AF = 5$

    (2) $AC = 6$; $DE = 3$.

10. For x, y integers, is xy odd?

    (1) $x^2 + y^2$ is odd.

    (2) $x + y$ is even.

11. In Iran 2% of the pre-war population have died during the war. What is the population of Iran right after the war?

    (1) One million people have died during the war.

    (2) The population right after the war is 103% of the pre-war population.

12. If $x \neq 0$ and $y \neq 0$, what is the value of $\dfrac{xy}{x^2 + y^2}$?

    (1) $y = 1/x$.

    (2) $y = -2x$.

13. If $\square$ represents a digit, what is the value of $\square$?

    (1) $10^\square \times 2 \times 674\square$ is an integer.

    (2) $(10^\square \times 2 \times 674\square) \div (10^{\square/2})$ is an integer.

14. The average age of passengers on a certain bus trip, at departure, was 60. While halfway on the trip two passengers were added, which changed the average age to 59. If one of the new passengers was 20 years older than the other, how old were the two?

    (1) There were 30 passengers at departure.

    (2) The sum of the ages of the passengers at departure was 1800.

15. Is $x^2 - 1 > 0$?

    (1) $x^3 - 1 < 0$.

    (2) $x + 1 > 0$.

16. If $x \neq 0$, is $x \mid x \mid > 0$?

    (1) $x + \mid x \mid = 0$.

    (2) $x^2 < 1$.

17. Box A contains 55 green and 45 blue marbles. Box B contains 45 green and 55 blue marbles. A certain number of marbles were exchanged between the boxes. How many marbles were exchanged?

    (1) There are 45 green and 55 blue marbles in Box A after the exchange.

    (2) There are 55 green and 45 blue marbles in Box B after the exchange.

18. A father said to his son, "If it is warm, I will take you to the lake." Did the father tell the truth?

    (1) It is cold.

    (2) The father takes his son to the lake.

19. The number 14 _ _ 61 has two missing digits. What is the number?

    (1) The sum of the number's digits is 28 and the second missing digit is a perfect square.

    (2) The missing digits differ by two.

20. "All squares are rhombi" is a true statement. Is figure A a square?

    (1) Figure A is not a rhombus.

    (2) Figure A is a quadrilateral.

21. Two cans of Catties Cat Chow cost 49 cents. How much will it cost Mrs. Smith to feed her cat for 1 week?

    (1) The cat eats 8 ounces each day.

    (2) If more than 10 cans are purchased at any one time, a 10% discount is given.

22. For what value of x is $(ax^2 + bx + c) / (cx + 2)$ not a real number?

    (1) $(ax^2 + bx + c) / (cx + 2) = 2.5$ when $x = 0$.

    (2) $b^2 - 4ac = 0$ and $b = 10$, $a = 5$.

23. A mirror is placed at point C and John, whose eye is at point A, backs away from the mirror until he sees the top of the tree in the mirror. How tall is the tree?

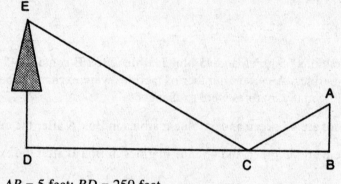

    (1) $AB = 5$ feet; $BD = 250$ feet.

    (2) $BC = 10$ feet.

24. If $x = \log a$ and $y = \log b$, what is ab?

    (1) $x = 3$ and $y = 2$.

    (2) $a/_b = 10^{x-y}$.

25. What are the factors (over the set of integers) of $a^2b^2 - 4a^2 - hb^2 + k$?

    (1) $k = 4h$, h is an integer.

    (2) $h = 4$, k is an integer.

DATA SUFFICIENCY PRACTICE TEST

ANSWER KEY

1. (E)	6. (D)	11. (C)	16. (A)	21. (E)
2. (D)	7. (B)	12. (B)	17. (E)	22. (D)
3. (E)	8. (E)	13. (B)	18. (D)	23. (C)
4. (B)	9. (C)	14. (D)	19. (A)	24. (A)
5. (C)	10. (A)	15. (C)	20. (A)	25. (A)

DETAILED EXPLANATIONS
OF ANSWERS

1. **(E)** Say the number of books he ordered is x and the price of each book is $\$y$. According to Statement (1) the sales tax per book is 8%. According to Statement (2) payment for postage and handling was $1.25 per book. Therefore, of the payment he enclosed the total expense per book is $\$y + \$0.08y + \$1.25$. Since the payment he enclosed is $91.40 we will have the equation

$$(\$y + \$0.08y + \$1.25)x = \$91.40.$$

Since neither Statement (1) nor (2) gives us the value of x we cannot solve for y (i.e., for the price per book). Hence (1) and (2) together are not sufficient.

2. **(D)** According to (1) $y = 4$; therefore, by substituting $y = 4$ in the given equation

$$\frac{x+1}{y-2} = 1$$

we can solve for x. Thus, the value of

$$\frac{x}{y-2}$$

can be determined. So (1) alone is sufficient.
   According to (2),

$$\frac{3}{2-y} = \frac{1}{5};$$

therefore multiplying both sides by $-\frac{1}{3}$, we will get:

$$\frac{1}{y-2} = -\frac{1}{15}.$$

Since it is given that

$$\frac{x+1}{y-2} = -1$$

it follows that

$$\frac{x}{y-2} + \frac{1}{y-2} = -1, \text{ i.e., } \frac{y}{y-2} = -1 - \frac{1}{y-2}.$$

Hence, (2) alone is also sufficient.

3. **(E)** According to (1), a round trip ticket costs $81.25, according to (2) the train fare is $.50 per mile; therefore, the round trip is 162.5 miles long. Since (1) and (2) do not give the time the trip takes, you cannot find the speed. (1) and (2) taken together are not sufficient.

4. **(B)** According to Statement (1) AC = 100 miles. Since (1) alone does not help to find the distance AB you cannot find the time it took to go from A to B using (1) alone. However, by Statement (2) BC = .3 miles; since we know the speed used to go from B to C, we can figure out the time it took to go from B to C. Moreover, the total time is known. So, (2) alone is sufficient to find the time it took to go from A to B.

5. **(C)** Statement (1) just says that ($^1/_3$) of the girls in public schools are 10th graders. (1) alone does not help to find the number of girls and boys in the 10th grade; you cannot find the percentage of girls in 10th grade using (1) alone. For similar reasons (2) alone is not sufficient. However, if we let x be the total number of students in public school, it is given that $.4x$ of them are boys, while the number of girls is $.6x$. Therefore, according to Statement (1), the number of girls in 10th grade is $^1/_3$ of $0.6x$, i.e., $0.2x$, and the number of boys in 10th grade is $^3/_5$ of $0.4x$, i.e., $0.24x$. As a result, the percentage of girls in 10th grade is

$$\frac{0 \cdot 2x}{0 \cdot 2x + 0 \cdot 24x} \ x \ 100\%.$$

Hence. (1) and (2) together are sufficient.

6. **(D)** According to Statement (1)

$$|AB| = 4 \text{ and } |BC| = |AC|.$$

Since A is the center of the circle, $|AB| = |AC|$ = the radius of the circle, i.e., 4 units. Since $|BC| = |AC|$, then

$$|AB| = |AC| = |BC| = 4 \text{ units.}$$

So, (1) alone is sufficient. According to Statement (2) $|AB|$ = 4 and $\angle BAC$ = 60°. Since A is the center $|AB| = |AC|$, therefore, $|AC|$ = 4. But, if

$$|AB| = |AC|, \text{ then } \angle ABC = \angle ACB.$$

Moreover,

$$\angle ABC + \angle ACB + \angle BAC = 180° \text{ and } \angle BAC = 60°.$$

Therefore, $\angle ABC = \angle ACB = \angle BAC = 60°$, i.e., $\triangle ABC$ is an equilateral triangle with side 4 units, and the perimeter is 12 units. Hence, (2) alone is also sufficient.

7. **(B)** According to Statement (1)

$$y + |x| > 0, \text{ i.e., } y > -|x|.$$

Since in the region (refer to the figure shown) $y > -|x|$, x can be less than y or x

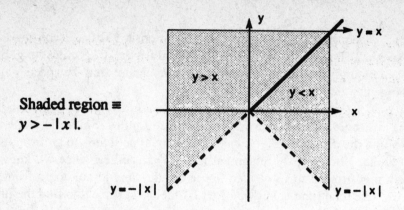

Shaded region ≡
$$y > -|x|.$$

can be greater than y, Statement (1) by itself is not sufficient. According to Statement (2)

$$y - |x| > 0, \text{ i.e., } y > |x|.$$

Since $|x| \geq x$, then $y > x$, i.e., x is less than y. Therefore, Statement (2) alone is sufficient to decide if x is less than y.

8.   **(E)**   According to Statement (1) the average income of the ten people in 1987 is $80,000. Therefore their combined income in 1987 is $800,000. According to Statement (2), five of the people have doubled their income in 1988 while the other five had the same income in 1987 and 1988. Since neither Statement (1) nor Statement (2) tells us what the incomes of these people were in 1988 we cannot determine the average using Statement (1) and (2) together.

9.   **(C)**   According to Statement (1) $AF = 5$. Since Statement (1) does not suggest the length of EF you cannot find the area using Statement (1) alone. According to Statement (2) $AC = 6$; $DE = 3$. Since the information in (2) helps to find neither AF nor EF, Statement (2) alone is not sufficient. However, since $\triangle ACF$ is similar to $\triangle EFD$, using (1) and (2) we get

$$\frac{AF}{DE} = \frac{AC}{EF}$$

from which we can determine the value of EF.

10.   **(A)**   According to Statement (1), $x^2 + y^2$ is odd. Since x and y are integers, then one of x^2 and y^2 is odd while the other is even, i.e., one of x and y is odd and the other is even. Therefore, the product of xy is odd. (1) alone is sufficient. However, according to Statement (2), $x + y$ is even; therefore, both x and y are odd. Both x and y are even. So, Statement (2) is not conclusive.

11.   **(C)**   By Statement (1), one million people have died during the war; therefore, the pre-war population of Iran was 50 million. Since (1) does not give the post-war population it alone is not sufficient. According to Statement (2) the population right after the war is 103% of the pre-war population. Since (2) does

not give the pre-war population, it, by itself, is not sufficient to answer the question. However, using (1) and (2) together we can figure out the population right after the war.

12.   **(B)**   According to Statement (1), $y = \frac{1}{x}$; therefore, substituting $y = \frac{1}{x}$ in

$$\frac{xy}{x^2 + y^2}$$

we will get

$$\frac{xy}{x^2 + y^2} = \frac{x^2}{x^4 + 1}.$$

Since Statement (1) does not give us the value of x, it alone is not sufficient to find the value of

$$\frac{xy}{x^2 + y^2}.$$

However, according to statement (2), $y = -2x$, and substituting $y = -2x$ in

$$\frac{xy}{x^2 + y^2}$$

we will get

$$\frac{-2x^2}{x^2 + 4x^2} = -\frac{2}{5}.$$

Hence, Statement (2) alone is sufficient to find the value of

$$\frac{xy}{x^2 + y^2}.$$

13.   **(B)**   According to Statement (1),

$$10^\square \times 2 \cdot 674\square,$$

is an integer; therefore $\square$ has to be one of the digits 4, 5, ..., 9. So, Statement (1) by itself is not sufficient to figure out the value of $\square$. According to Statement (2),

$$(10^\square \times 2 \cdot 674\square) + (10^{\square/2})$$

is an integer. But this is true only if the digit $\square$ is 8. Hence, Statement (2) alone is sufficient to find the value of $\square$.

14.   **(D)**   According to Statement (1) there were 30 passengers at departure. Since the average age was 60, using (1), the sum of the ages at departure is 1800. When two new passengers of age x and $x + 20$ joined the trip, average age is given by the formula

$$\frac{1800 + x + (x + 20)}{32}.$$

This average equals 59, so you can solve for x. Using just (2) you get the same equation

$$\frac{1800 + x + (x + 20)}{32} = 59.$$

which also enables you to solve for x.

15. **(C)** (1) says $x^3 - 1 < 0$; therefore

$$(x - 1)(x^2 + x + 1) < 0.$$

Since $x^2 + x + 1$ is positive for every x, $x - 1 < 0$. Since

$$x^2 - 1 = (x - 1)(x + 1),$$

and Statement (1) does not indicate the sign of (1), you cannot answer the question using Statement (1) alone. According to Statement (2), $x + 1 > 0$. Since Statement (2) does not suffice to find the sign of $x - 1$, it is not sufficient to find the sign of $x^2 - 1$. However, using (1) and (2) together you can answer the question.

16. **(A)** By Statement (1)

$$x + |x| = 0;$$

therefore, $|x| = -x$. Since $x \neq 0$, this says x is negative and therefore (1) is sufficient to answer the question. Since Statement (2) does not indicate the sign of x, (2) alone is not enough to answer the question.

17. **(E)** Since the total number of green marbles in boxes A and B remains 100, when A contains 45 green marbles, B will contain 55 green marbles (similarly for blue marbles). Therefore Statements (1) and (2) say the same thing. Moreover, for different amounts of exchange the compositions given in (1) and (2) can be achieved: if 20 green and 15 blue from Box A is exchanged for 10 green and 25 blue from Box B; 10 green and 10 blue from Box A for 20 blue from Box B, and so on. Hence, (1) and (2) are not sufficient to determine the number of marbles exchanged.

18. **(D)** A conditional statement can be false only if the "if part" (hypothesis) is true and the "then part" (conclusion) is false. Statement (1) says the hypothesis is false. Therefore whether or not the father takes his son to the lake is immaterial—the father has told the truth. Statement (2) is sufficient to answer the question. The father is telling the truth. Whenever the conclusion is true, a conditional statement is always true. Therefore, each statement alone is sufficient.

19.   **(A)**   Since the sum of the digits is 28, the missing digits must sum to 16. (28 − 12 = 16). The second digit has to be either 1, 4, or 9. Only 9 plus 7 equals 16, hence the number is 147961. There exists no single digit which can be added to 1 or 4 so that the sum is 16. Statement (2) is insufficient. We can deduce that the missing digits are 7 or 9 but there is no way to determine whether the given number is 147961 or 149761.

20.   **(A)**   Look at a Venn diagram, where

Q = quadrilaterals

R = rhombi

S = squares

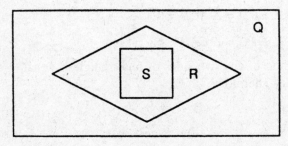

Statement (1) implies that A is not a square. So Statement (1) gives sufficient information to answer the question. Statement (2) only permits one to conclude A is in the set of Q but we cannot answer whether A is a square.

21.   **(E)**   To answer this question, we must know how much food the cat eats in one day and how much food is in each can of Catties Cat Chow. This would permit us to calculate the number of cans needed and by multiplying by the price per can we get the weekly cost. But we cannot find the information from Statements (1) or (2), thus, both statements together are not sufficient.

22.   **(D)**   The given fraction is not real only if $cx + 2$ is zero. Statement (1) implies that $c = 5$. Now

$5x + 2$ 0 only if $x = -\,^2/_5$.

Statement (2) gives

$100 - 4(5)c = 0$

which leads to $c = 5$. Again $x = -\,^2/_5$. Therefore, each statement alone is not sufficient.

23.   **(C)**   Basically we know from the main body of the problem that ΔEDC and ΔACB are similar, i.e., they have the same angles. Specifically, (see the figure)

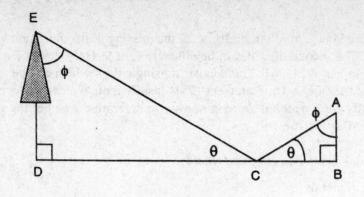

(a) $\angle EDC = \angle ABC = 90°$

(b) $\angle ECD = \angle ACB = \theta$

(c) $\angle DEC = \angle CAB = \phi.$

Hence the ratio of any two sides of one triangle is equal to a similar ration in the other triangle. Therefore

$$\frac{ED}{DC} = \frac{AB}{BC}.$$

From this relation, we can compute one unknown if we know the other three sides (four sides are involved).

Statement (1) supplies us with the length of one side $AB = 5$ ft, but overall length $BD = 250$ ft. This is useless unless we know the individual length of either DC or BC. Note $BD = DC + BC$. Hence Statement (1) by itself cannot solve the problem.

Statement (2) gives us the length $BC = 10$ ft. Hence, as

$$BD = DC + BC \quad \text{and} \quad BD = 250$$

$$\therefore 250 = DC + 10 \text{ or } DC = 240 \text{ ft.}$$

Therefore, we now know $BC = 10$ ft and $DC = 240$ ft. Together with $AB = 5$ feet from Statement (1) we know three sides in the relation

$$\frac{ED}{DC} = \frac{AB}{BC} \quad \text{or} \quad \frac{ED}{240} = \frac{5}{10}$$

or $ED = 120$ feet.

24.   **(A)**

$$x + y = \log a + \log b = \log ab.$$

When $x = 3$ and $y = 2$, we have $5 = \log ab$ which implies $ab = 10^5 = 100,000$. Statement (2) is true but by itself we cannot determine ab.

25.   **(A)**   From Statement (1) we have

$$a^2b^2 - 4a^2 - 4b^2 + 4h = a^2(b^2 - 4) - h(b^2 - 4)$$

$$= (a^2 - h)(b^2 - 4) = (a^2 - h)(b - 2)(b + 2).$$

So Statement (1) is sufficient.

According to Statement (2), $h = 4$, but k cannot be found, and its relationship to h, a and b is not known. So, Statement (2) alone is not sufficient.

CHAPTER 9

Mini-Tests

MINI TEST 1

1. Ⓐ Ⓑ Ⓒ Ⓓ Ⓔ
2. Ⓐ Ⓑ Ⓒ Ⓓ Ⓔ
3. Ⓐ Ⓑ Ⓒ Ⓓ Ⓔ
4. Ⓐ Ⓑ Ⓒ Ⓓ Ⓔ
5. Ⓐ Ⓑ Ⓒ Ⓓ Ⓔ
6. Ⓐ Ⓑ Ⓒ Ⓓ Ⓔ
7. Ⓐ Ⓑ Ⓒ Ⓓ Ⓔ
8. Ⓐ Ⓑ Ⓒ Ⓓ Ⓔ
9. Ⓐ Ⓑ Ⓒ Ⓓ Ⓔ
10. Ⓐ Ⓑ Ⓒ Ⓓ Ⓔ
11. Ⓐ Ⓑ Ⓒ Ⓓ Ⓔ
12. Ⓐ Ⓑ Ⓒ Ⓓ Ⓔ
13. Ⓐ Ⓑ Ⓒ Ⓓ Ⓔ
14. Ⓐ Ⓑ Ⓒ Ⓓ Ⓔ
15. Ⓐ Ⓑ Ⓒ Ⓓ Ⓔ
16. Ⓐ Ⓑ Ⓒ Ⓓ Ⓔ
17. Ⓐ Ⓑ Ⓒ Ⓓ Ⓔ
18. Ⓐ Ⓑ Ⓒ Ⓓ Ⓔ
19. Ⓐ Ⓑ Ⓒ Ⓓ Ⓔ
20. Ⓐ Ⓑ Ⓒ Ⓓ Ⓔ
21. Ⓐ Ⓑ Ⓒ Ⓓ Ⓔ
22. Ⓐ Ⓑ Ⓒ Ⓓ Ⓔ
23. Ⓐ Ⓑ Ⓒ Ⓓ Ⓔ
24. Ⓐ Ⓑ Ⓒ Ⓓ Ⓔ
25. Ⓐ Ⓑ Ⓒ Ⓓ Ⓔ

MINI TEST 1

DIRECTIONS: Choose the best answer for each of the 25 problems below.

1. If $x = -3$ then $x^x =$

   (A) $-\frac{1}{27}$ (B) $\frac{1}{27}$ (C) 27

   (D) -27 (E) 9

2. If an item is sold for x dollars, there is a profit of 20%; and if the same item is sold for y dollars, there is a loss of 20%. Then $x/y =$

   (A) $\frac{2}{3}$ (B) $\frac{3}{4}$ (C) $\frac{4}{3}$

   (D) $\frac{5}{4}$ (E) $\frac{3}{2}$

3. Joe and Bob were playing marbles. Bob said, "Give me two of your marbles and I'll have as many as you." Joe answered, "But if you give me two of yours, I'll have twice as many as you." With how many marbles did Bob start out?

   (A) 14   (B) 12   (C) 6

   (D) 8   (E) 10

For problems 4 and 5, use the following information:

A company earns a weekly profit according to the formula

$$P(x) = -.5x^2 + 200x - 1800.$$

4. Find the number of items the company must sell each week in order to obtain the largest possible profit.

   (A) 20   (B) 50   (C) 100

   (D) 150   (E) 200

5. Find the largest possible profit.

   (A) $18,200   (B) $16,950   (C) $13,200

   (D) $6,950   (E) $2,000

6. How many sides does a regular polygon have, each of whose interior angles is 150°?

    (A) 10   (B) 12   (C) 14

    (D) 6   (E) 16

7. If $X + Y = 8$ and $3X + Y = 12$ then $2X - Y$ is

    (A) -2 (B) 2   (C) 4

    (D) 8   (E) 10

8. Sherry wishes to leave a 15% tip for her waiter. If she paid a total of $24.15 for her meal and the tip, how much was the cost of the meal?

    (A) $20.00   (B) $21.00   (C) $22.00

    (D) $23.00   (E) $24.15

9. The smallest even integer n for which $(.5)^n$ is less than 0.01 is

    (A) 2   (B) 4   (C) 6

    (D) 8   (E) 10

10. Mr. Wheeler can purchase a television set for $395 cash or he can purchase it for $50 down and 12 monthly payments of $35 each. The cost of credit is

    (A) $25   (B) $30   (C) $35

    (D) $50   (E) $75

11. Which of the following figures has exactly two lines of symmetry?

    (A) a trapezoid which is not a parallelogram

    (B) a parallelogram which is not a rectangle

    (C) a rectangle which is not a square

    (D) a square

    (E) an equilateral triangle

12. If $x + y = 12$ and $x^2 + y^2 = 126$ then $xy =$

    (A) 9   (B) 10   (C) 11

    (D) 13   (E) 16

13. Points *A, B* and *C* are noncolinear. Line segment *AC* has length 24 inches, *AB* has length 13 inches and *BC* has length 13 inches. The shortest distance between *B* and line segment *AC* is

    (A) 5 inches   (B) $2\sqrt{12}$ inches   (C) $\sqrt{313}$ inches

    (D) $\sqrt{407}$ inches   (E) 25 inches

14. If $x + 2y = 10$ and $^x/_y = 3$, then $x =$

    (A) – 2   (B) 2   (C) 4

    (D) 6   (E) 8

15. The area of this right-angled plane figure is

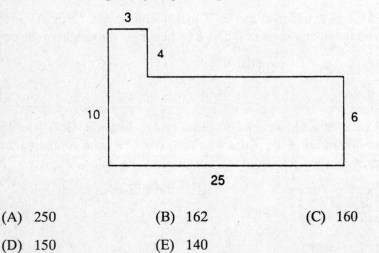

    (A) 250   (B) 162   (C) 160

    (D) 150   (E) 140

16. John's beginning six month salary was $15,000. At the end of each six month period, his salary was increased by $500. His annual salary during his fourth year of employment was

    (A) $18,500   (B) $19,000   (C) $33,500

    (D) $35,500   (E) $36,500

17. The diameter of an automobile tire is 24". How many revolutions does the tire make in traveling a mile? (1 mile = 5,280 feet).

    (A) $\dfrac{220}{\pi}$ (B) 2640π (C) $\dfrac{2640}{\pi}$

    (D) $\dfrac{440}{\pi}$ (E) 440π

18. A publisher's clearing house contest claims it will pay the winner some money every day for a month. The amounts are $25 the first day, $50 the second day, $75 the third day, and so on. In a 30 day month, how much will the winner receive?

    (A) $20,000   (B) $12,500   (C) $19,125

    (D) $11,625   (E) $10,200

19. A cone of radius 3 inches and a cylinder of radius 4 inches have equal volumes. Find the ratio of the height of the cone to that of the cylinder.

    (A) $^{16}/_9$ (B) $^{16}/_3$ (C) $^9/_{16}$

    (D) $^3/_4$ (E) $^3/_{16}$

20. A solid metal cylinder of radius 4 inches and height 12 inches is melted down and recast as a cone of radius 8 inches. Find the height of the cone.

    (A) 12 in.   (B) 9 in.   (C) 6 in.

    (D) 36 in.   (E) 24 in.

21. Cheryl covered a distance of 50 miles on her first trip. On a later trip she traveled 400 miles going 4 times as fast. Her new time compared with the old time was

    (A) four times as much   (B) three times as much

    (C) twice as much   (D) the same

    (E) half as much

22. If $z = \dfrac{xy}{x + y}$, then $x =$

    (A) $\dfrac{zy}{y - z}$ (B) $\dfrac{zy}{z - y}$ (C) $\dfrac{y - z}{zy}$

    (D) $\dfrac{z - y}{zy}$ (E) $\dfrac{z - y}{y}$

23. Tickets to a high school basketball game cost $4 for adults and $2 for students. 1,000 tickets were sold. If the total receipts from the sale of tickets were $3,200, how many student tickets were sold?

    (A) 400   (B) 600   (C) 800

    (D) 1,000   (E) 1,600

24. A rectangular tank with base dimensions of 120 inches and 80 inches is filled with water to a depth of 50 inches. The water rises $6^2/_3$ inches when a solid metal cube is submerged in the tank. Find the length of an edge of the cube.

    (A) 18.9   (B) 16.5   (C) 82

    (D) 40   (E) $6^2/_3$

25. Exactly one of the following sentences is true. Which one is true?

    (A) $\left(\frac{1}{2}\right)^{33} < \left(\frac{1}{3}\right)^{22} < \left(\frac{1}{7}\right)^{11}$

    (B) $\left(\frac{1}{7}\right)^{11} < \left(\frac{1}{2}\right)^{33} < \left(\frac{1}{3}\right)^{22}$

    (C) $\left(\frac{1}{3}\right)^{22} < \left(\frac{1}{7}\right)^{11} < \left(\frac{1}{2}\right)^{33}$

    (D) $\left(\frac{1}{2}\right)^{33} < \left(\frac{1}{7}\right)^{11} < \left(\frac{1}{3}\right)^{22}$

    (E) $\left(\frac{1}{3}\right)^{22} < \left(\frac{1}{2}\right)^{33} < \left(\frac{1}{7}\right)^{11}$

MINI TEST 1

ANSWER KEY

1.	(A)	6.	(B)	11.	(C)	16.	(E)	21.	(C)
2.	(E)	7.	(A)	12.	(A)	17.	(C)	22.	(A)
3.	(E)	8.	(B)	13.	(A)	18.	(D)	23.	(A)
4.	(E)	9.	(D)	14.	(D)	19.	(B)	24.	(D)
5.	(A)	10.	(E)	15.	(B)	20.	(B)	25.	(E)

DETAILED EXPLANATIONS
OF ANSWERS

1.   **(A)**

$$-3^{-3} = \frac{1}{(-3)^3}$$

$$= \frac{1}{-27}$$

$$= \frac{-1}{27}$$

2.   **(E)**   Let c = the original cost of the item. Then

$$\frac{x}{y} = \frac{c + .20c}{c - .20c}$$

$$= \frac{1.2c}{.8c}$$

$$= \frac{3}{2}.$$

3.   **(E)**   Let x = # of Bob's marbles and let y = # of Joe's marbles. If Joe gives two of his marbles to Bob, then the equation

$$x + 2 = y - 2$$

is true. If bob gives two of his marbles to Joe, then the equation

$$2(x - 2) = y + 2$$

is true. Simplifying both equations we have the following system:

$$x - y = -4$$

$$2x - y = 6$$

Subtracting the first from the second, gives $x = 10$. To check, we find that $y = 14$ so if Bob gives 2 of his marbles to Joe, he will have 8 and Joe will have 16, which verifies Joe's comment that he will have twice the number Bob has.

4.   **(E)**   The profit equation represents a parabola which opens downward. The x-coordinate of its vertex is the maximum number of items needed to be sold. The easiest way to find x is by using the formula $x = -^b/_{2a}$ where $b = -200$

and $a = .5$. So,

$$x = \frac{-200}{2(-.5)} = 200$$

5.　　**(A)**　Evaluating $P(x)$ when $x = 200$ gives the largest possible profit. That is, $P(200)$ is the y-coordinate of the vertex of the parabola.

$$p(200) = -.5(200)^2 + 200\,(200) - 1800$$
$$= -.5(40,000) + 40,000 - 1800$$
$$= 18,200.$$

6.　　**(B)**　Let n = the number of sides of the polygon. Then

$$\frac{(n-2)\,180°}{n} = 150°,$$

$$(n-2)180° = 150°n,$$

$$180°n - 360° = 150°n,$$

$$30n = 360, \ n = 12.$$

7.　　**(A)**　If $X + Y = 8$ and $3X + Y = 12$, then

$$(3X + Y) - (X + Y) = 12 - 8.$$

Therefore, $2X = 4$, $X = 2$ and $Y = 8 - X = 6$. Hence $2X - Y = 4 - 6 = -2$.

8.　　**(B)**　If X is the cost of Sherry's meal, then her tip is $.15X$. Thus her total meal cost (including the tip) is

$$X + .15X = \$24.15$$

so that X is $24.15/1.15 = \$21$.

9.　　**(D)**　Since

$$(.5)^2 = .25, (.5)^4 = (.25)^2 = .0625,$$

$$(.5)^6 = .015625 > .01,$$

$$(.5)^8 = (.25)\,(.015625) < .01,$$

and n is an even integer, n must equal 8.

10.　　**(E)**　If Mr. Wheeler chooses to pay $50 down and $35 each in 12 monthly payments, his total cost is $50 + 12(35) = \$470$. Since the cash price is $395, the cost of credit is $\$(470 - 395) = \$75$.

11. **(C)** Trapezoids and parallelograms have zero lines of symmetry, squares have four lines of symmetry, equilateral triangles have three lines of symmetry, and rectangles which are not squares have two lines of symmetry.

12. **(A)**

$$x + y = 12$$
$$(x + y)^2 = 12^2$$
$$x^2 + 2xy + y^2 = 144$$
$$x^2 + y^2 = 126$$
$$2xy = 18$$
$$xy = 9.$$

13. **(A)** Since line segments AB and BC have the same length, ABC is an isosceles triangle. The shortest distance between B and AC is the length of the perpendicular from B to AC. If BD is perpendicular to AC, it must be the perpendicular bisector of AC. Thus AD and DC have length 12 inches each. By Pythagorus' theorem length of

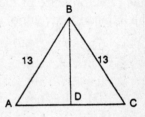

$$BD = \sqrt{13^2 - 12^2} = \sqrt{25} = 5 \text{ inches.}$$

14. **(D)** If $x/y = 3$, then $x = 3y$. Substituting $x = 3y$ in

$$x + 2y = 10$$

we get

$$3y + 2y = 10,$$

or, $y = 2$. Since $x = 3y$, $x = 3(2) = 6$.

15. **(B)** Complete the diagram as shown to give two rectangles. The smaller rectangle has sides 3 and 4 and the larger has sides 6 and 25. The area of the figure

$$= 3 \times 4 + 6 \times 25 = 162.$$

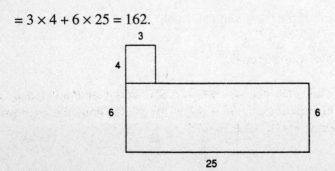

16. **(E)** During the first year John earns

$$15,000 + 15,500 = \$30,500.$$

During the second year he earns

$$16,000 + 16,500 = \$32,500;$$

during the third year he earns

$$17,000 + 17,500 = \$34,500,$$

and during the fourth year he earns

$$18,000 + 18,500 = \$36,500.$$

17. **(C)**

One mile $= 5,280$ ft $\times 12$ in/ft $= 63,360$ inches.

The circumference of the tire is found by the formula $c = \pi d$ or 24π. Therefore, the number of revolutions is

$$\frac{63,360}{24\pi} = \frac{2,640}{\pi}.$$

18. **(D)** It is necessary to find the sum of the arithmetic series

$$25 + 50 + 75 + \ldots$$

the 30th term of which a_{30} is found, using $n = 30$:

$$a_{30} = a_1 + (n-1)d, \, a_{30} = 25 + 29(25) = 750.$$

Then we sum the numbers 25, 50, 75, ..., 750 by taking the average of the first and last terms and multiplying that by 30, the number of terms:

$$\frac{30(25+750)}{2} = 11,625.$$

19. **(B)** Set V (cylinder) $= V$ (cone).

$$\pi r_1^2 h_1 = \frac{1}{3}\pi r_2^2$$

Cancel the pi's and substitute the given values of r:

$$16h_1 = \frac{1}{3}9h_2 \,, 16h_1 = 3h_2 \,, \frac{16}{3}h_1 = h_2$$

so that

$$\frac{16}{3} = \frac{h_2}{h_1}.$$

Choice (A) comes from not taking $^1/_3$ of the core radius. Choice (C) comes form the mistake in part (A) and also, taking the ratio of the cylinder to the cone. Choice (D) comes from taking the ratio of the radii. Choice (E) has the correct numbers but is the ratio of the height of the cylinder to the height of the cone.

20. **(B)**

$$V \text{ (cylinder)} = \pi 4^2(12) = 192\pi.$$

Since the volumes are the same,

$$V \text{ (cone)} = 192\pi = \frac{1}{3}\pi r^2 h = \frac{1}{3}\pi(64)h.$$

Canceling the pi's and multiplying 192 by 3 gives $64h = 576$ or $h = 9$. Choice (A) equates the heights of the cone and cylinder. Choice (C) is half the height of the cylinder. Choice (D) comes from taking 3 times the height of the cylinder.

21. **(C)** $t = {}^d/_r$, let t_1 be her old time and t_2 be her new time so that

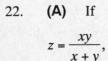

$$t_1 = \frac{50}{r} \quad \text{and} \quad t_2 = \frac{400}{4r} = \frac{100}{r}.$$

Therefore, comparing, we see that $t_2 = 2 \cdot t_1$.

22. **(A)** If

$$z = \frac{xy}{x+y},$$

then $z(x + y) = xy,$

or $zx + zy = xy.$

Thus $zy = xy - zx,$

or $x(y - z) = zy,$

giving $x = zy/(y - z)$.

23. **(A)** If X student tickets were sold, then $1000 - X$ adult tickets were sold. The total receipts would be

$$2(X) + 4(1000 - X) = 400 - 2X.$$

Therefore,

$$4000 - 2X = 3200, \text{ or } X = 400.$$

24. **(D)**   Volume of cube = volume of displaced water

= 120(80) (6²/₃) = 64,000.

V(cube) = e^3 and e^3 = 64,000, e = 40.

Choice (A) comes from 120(56²/₃) = 6800 and e^3 = 6800, e = 18.9.

Choice (B) comes from 80(56²/₃) = 4533 and e^3 = 4533, e = 16.5.

Choice (C) comes from 120 (80) (56²/₃) = 544,000 and e^3 = 544,000, e = 81.6 ≈ 82.

25. **(E)**   Applying the exponent law

$x^{mn} = (x^m)^n$,

$$\left(\frac{1}{2}\right)^{33} = \left[\left(\frac{1}{2}\right)^{3}\right]^{11} \quad \text{and} \quad \left(\frac{1}{3}\right)^{22} = \left[\left(\frac{1}{3}\right)^{2}\right]^{11}$$

$$= \left(\frac{1}{8}\right)^{11} \qquad\qquad = \left(\frac{1}{9}\right)^{11}$$

Since $\dfrac{1}{9} < \dfrac{1}{8} < \dfrac{1}{7}, \left(\dfrac{1}{9}\right)^{11} < \left(\dfrac{1}{8}\right)^{11} < \left(\dfrac{1}{7}\right)^{11}$ and $\left(\dfrac{1}{3}\right)^{22} < \left(\dfrac{1}{2}\right)^{33} < \left(\dfrac{1}{7}\right)^{11}$

MINI TEST 2

1. (A) (B) (C) (D) (E)
2. (A) (B) (C) (D) (E)
3. (A) (B) (C) (D) (E)
4. (A) (B) (C) (D) (E)
5. (A) (B) (C) (D) (E)
6. (A) (B) (C) (D) (E)
7. (A) (B) (C) (D) (E)
8. (A) (B) (C) (D) (E)
9. (A) (B) (C) (D) (E)
10. (A) (B) (C) (D) (E)
11. (A) (B) (C) (D) (E)
12. (A) (B) (C) (D) (E)
13. (A) (B) (C) (D) (E)
14. (A) (B) (C) (D) (E)
15. (A) (B) (C) (D) (E)
16. (A) (B) (C) (D) (E)
17. (A) (B) (C) (D) (E)
18. (A) (B) (C) (D) (E)
19. (A) (B) (C) (D) (E)
20. (A) (B) (C) (D) (E)
21. (A) (B) (C) (D) (E)
22. (A) (B) (C) (D) (E)
23. (A) (B) (C) (D) (E)
24. (A) (B) (C) (D) (E)
25. (A) (B) (C) (D) (E)

MINI TEST 2

DIRECTIONS: Choose the best answer for each of the 25 problems below.

Use the following table for questions 1–2.

ANNUAL INCOME BY SEX OF HEAD
OF THE HOUSEHOLD

| Sex | Number of heads of households with income | | | |
	Less than $15,000	$15,000 – $35,000	$35,000 – $50,000	$50,000 and above
Male	12	25	35	8
Female	22	10	6	2

1. What percent of the males earn less than $35,000?

   (A) 31   (B) $46^1/_4$ (C) $57^1/_2$

   (D) 60   (E) 90

2. The number of heads of the household who are males is x times the number of heads of household who are females, where x is

   (A) 1.5   (B) 2   (C) 2.5

   (D) 3   (E) 4

3. A rectangle is 3 feet long and 6 feet wide. The number of squares with sides 3 inches long that are needed to cover the rectangle is

   (A) 6   (B) 72   (C) 144

   (D) 288   (E) 864

4. The side of a square increases 10% and the area increases $5.25(ft)^2$. What was the original value of the side of the square?

   (A) 3 ft   (B) 2 ft   (C) 1 ft

   (D) 4 ft   (E) 5 ft

5. A used car dealer reduced the price of all the cars on his lot by $300. If a car was originally priced at $1,195, what percent (to the nearest tenth) is the markdown on the sale price?

(A) 29.3%   (B) 8.4%   (C) 37.7%

(D) 25.1%   (E) 33.5%

6. In which of the following alternatives can we simplify a without changing the expression?

(A) $\dfrac{x/a}{a/x}$ (B) $\dfrac{x+a}{x-a}$ (C) $\dfrac{ax-a}{a}$

(D) $\dfrac{x^a}{2^a}$ (E) $ax + a$

7. In College Bookstore, $a + b$ books are selling for $1,000. Myron buys 12 books and for each one has a discount of $1. How much does Myron need to pay?

(A) $[(a + b) - 1] \times 12$ (B) $[(a + b)/1000 - 1] \times 12$

(C) $[(1000/(a + b)) - 1] \times 12$ (D) $[a + b] \times 12$

(E) $(a + b)$

8. A square is inscribed in a circle of area 18π. What is the length of a side of the square?

(A) 6   (B) 3   (C) $3\sqrt{2}$

(D) $6\sqrt{2}$ (E) Cannot be determined

Questions 9–10 are based on the following table.

Payroll Summary of R.S.E.T.T. Company, 1989

Position Title	Number in Position	Total Amount Paid to Employees in the Position
Vice President/Manager	5	$ 110,000
Team Leader/Coordinator	25	350,000
Assembly Line Worker	500	600,000
Total	530	$1,060,000

9. What is the ratio of wages earned by a vice president/manager to the wages earned by an assembly line worker?

    (A) 60 to 11   (B) 11 to 6   (C) 10 to 6

    (D) 55 to 3   (E) None of these

10. What percent (to the nearest tenth) make up the wages paid to the vice presidents/managers?

    (A) 5.2   (B) 9.5   (C) 10.4

    (D) 11.4   (E) 42

Questions 11–14 are based on the following information.

You have been provided a string that is 31.4 inches long. Your assignment is to form the string into an enclosed geometric shape that will create the largest area within the sides of the figure you create.

11. Which of the following geometric shapes will include the largest area?

    (A) Triangle   (B) Square   (C) Circle

    (D) Hexagon   (E) Rectangle

12. If the string is formed into a circle, what is the approximate radius of the circle?

    (A) 10 inches   (B) 5 inches   (C) 7.5 inches

    (D) 16.7 inches   (E) 12.5 inches

13. If the length of the string is doubled and formed into a square, how much larger area would be enclosed than if a square was formed with the original length of 31.4 inches?

    (A) The area would double.

    (B) The area would triple.

    (C) The area would quadruple.

    (D) The area would be eight times larger.

    (E) The area would be six times as large.

14. If the string was formed into an equilateral triangle, approximately how many square inches would be enclosed in the area of the triangle?

    (A) 35   (B) 40   (C) 45

    (D) 50   (E) 55

15. $\dfrac{x+y}{y} = a; \dfrac{y}{x} = ?$

    (A) 1   (B) a (C) $1/a$

    (D) $a - 1$ (E) $1/(a - 1)$

16. If $x - (4x - 8) + 9 + (6x - 8) = 9 - x + 24$, then $x =$

    (A) 4   (B) 2   (C) 8

    (D) 6   (E) 10

17. Two dice are thrown, one red and one green. The probability that the number on the red exceeds the number showing on the green by exactly two is

    (A) $\dfrac{1}{18}$ (B) $\dfrac{1}{4}$ (C) $\dfrac{1}{9}$

    (D) $\dfrac{1}{36}$ (E) $\dfrac{1}{24}$

18. If $3^x > 1$ then x

    (A) $0 < x < 1$ (B) $x \geq 0$ (C) $x \geq 1$

    (D) $x > 0$ (E) $x > 1$

19. In how many ways can 5 prizes be given away to 4 boys, when each boy is eligible for all the prizes?

    (A) 64   (B) 120   (C) 1024

    (D) 5   (E) 20

20. In the figure, if $BD \mid\mid AE$, then the following must be true:

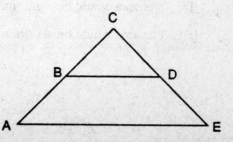

(A) $\angle CBD = \angle CDB$

(B) $\angle CAE = \angle CEA$

(C) $\dfrac{CB}{CA} = \dfrac{CD}{AE}$

(D) $\dfrac{CD}{CE} = \dfrac{BD}{AE}$

(E) $\dfrac{CB}{BD} = \dfrac{CD}{CA}$

21   A man who is 40 years old has three sons, ages 6, 3, and 1. In how many years will the combined age of his three sons equal 80% of his age?

(A) 5

(B) 10

(C) 15

(D) 20

(E) 25

Questions 22 – 25 refer to the following table.

Adapted from *Scholastic Update*, 5/5/89. Vol. 121, N. 17.

TWO GIANTS

	China	Soviet Union
Area (sq. mi)	3.7 million	8.7 million
Population	1.1 billion	289 million
Percentage Under 15	39% (1960)	31% (1960)
	25% (1990)	25% (1990)
Percent Who Live in Cities	19% (1960)	49% (1960)
	21% (1990)	68% (1990)
Life Expectancy	60 (1970)	70 (1970)
	69 (1990)	72 (1990)
Infant Mortality	81 (1970)	26 (1970)
(deaths per 1000 births)	32 (1990)	22 (1990)
Birth Rate	37 (1970)	18 (1970)
(births per 1000 pop.)	18 (1990)	18 (1990)
Citizens per Doctor	1,757	267
Students (Ages 9–15) per teacher	42	25
Literacy	70%	99%
Gross National Product (GNP)	$315 billion	$2 trillion
Percent of GNP to Military	7%	11.5%
Exports to U.S.	$9.3 billion	$470 million
Imports from U.S.	$5.03 billion	$1.5 billion

22.   What is the annual per capita income in China (approximately)?

(A) $2,864

(B) $286.4

(C) $300

(D) $3,000

(E) $315

23. How many persons are older than 15 years old in China (1990)?

    (A) 825 million   (B) 8.25 billion   (C) .0825 billion

    (D) 671 million   (E) 216.75 million

24. How many new borns will die in the Soviet Union (1990)?

    (A) 11,444   (B) 114,000

    (C) 1,144,444   (D) Cannot be determined

    (E) 114,444

25. What is the ratio of doctors between Soviet Union and China respectively? (approximately)

    (A) .578   (B) 1.729   (C) .152

    (D) 6.58   (E) .263

MINI TEST 2

ANSWER KEY

1. (B)	6. (C)	11. (C)	16. (D)	21. (B)
2. (B)	7. (C)	12. (B)	17. (C)	22. (B)
3. (D)	8. (A)	13. (C)	18. (D)	23. (A)
4. (E)	9. (D)	14. (C)	19. (C)	24. (E)
5. (E)	10. (C)	15. (E)	20. (D)	25. (B)

DETAILED EXPLANATIONS
OF ANSWERS

1. **(B)**   The number of males

    $$= 12 + 25 + 35 + 8 = 80.$$

Of these $12 + 25 = 37$ earn less than \$35,000. Therefore, the percent of males earning less than \$35,000 is $(37/80)100 = 46^{1}/_{4}$.

2. **(B)**   The number of males = 80, and those of females

    $$= 22 + 10 - 6 + 2 = 40.$$

Thus $80 = 40x$, or $x = 2$.

3. **(D)**   The area of the rectangle in square inches is

    $$(3 \times 12)\,(6 \times 12)$$

and the area of each square of sides 3 inches is $3 \times 3 = 9$ square inches. If X is the number of 3×3 squares needed to cover the rectangle, then

$$9X = (3 \times 12)\,(6 \times 12), \quad \text{or} \quad X = 36(72)/9 = 288.$$

4. **(E)**   The original square is below left and when the side increases by 10% is below right.

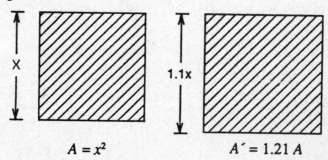

$$A = x^2 \qquad\qquad A' = 1.21\,A$$

The difference in Areas is 5.25 (ft)^2, therefore

$$
\begin{aligned}
1.21x^2 - x^2 &= 5.25 \\
.21x^2 &= 5.25 \\
x^2 &= 5.25/.21 \\
x^2 &= 25 \\
x &= 5.
\end{aligned}
$$

5.   **(E)**   This question requires the calculation of the percent of the mark-down of the sale price. We can start by letting $x\%$ = the required percent.

Since the original price of the car is $1,195 and the markdown is $300, it follows that the sale price of the car is equal to $1,195 − $300 = $895. Thus, we need to find what percent 300 is of 895. This can be found by a direct proportion as follows:

$$\frac{\text{markdown } x}{\text{sale price } x} = \frac{\text{markdown } y}{\text{sale price } y}$$

Since percent means the number of parts per 100 parts, we have,

$$\frac{x}{100} = \frac{300}{895}$$

Crossmultiplication yields

$$895x = (300)(100)$$

$$x = \frac{(300)(100)}{895} = 0.335$$

Thus, $x\% = 0.335 \times 100\% = 33.5\%$.

Another way of attacking this problem is to divide 300 by 895, then multiply the result by 100%. This yields,

$$x\% = \left(\frac{300}{895}\right)100\% = 33.5\%.$$

Yet a third way to solve this problem is to test each of the percents given in the answer choices as possible answers. This can be done by calculating the given percent of $895. If the result is $300, the given percent is correct, otherwise, the given percent is the wrong answer. Thus,

(A)   29.3%: $(.293)(\$895) \cong \$262 \neq \$300$

(B)   8.4%: $(.84)(\$895) \cong \$75 \neq \$300$

(C)   37.7%: $(.377)(\$895) \cong \$377 \neq \$300$

(D)   25.1%: $(.251)(\$895) \cong \$225 \neq \$300.$

(E)   33.5% $(.335)(\$895) \cong \$300.$

6.   **(C)**   We can simplify a in alternative (C) as shown below.

$$\frac{ax - a}{a} = \frac{a(x - 1)}{x} = x - 1$$

In all of the other choices, simplification of a changes the expression.

7.   **(C)**

$a + b$ books = $1,000.

Let 1 book = x.

$$x = \frac{1000}{a+b} \text{ ($/book)}$$

Myron bought each one for $1 less. He paid

$$\frac{1000}{a+b} - 1 \text{ ($/book)}$$

Therefore for 12, he paid

$$\left(\frac{1000}{a+b} - 1\right) \times 12.$$

8. **(A)** The formula for the area of a circle is

$A = \pi r^2$.

Since the area of the square is 18π, then it is true that

$$\pi r^2 = 18\pi \quad \text{or} \quad r^2 = 18 \quad \text{or} \quad r = \sqrt{18} = 3\sqrt{2}.$$

Then, the diameter of the circle is

$$2r = 2(3\sqrt{2}) = 6\sqrt{2}.$$

The diameter of the circle bisects the inscribed square into two equal triangles. which are $45° - 45° - 90°$ triangles. Since the diameter of the circle is also the hypotenuse of each of the triangles, $6\sqrt{2}$, and the sides x of each are equal, one can write the following using the Pythagorean Theorem:

$$x^2 + x^2 = \left(6\sqrt{2}\right)^2$$
$$2x^2 = 36(2)$$
$$x^2 = 36$$
$$x = 6,$$

the length of a side of the square.

So, the correct answer choice is (A). The other answer choices are obtained by failing to find the correct diameter of the circle or failing to use the Pythagorean Theorem correctly.

9. **(D)** First, find the average wages earned by a vice president/manager by dividing 5 into $110,000, which yields $22,000. Similarly, find the average wages earned by an assembly line worker by dividing 500 into $600,000 which is $1,200. Then, the ratio is given by

$$\frac{22,000}{1,200} = \frac{220}{12} = \frac{55}{3}$$

which also can be written as 55 to 3.

10.   **(C)**   Since the total amount of the payroll for the company is $1,060,000 and the wages paid to vice presidents/managers amount to $110,000, then the percent of wages paid to this position group is found as follows:

$$\frac{110,000}{1,060,000} = \frac{11}{106} = 0.104 \quad \text{or} \quad 10.4\%$$

11.   **(C)**;   12.   **(B)**;   13.   **(C)**;   14.   **(C)**

   There are several ways to answer this series of questions. One might calculate the area of the square (which would be about 8 × 8 = 64) which is only one of the three shapes for which sufficient information is given to do so. The second most obvious shape is a circle. The length of the string would form a circle whose diameter is 10 inches (31.4/3.14) and whose radius is 5 inches. Since $\pi r^2 = 25\pi =$ about 78 square inches is larger than the square, the circle appears to be the largest. One might infer from this (correctly) that a smooth edge with no corners encloses a larger area than one with corners. Experimenting with various lengths for the rectangle, the triangle, and the hexagon should soon make it evident that the circle is the best answer. This is not so much a mathematical question as it is one that calls for logical inference from the data provided. Item 6 was answered in the previous discussion and 7 can be answered with a brief calculation. If the original square had sides of about 8 inches, then a string twice as long would form sides of about 16 inches. 8 squared is 64 and 16 squared is 256, or 4 times as much area. Item 8 calls for a triangle whose sides are each about $10^1/_2$ inches. The area of a triangle is $^1/_2$ the base (about 5.25 inches) times the height (about 9 inches) or about 45. Again, this is not so much a mathematical question as it is one of estimating logically. Sketching the geometric figures in this question should help. Approximate answers are all you need to determine to select the correct response.

15.   **(E)**   What is an expression for y/x as a function of a if

$$\frac{x+y}{y} = a?$$

$$\frac{x+y}{y} = a$$

$$\frac{x}{y} + \frac{y}{y} = a$$

$$\frac{x}{y} + 1 = a$$

$$\frac{x}{y} = a - 1$$

$$\frac{y}{x} = \frac{1}{a-1}$$

16.   **(D)**   The most direct way to solve this problem is to perform the indicated operations in the given equation and solve it for x. Thus,

$$x - (4x - 8) + 9 + (6x - 8) = 9 - x + 24$$

$$x - 4x + 8 + 9 + 6x - 8 = 9 - x + 24$$

$$(x + 6x - 4x) + (8 - 8 + 9) = (9 + 24) - x$$

$$(7x - 4x) + 9 = 33 - x$$

$$3x + x = 33 - 9$$

$$4x = 24$$

$$x = 6.$$

17.   **(C)**   The total number of possible combinations on a pair of dice is $(6)^2$ = 36 combinations.

We are looking for combinations where the number showing on the red die exceeds the number on the green die by 2. This occurs only for the following combinations.

Red	Green
3	1
4	2
5	3
6	4

Thus there are four combinations that satisfy the constraints, out of 36 possible combinations.

The probability is equal to $^4/_{36} = ^1/_9$.

18.   **(D)**   We need to find the value of x, where $3^x > 1$.

If $x = 0$ then $3^0 = 1$

If $x = 1$ then $3^1 = 3$

given that 3^x must be bigger than 1, $x > 0$.

19.   **(C)**   Any one of the prizes can be given in 4 ways; and then any one of the remaining prizes can also be given in 4 ways, since it may be obtained by the boy who has already received a prize. Thus two prizes can be given away in 4^2 ways, three prizes in 4^3 ways, and so on. Hence, the 5 prizes can be given away in 4^5, or 1024 ways.

20.   **(D)**   We are told that segments BD and AE are parallel. This implies that

$$\angle CBD = \angle CAE \text{ and } \angle CAE \text{ and } \angle CDB = \angle CEA$$

(corresponding angles formed by parallel lines cut by a transversal are congruent).

$\angle ACE = \angle BCD$ (same angle).

Thus $\triangle BCD$ and $\triangle ACE$ are equiangular and similar. From a theorem, we know that the sides of similar triangles that correspond to each other are proportional. Sides CD and CE and BD and AE are corresponding sides and are thus proportional:

$$\frac{CD}{CE} = \frac{BD}{AE}$$

21.   **(B)** n years later, the ages will be

father $40 + n$

son # 1 $6 + n$

son # 2 $3 + n$

son # 3 $1 + n$

Therefore

$$6 + n + 3 + n + 1 + n = (80/100) * (40 + n)$$
$$10 + 3n = .8(40 + n)$$
$$10 + 3n = 32 + .8n$$
$$2.2n = 22$$
$$n = 10.$$

22.   **(B)**   The annual per capita income is:

$$\frac{\text{Gross National Product (GNP)}}{\text{Population}}$$

In this case

$$\frac{\$315 \text{ billion}}{1.1 \text{ billion (citizens)}} = 286.4 \ (\$ / \text{citizen})$$

23.   **(A)**   In 1990 the percentage under 15 in China will be 25%, therefore 75% will be older than 15. Then

$$\frac{75}{100}(1.1 \text{ billion}) = .825 \text{ billion}$$

or 825 million.

24. **(E)** To solve the problem we need to know

a) Population

b) Birth rate, and

c) Infant Mortality

$$\text{New Born in 1990} = \text{Birth Rate} \times \text{number of citizens}$$

$$= 18/1000 \times 289,000,000$$

$$= 5.202 \times 10^6.$$

$$\text{New Born that will die} = \text{Infant Mortality Rate} \times \text{New Born in 1990}$$

$$= 22/1000 \times 5.202 \times 10^6$$

$$= 1.14444 \times 10^5 = 114,444.$$

25. **(B)** First calculate the number of doctors in each country.

Soviet Union:

$$\frac{289 \text{ million (citizens)}}{267 \text{ (citizens / doctor)}} = 1.082397 \times 10^6 \text{ doctors}$$

China:

$$\frac{1.1 \text{ billion (citizens)}}{1757 \text{ (citizens / doctor)}} = 626,067 \text{ doctors}$$

$$\frac{\text{No. of Drs., USSR}}{\text{No. of Drs., China}} = \frac{1.082397 \times 10^6}{626,067} \approx 1.729$$

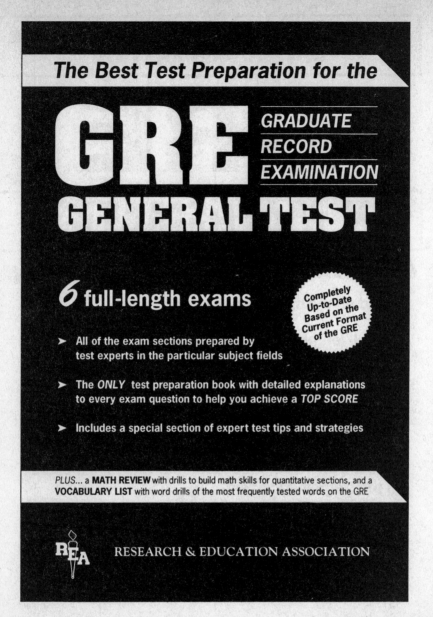

The Best Test Preparation for the

GMAT

Graduate Management Admission Test

6 full-length exams

Completely Up-to-Date Based on the Current Format of the GMAT

➤ Prepares you for admission to MBA programs and graduate business schools

➤ All of the exam sections prepared by test experts in the particular subject fields

➤ The *ONLY* test preparation book with detailed explanations to every exam question to help you achieve a *TOP SCORE*

➤ Includes a special section of expert test tips and strategies

PLUS... a COMPREHENSIVE MATH REVIEW with drills to build math skills for quantitative sections.

R E A **Research & Education Association**

Available at your local bookstore or order directly from us by sending in coupon below.

"The ESSENTIALS" of
ACCOUNTING & BUSINESS

Each book in the **Accounting and Business ESSENTIALS** series offers all essential information about the subject it covers. It includes every important principle and concept, and is designed to help students in preparing for exams and doing homework. The **Accounting and Business ESSENTIALS** are excellent supplements to any class text or course of study.

The **Accounting and Business ESSENTIALS** are complete and concise, with quick access to needed information. They also provide a handy reference source at all times. The **Accounting and Business ESSENTIALS** are prepared with REA's customary concern for high professional quality and student needs.

Available titles include:

Accounting I & II

Advanced Accounting I & II

Advertising

Auditing

Business Law I & II

Business Statistics I & II

Corporate Taxation

Cost & Managerial Accounting I & II

Financial Management

Income Taxation

Intermediate Accounting I & II

Microeconomics

Macroeconomics I & II

Marketing Principles

Money & Banking I & II

If you would like more information about any of these books,
complete the coupon below and return it to us or go to your local bookstore.